Easing *the* Teasing®

Helping Your Child Cope with Name-Calling,
Ridicule, and Verbal Bullying

Easing *the* Teasing ®

Judy S. Freedman, M.S.W., L.C.S.W.

Contemporary Books

Chicago   New York   San Francisco   Lisbon   London   Madrid   Mexico City
Milan   New Delhi   San Juan   Seoul   Singapore   Sydney   Toronto

Library of Congress Cataloging-in-Publication Data

Freedman, Judy S.
    Easing the teasing : helping your child cope with name-calling, ridicule, and
verbal bullying / Judy S. Freedman.
        p.   cm.
    Includes bibliographical references and index.
    ISBN 0-07-138175-9 (alk. paper)
    1. Teasing.   2. Child rearing.   I. Title.

    BF637.T43.F74   2002
    649'.1—dc21   2002020764

Contemporary Books

A Division of The McGraw·Hill Companies

2 3 4 5 6 7 8 9 0   AGM/AGM   1 0 9 8 7 6 5 4 3 2

ISBN 0-07-138175-9

This book was set in Sabon
Printed and bound by Quebecor Martinsburg

Cover and interior design by Nick Panos
Cover photograph © MacGregor & Gordon/Photonica

McGraw-Hill books are available at special quantity discounts to use as premiums and
sales promotions, or for use in corporate training programs. For more information, please
write to the Director of Special Sales, Professional Publishing, McGraw-Hill, Two Penn
Plaza, New York, NY 10121-2298. Or contact your local bookstore.

The examples in this book are pulled from more than seventeen years of experience as a
school social worker as well as private practice and from experiences parents and
colleagues have shared with me. All the names and identifying details have been
changed to protect the privacy of the children and families involved.

This book is printed on acid-free paper.

*To the children whom I have
counseled and taught how to cope with teasing.*

Contents

I will cook the teases away in the steam of my pasta.

Acknowledgments

This book became a reality with the guidance, support, and contributions from an all-star team of family, friends, and colleagues.

I want to thank the teachers at Harper and Prairie schools, who welcomed me into their classrooms over the last seventeen years. We all learned that classroom intervention was a very effective and exciting way to address many of the social and emotional needs of most children. Helping kids deal with the recurring issue of teasing led to the creation of *Easing the Teasing*. I am grateful to my "team captains," former principals, Barbara Savitt and Alice Gruenberg, and current principal, Paul Louis. They gave me the opportunities and encouragement that enabled me to help kids in more creative ways. I also appreciate the support of the administration and school board of Kildeer Countryside District 96 in Buffalo Grove, Illinois.

This team effort includes the contributions of many colleagues, relatives, friends, and students, who have shared opinions, ideas, and experiences. I extend my heartfelt thanks to Marley Stein, Myrna Halpern, Emily Kline, Marcia Anderson, Susan Weller, Lou Mongillo, Deborah Hermalyn, Liz Androyna, Stephanie Novak, Bobbie Kott, Jeanette Saltzberg, Maureen Stolman, Barbara Borden, and Carrie Dyer. I sincerely appreciate the ongoing support of Susan Mendenhall, Gretchen Borowki, and Kim Martinson. I also want to thank Kay Katz, who enthusiastically welcomed my idea to bring stress education into her fourth grade classroom when I first began school social work. I am very grateful for all the wonderful contributions made by many Prairie School students.

I also thank my sister, Lesley Samuels Marks, for being such a good sport as I continue to tell how I used to tease her about cows.

I am thrilled and flattered that the Imagination Theater has brought many pages of this book "to life" in their outstanding performances to thousands of children. I extend my heartfelt gratitude to Aimee-Lynn Simpson, Don Schroeder, and the entire ensemble.

The cheerleader for this project from the very beginning has been Gail Reichlin, executive director of Parents Resource Network and author of *Pocket Parent* (Workman, 2001). Gail has continued to offer encouragement, inspiration, and advice. I am deeply indebted to her for introducing me to her literary agent, Nancy Crossman. Nancy's immediate interest and belief in my work led to her finding the right publishing team. It has been a pleasure to work with Contemporary Books' senior editor, Judith McCarthy, and her assistant, Michele Pezzuti. Their enthusiasm and respect for my work have meant a great deal to me. Nancy Crossman also found an extraordinary coach to help me reach the finish line, Chris Benton. Chris's insightful understanding of my ideas and thoughts, her gifted writing, and her expert knowledge of the publishing process were invaluable. I appreciate Chris being so understanding, patient, caring, concerned, and supportive—truly the qualities of a good friend, as described in Chapter 8. Reaching the finish line would not have been possible without the guidance and efforts of Nancy Hall, the associate project editor at Contemporary Books, who oversaw the production of this book.

I am indeed grateful to my parents, Helen and Henry Samuels—my role models and Memphis "cheerleaders." They have inspired me with their extraordinary examples of hard work, dedication, success, and accomplishments.

No team would be complete without devoted fans, such as my dear mother-in-law, Blossom Lowenstein; special aunts, Jeanie Cooper and Phyllis Heyman; and my lifelong friend Wendy Dan. I thank them for always being there with their cheers and applause.

Words cannot convey my deep gratitude for the love, constant support, and encouragement from my husband, Ken, and our sons, Matt, Jeff, and Lee. I could not have done this without their patience, ideas, and computer instruction.

I am deeply indebted to my whole team of players, supporters, captains, coaches, cheerleaders, and fans for making this book possible. What an all-star team effort!

Introduction

———◆———

Teasing hurts. I know an eight-year-old boy who cannot attend school because teasing caused him severe distress and his school failed to intervene. I know a seventh-grade girl who requires medication and psychotherapy for depression that resulted from ridicule and exclusion by her classmates. Studies have shown that children recovering from cancer have found the ridicule over their chemotherapy's side effects to be more painful than the physical pain of the treatments themselves. I've known far too many kids who have skipped school, feigned illness, bypassed lunch, and clammed up in class because they could not cope with teasing that had begun to feel like torture to them. And we've all watched the news in horror as children commit shocking acts of violence that are later attributed to their anger and desire for revenge against peers who tormented them.

Fortunately, extreme responses to teasing among children seem to be rare. Not so rare, however, are the chronic stress, anxiety, aggressive behavior, depression, and physical illness suffered by children who are regularly taunted, verbally abused, or excluded. Childhood teasing can be highly stressful and often leaves lasting emotional scars.

If you're the parent of a child who is being hurt by teasing, you're hurting too. In my seventeen years as a school social worker, I've met mothers and fathers who have been devastated by the pain and bewilderment that their teased children bring home. The parents of the eight-year-old I just mentioned decided to home-school their son. The mother of the depressed seventh-grader cried when she told me about her daughter's plight. Sometimes, parents are all too aware of what their children are going through. Is there an adult among us who hasn't been teased or witnessed its painful effects? During just the last couple of years, I've received requests for help from parents all over the country who are anticipating that their children will be teased simply because they are in some way "different." Caucasian parents who had adopted Chinese children have asked me how they can head off any teasing their children might experience as they get older. The mother of a gifted child suggested that all gifted kids learn coping strategies because they are frequently targeted. Parents of kids with special needs also ask me for advice in helping their children cope with the verbal aggression frequently aimed at them.

Today, adults know that teasing is a big problem. The National Association of School Psychologists estimates that 160,000 students miss school daily because they are afraid of intimidation or attack by other students. Parents and educators realize that they're up against a significant problem. They just don't always know what to do about it. How seriously should they take the child's complaint? What should they say to the child? How should they intervene—or should they just stay out of it and let kids fight their own battles? How can they tell when a child is truly being hurt rather than just temporarily irritated? Are there ways to eliminate teasing altogether from the classroom, Scout troop, playground, school bus, and summer camp?

Research and my own professional experience have demonstrated that we can't completely prevent teasing, as it is universal and widespread. Instead, we can teach children how to react so that they don't suffer. A pile of evidence reveals that children need adult assistance with true bullying situations, which are repeated and intentional acts of aggression that occur over an extended period of time. But most kids are able to handle teasing, name-calling, and ridicule without adult help when they are equipped with the skills and strategies to do so. Dorothea Ross, research psychologist at the University of California in San Francisco, reported on the pain of ridicule felt by childhood cancer victims. She has done extensive study on bullying and teasing and stated, "Teasing merits separate consideration when it occurs in the absence of any other components of bullying. . . . Most teasing victims can learn to cope with teasing and manage teasing incidents without adult help when no other components of bullying are involved." SuEllen Fried and Paula Fried, authors of *Bullies and*

Victims, emphasize the importance of kids having a repertoire of strategies to deal with verbal abuse. The conclusion reached by these and many other experts today coincides with mine.

Before school begins, we take our kids shopping for new clothes, shoes, and school supplies. I strongly believe we must send kids to school with some other essentials that they cannot purchase at the mall—coping skills.

That's what this book is all about: teaching children strategies for easing the teasing that they can take with them into every arena of their lives, from classroom to school bus, from playground to campground, from home to far away. I have successfully used this program to help thousands of children—elementary school age and what is variously called middle school and junior high. It is based on the reality that teasing cannot be prevented altogether. Children—and their parents and teachers—need to understand that although they cannot always control what other people say, they can learn to control their own reactions. Parents and educators can teach simple strategies that will empower children and reduce their feelings of helplessness. When kids realize that they can use effective strategies in teasing situations, their confidence increases, and their coping skills are strengthened. The strategies will "ease the tease" for most children, which will ease the stress of most parents.

This book is an outgrowth of more than thirty years of experience as a social worker, seventeen of them working with children, parents, and educators in elementary schools. One fact became inescapable as I worked with children growing up in our challenging era: all children—not just those referred to a social worker—experience stress. Some learn to cope; others do not. Much depends on their self-esteem, their general coping skills, and the extent and duration of the stressor. I quickly found that teasing, ridicule, and verbal aggression are among the most predictable stressors for children of elementary school age. And I learned over time that a majority of children can deal with teasing once they are given empowering tools and the words to use in individual situations.

I have found that children are eager and receptive to learning these easy strategies. Young children who learn these coping skills will be better prepared for the more significant social challenges and conflicts in their preteen and teen years. Older kids and teens who haven't yet learned to deal with teasing will find that these skills can ease their more intense stress and pain that often result from verbal aggression.

My goal—in this book and in the program I have presented at workshops across the country—is to empower parents to help kids cope with the widespread and universal problem of teasing. Although most parents do not have a degree in education, all parents are teachers. We teach our children valuable life lessons every day—what is safe and what is dangerous, what is right and what is wrong, and what is good and what is bad. We instruct our sons and daughters in how to take care of themselves, how to fulfill daily household responsibilities, and how to treat others. We program their lives with numerous activities and lessons to enhance their social, cognitive, and physical skills. Where do they learn coping skills? Parents must intentionally and proactively teach their kids strategies to deal with teasing to reduce helplessness and increase empowerment. If they don't, the mild effects of occasional teasing can erupt into enduring damage from prolonged teasing. Inability to cope effectively with chronic teasing can lead to increased difficulties in peer relationships and an inability to withstand peer pressure. Stress-related academic difficulties might become chronic learning problems. Feelings of helplessness may be transformed into hopelessness. Parents are in the ideal position to break this cycle or to prevent it from beginning in the first place.

Make no mistake about it, however. The task is not the responsibility of parents alone. The ideal prescription for easing the teasing includes implementing an "anti-teasing" campaign at school, consistent dialogue about teasing in the classrooms, and instruction from parents at home. Many parents have complained to me over the years that their kids' schools have been unresponsive to their pleas for help and intervention. In return, I have heard from school personnel that they need to learn ways to address this in the school setting. It's not that educators don't care about the problem; many simply do not know how to intervene, especially when the incident occurs in unsupervised situations.

To address this need, this book also contains a section of activities and suggestions that parents can present to their child's school administrator or teacher. This provides an opportunity for parents and school personnel to work in partnership to address this problem. I can't emphasize enough that the school component is essential. *A schoolwide campaign against teasing is more effective in decreasing these behaviors than individual intervention with the teasers.* Positive peer pressure is very powerful in discouraging teasing and taunting behaviors.

So, how can you use this book? Whether you're a parent, an educator, a social worker like me, a caregiver, a counselor, a psychologist, a coach, or a Scout leader, you can adapt each section to your own needs. The first three chapters will tell you what we know about teasing: what it is and is not; how to distinguish it from bullying; when, where, and why it hurts—and how much; what kids are teased about and why teasers tease. Not all teasing is hurtful, but it's critical that we adults avoid making too little of it. What starts out as a joke might grow into ridicule depending on a variety of factors.

The next three chapters help you take action once you're made aware of teasing. First you need to explore the situation: how can you take a good look at your child's behavior, your family's behavior at home, and other factors to see what's really going on as clearly as possible? Once you have as firm a handle on the circumstances as you can get, you can talk to your child about it—always with openness and attentiveness, empathy and equanimity. In Chapter 6, you can help your child learn to cope, with the ten strategies that I've found so helpful with children of many ages, all over the country. In this central chapter you'll learn how, when, and where kids can best use the strategies and also how to practice them so that they become a part of the child's core skills for living.

The remainder of the book addresses a variety of circumstances. Chapter 7 is full of tips and tools for establishing a fruitful Easing the Teasing partnership between parents and educators. Chapter 8 helps children build healthy friendships that will insulate them from cruelty and teach them zero tolerance for it themselves, and Chapter 9 furthers the latter goal by presenting ways to enhance children's innate empathy and compassion and helping them learn to stand up for each other. I hope these chapters will illustrate without a doubt that, while teasing cannot be prevented entirely, there is an awful lot that we can do to discourage it and to shape a world that is much more conducive to compassion and empathy and much less tolerant of cruelty and victimization. Chapter 10 holds a wealth of success stories, told—and drawn—by children themselves; parents and educators will find these gems inspiring to kids when they're down and need a boost. Chapter 11 is for the parents of teasers who are concerned and dismayed by the discovery that their children have been hurting others and wish to do something about it.

I hope these tools help your children ease the teasing. If they do, please send me their success stories to add to the ones in this book!

Easing *the* Teasing®

1

What Is Teasing and Why Does It Hurt So Much?

"How did school go today, honey?"

"Fine, Mom. Some of the kids who hadn't seen my braces yet called me 'Metal Mouth,' but that was OK. They were only teasing."

"How did school go today, sweetie?"

"It was *awful*! I'm never going back! The other kids were teasing me about my accent all day. They kept telling me to go back where I came from, and I hate them!"

Both children in these two scenarios used the word *teasing*, but clearly they were talking about two entirely different experiences. Or were they? Teasing can be fun and friendly or cruel and hurtful—and a wealth of variations in between—but for parents it's not always easy to tell exactly what may have happened when a child reports being teased. The kids who called Nancy "Metal Mouth" might have intended to humiliate her just as the New York kids wanted to demean Lonnie by telling him to go back to Alabama. Or both groups may have meant the teasing lightly and harmlessly. The problem with interpreting these incidents is that their impact depends just as much on the victim's response as on the teaser's intent.

To complicate matters, as parents we're governed not only by love and protectiveness toward our children but also by preconceived notions about teasing that we formed from our own experiences. When you see your child trudging home, looking like she has the weight of the world on her shoulders, your instinctive reaction is, of course, concern. But what happens when she tearfully tells you that someone laughed at her leg brace and called her "Stumpy," and someone else acted disgusted by the sushi she brought for lunch? Some parents will continue to express concern and gently try to comfort the child, feeling distressed themselves because they don't know what else to do. Others express outrage and immediately encourage the child to "get even." And some parents try to shrug off the incident, telling the child not to worry about it because the teaser is "just jealous."

None of these reactions may be particularly helpful to the child beyond the moment. It will help, however, if you understand exactly what happened and then teach the child skills for coping with these types of situations. I'll tell you how to explore the incident in Chapter 4, and coping skills are offered in Chapter 6. But first, let's gain an objective understanding of what teasing is; how it differs from bullying and other types of abuse; and how, when, and why it can hurt so much.

What Is Teasing?

Teasing can take different forms, from jocular to demeaning and all the way to hateful and abusive. When I try to explain the differences to kids, I usually start by focusing on the intention of the teaser, because kids generally view teasing as something done to them. When they have been hurt by teasing, they don't want to hear that how they're feeling is at least partly in their power—and is partly their responsibility—even though that is true. I've found it very effective to explain to children that one kind of teasing, the fun and friendly variety, involves *having fun with* someone, while the other, including both the hurtful kind and the stronger abusive type, involves *making fun of* someone.

Having Fun Versus Making Fun

Having fun with someone is good-humored or playful teasing—what one first-grader referred to as "happy." Friendly teasing causes everyone to smile or laugh, including the "teasee," the person who is teased. It is kidding and joking around. Everyone thinks it's funny. Fun and friendly teasing is a sign of friendship. It's not offensive and does not damage a child's self-esteem.

Most children know that if a friend is joking around, it is usually good-humored. Also, they usually pick up the teaser's subtle cues via the tone of voice and facial expressions, such as winking or smiling. When Jimmy was giving his book report in front of the class, his best friend, Jonas, made faces at him. Afterward, they both laughed about it, but Jimmy might have found these funny faces distracting and annoying if delivered by someone else. The existing relationship definitely matters. Two fifth-grade boys who are best friends recently told me that they constantly tease each other for fun. They enjoy each other's sense of humor and they're having fun.

I probably don't have to tell you that you're not likely to hear about this kind of teasing from your children. Obviously, children don't come home upset about the humorous bantering or joking that is often part of their daily interactions with friends. Most children, in fact, wouldn't put this kind of joking and clowning around in the same category as what they view as teasing. When I ask young children if teasing is ever fun and friendly, the majority say "no." They're often surprised to learn that joking around can be called friendly teasing, because they generally perceive the act as negative and hurtful. It's important, however, for kids—and parents—to understand that there is a positive kind of teasing because it is often part of successful social intercourse.

One particularly beneficial form of teasing can even bond a group together. It involves drawing attention to the lighter side of a situation and helping people share their humanity with each other. A teacher might set an example for her class by poking fun at herself. She might say, "I guess I forgot to eat my Power Bar this morning," when she drops all the books on the floor, or "Yes, boys and girls, we seniors are incredibly sharp at all times," when she forgets to collect yesterday's homework assignment and pass out today's. Adults in a group setting can aim the same kind of affectionate "we're all in this together" teasing at a child, but they have to take great care that everyone is in on the joke and that the teasing does not in any way denigrate the child's character, personality, or physical flaws. Obviously this takes wisdom and finesse, and many teachers are afraid to try this for fear of failing and hurting the child.

The benefits can be sizable, however, and for this reason all adults should help children distinguish between the benevolent and malevolent forms of teasing by modeling humanity-sharing, gentle teasing. Children who learn to laugh at themselves have a powerful weapon for fending off teasing by others. Beating others to it by making fun of yourself is one of the best ways I know to protect yourself and earn the affection and admiration of others. Being able to laugh at yourself demonstrates a very likable humility. I know a teacher named Bobbie Kott who describes how this kind of teasing benefits a group. "It can lighten the load of a rainy, work-filled day. It can bring a smile to a child who may have serious problems at home. It relaxes the atmosphere in the classroom, which makes true learning possible."

In contrast, if your child comes home upset that a classmate made fun of him on the playground or gave him a hard time on the bus, you can assume that he has either experienced hurtful teasing or has taken it in a belittling or degrading way. What we usually mean when we talk about negative teasing is making fun of someone with the intent to hurt or provoke a painful, emotional response, though it's important to understand that not all teasing that stings is intended to do so. Hurtful or cruel teasing includes ridicule, name-calling, put-downs, verbal insults, and gesturing, as well as annoying actions. Cruel teasing occurs when the teaser successfully finds the sore spot of his intended victim. Unlike the friendly and good-humored variety, hurtful teasing often causes the victim to feel sad, angry, upset, afraid, embarrassed, or helpless. It becomes harmful if it causes distress and pain for the teasee.

The Teasing Continuum

Unfortunately, no general rule of thumb exists for when teasing is likely to become harmful because not all kids will take the same statement, gesture, or other behavior the same way. If we view teasing along a continuum, we'll find plainly affectionate, friendly teasing on one end and hostile teasing on the other. In the middle might be teasing that can be either friendly or unfriendly, depending in part on how the teased child reacts. Some kids will tease a classmate or playmate as a type of test of the child's mettle. If the child reacts with poise or humor and obviously refuses to be intimidated, the teasing might either end immediately or turn into joking banter. If the child cowers or cries, the teaser, encouraged by the sense of power gained, might turn cruel. Or if the child reacts aggressively, the teaser might feel challenged and push the teasing toward the meaner end of the continuum.

Teasing Versus Bullying

If we stretched the teasing continuum a little further to the hurtful end, we'd run into bullying. Some experts view the difference between teasing and bullying as only a matter of degree. The key difference that is emphasized in the literature is that bullying is characterized by the persistence of the attacks. When cruel teasing and taunting occur repeatedly over a period of time, they can be considered abusive. This hostile teasing includes tormenting, harassing, or verbal bullying. According to professional literature, bullying is ongoing and frequent and includes verbal taunting, name-calling, threats, stealing, and acts of physical aggression. Dan Olweus, who has researched bullying extensively, states that "a student is being bullied or victimized when he or she is exposed repeatedly and over time to negative actions on the part of one or more other students." Bullying is also characterized by an imbalance of power. The bully is usually bigger, older, stronger, or smarter, and the intent is to exert power over the victim.

Bullying may in fact begin with mild teasing as the bully carefully searches for a vulnerable target. Once the bully gets a rise out of his or her target, the teasing usually becomes more intense and persistent. This is why it is so important for parents to do what they can to accurately assess the situation when a child complains of being teased. A clear and thorough understanding of the situation will allow you to choose the appropriate, effective response. If your child is truly being teased in a hurtful way, now is the time to put a stop to it, before it turns into bullying. When children are able to respond to mild teasing with the tools and words that empower them to react quickly and confidently, they are not likely to become victims of bullies.

If your child is being bullied, your response should be different from the strategies proposed in this book. Kids can learn to handle most teasing situations, but they need adult assistance or intervention when they are subjected to repeated or prolonged hostile and aggressive behavior or when they do not feel physically or emotionally safe. Consult your child's teacher, school administrator, mental health professional, or local law enforcement official to help you develop an appropriate course of action to end the bullying or harassing behavior.

What Typical Hurtful Teasing Looks Like

In my observation over the last seventeen years in elementary school settings, the most typical teasing situations involve name-calling, ridicule, or put-downs. This type of incident is so common that when I ask students in first through fifth grades, "Who has ever been teased or made fun of?" almost every hand goes up. The prevalence of this behavior has been confirmed by virtually every teacher, administrator, and parent I've spoken to from other schools in Illinois and throughout the country.

Parents frequently ask me if teasing is in fact on the rise. This is very difficult to measure. Informally, however, I perceive that disrespect is on the rise in our society. Kids are more disrespectful to each other, and it is not uncommon for some kids to speak disrespectfully to adults such as parents and teachers. Colleagues have told me they have noticed more parents speaking disrespectfully to teachers and school administrators as well. It's not hard to imagine what kind of message this behavior sends to our kids. (More on how kids mimic the disrespectful, hurtful behavior—like teasing—that they see around them and what we can do to reshape such models can be found later in Chapters 3 and 11.)

Perhaps the prevalence of this kind of behavior explains why bullying has gotten so much attention lately. Where we have definitions of bullying, however, we lack them for teasing. (Some sources you will encounter as you read about teasing and bullying treat the two as synonymous, so even if you feel your child has a problem with teasing but not with bullying, you may be able to gain useful information from articles and books on bullying.) I think this is in part because the harm that teasing can do has only recently gained notice. It's also, however, due to the subjective nature of teasing. That's why when we are trying to define teasing, it's important to find out what kids think it is.

When I ask children to define teasing, their answers include "name-calling and being laughed at," "something that abuses another person," "being insulted," "being rude to another person," and "something someone says or does to another person that is hurtful." Most elementary school–age children explain that teasing is "when someone gets made fun of."

The type of teasing that you and I—and our children—are concerned about is cruel teasing, taunting done with an intent to hurt. Kids certainly understand that this form of teasing is undesirable and ideally should be stopped. What's a little harder for them to grasp is that whether teasing hurts is largely up to them. Sometimes they are hurt by teasing that wasn't intended to harm at all. And even teasing that is meant to hurt does not have to. So, while many of the ideas in this book are aimed at discouraging children from teasing, the intent of the teaser isn't the most important factor to consider. The strategies focus primarily on the response of the teased child. Children who learn these coping skills will feel less hurt when someone teases them with the intent to harm, and they will eventually learn not to overreact to teasing that falls toward the benign end of the continuum.

Why Teasing Hurts So Much

It doesn't take much thought to understand that teasing hurts because it makes us feel diminished, demeaned, devalued, and somehow unacceptable. But because we adults had to learn to deal with it in the school of hard knocks, and probably view it as one of those inevitable evils of growing up, we sometimes brush past how and why it stings in our rush to solve the problem. Yet a thorough understanding of why people react to teasing as they do is an essential ingredient to finding the best solutions.

Experiences in infancy, toddlerhood, and early childhood lay the foundation for a child's personality and identity. Obviously, a child who has had positive emotional and social experiences will emerge with a confident and assured sense of self. Positive feedback from others nurtures and shapes a child's developing identity and personality. Kids who are on the receiving end of frequent hurtful comments and negative feedback from others are at risk for emerging with a weaker sense of self and a lack of appreciation for who they are. Children are like dry sponges. They quickly absorb acceptance and approval, and they can be just as quick to soak up rejection and disapproval.

The development of identity in childhood is dependent on the feedback of others. Kids learn to see themselves as others see them. Parents, teachers, and classmates evaluate them. Their self-esteem is influenced by the positive regard and approval they receive from others. Children who hear remarks that make them feel they are not as "good" as others might develop a fragile self-concept. They will most likely be more vulnerable and susceptible to negative comments or criticism. They may begin to experience feelings of inadequacy and self-doubt. Parents who understand how damaging this can be will not minimize the hurt that teasing inflicts, expecting their children to "toughen up" or "shrug it off" on command. By the time Mom and Dad hear about it, their son or daughter may already believe too much of what a teaser says.

As parents, we may find this possibility hard to believe. Haven't we been lavishing praise and encouragement on our kids from the moment they were born? Don't our kids feel good about themselves because we take every opportunity to affirm their value and their uniqueness? Thanks to our love and care, many kids do start school with a background marked by automatic and unconditional acceptance by those around them. This arms them with strength and self-confidence, but it also leaves them unprepared for being perceived or judged according to their abilities, merits, and behaviors, without the soft filter of familial love.

Children begin to compare themselves to others in the classroom, on the playground, and in gymnastics or dance class to assess their own abilities. They also begin to identify and assess their peers' skills. A child might conclude that a classmate is a great reader but is terrible at baseball. Each child is jockeying for position in the classroom, on the playground, and elsewhere outside of home. We need to explain to them that everyone has unique strengths and weaknesses. They can't be good at everything, and they shouldn't be ashamed of their innate qualities. At the same time, we are in a unique position to help them find their niche. Children who don't find it are especially vulnerable to criticism and certainly to the perceived humiliation of any teasing aimed at them. The first inkling of teasing should be a cue to start boosting a child's self-worth.

But, even kids who do find a niche may be harmed by the unexpected blow of criticism or any remark that smacks of rejection. We need to ensure that our kids understand that people outside their family may be less inclined to be kind and affirming. We need to help them navigate the rough waters of peer scrutiny by assuring them that they *are* lovable and by telling them in no uncertain terms that no one has a right to treat them disrespectfully. More on how to talk to your children about being victims of teasing is in Chapter 5.

Oversensitivity and the feeling of not belonging can definitely stay with kids as they grow. Many adults, who have emotional scars from childhood ridicule and teasing or who do not feel good about who they are for other reasons, are more vulnerable to negative remarks in their adult life. On the other hand, one mother told me that she had endured so much harassment in her junior high years that the rest of her life has felt like "a piece of cake"!

I'd like to give children the skills that can make childhood too seem like a piece of cake. The strategies in Chapter 6, when learned and used proactively, not only help kids respond to teasing in a healthy way, but they also make them feel good about themselves in general. The coping skills contribute to self-esteem and self-confidence and help children find that happy place where they can retain their individuality while also fitting in.

What Makes Some Kids More Vulnerable to Teasing Than Others?

Nine-year-old Susan was the only girl on a park district baseball team. Not surprisingly, a few of the guys on the team made comments about this, from teasing her about hiding her ponytail under her baseball cap to looking like one of the guys in her uniform. Susan responded with a smile and later told her parents that she thought the attention the boys were giving her was "kind of neat." Her enthusiasm for the games continued, and her first Little League experience was very enjoyable and successful.

Susan's classmate, Alexandra, was the only girl on her team as well. She also was teased by her fellow players, but she found their remarks very annoying. Those comments also affected her ability to play. Alexandra complained to her parents that the boys on the team were giving her a hard time. She thought they were always staring at her when she was up to bat and secretly laughing at her, hoping she'd strike out, which made her nervous. Alexandra pleaded with her parents to let her quit.

What made Alexandra so much more sensitive than Susan? Why was she more susceptible to this somewhat typical teasing than Susan was? To put it simply, some kids have "thicker skin" than others. What is hurtful teasing for one child may not be hurtful for another. There can be several reasons for this.

How Is the Child's Self-Esteem?

A child's perception of and reaction to teasing often depend on his or her self-esteem. A child with a positive or healthy self-esteem usually demonstrates more effective coping skills in teasing situations. A child who feels good about himself is generally more socially secure and confident. If your child has been victimized by a teaser, you're probably already noticing the irony in this setup. Being teased can lower a child's self-esteem, but children with low self-esteem are more likely to be teased. If you can determine that any low self-esteem exhibited by your child is strictly a product of being teased, then the teasing should be your target. But low self-esteem in children can be caused by a variety of other factors (and, no, not all of them are your fault), and you might want to see what else in your child's life might be chipping away at his or her self-worth. See Chapter 4.

If you're not sure whether your child is suffering from low self-esteem, here are a few examples of behaviors to look for:

- Not being able to pat herself on the back
- Having difficulty accepting and believing compliments
- Being tentative and afraid to take risks
- Having trouble making decisions

Sensitive, passive, and vulnerable children tend to react to teasing with hurt feelings, crying, anger, physical complaints, fear, or feelings of helplessness. Their self-esteem may be weak, which means they are more likely to believe what the teaser is saying. This further reinforces their negative feelings about themselves. Kids who do not feel good about themselves are less secure and more anxious than other kids. They often lack social skills, or they are socially immature.

Does the Child Tend to Be Sensitive or Moody?

Self-esteem is not the only factor that can increase a child's vulnerability to teasing. Some kids might be called "high-strung" or "temperamental." These kids seem hypersensitive to many things—loud noises, changes in routine, and definitely criticism, which is likely how they will view teasing. A moody child might be unpredictably volatile—caught at the wrong moment, he may be infuri- ated by the mildest teasing. As part of a child's innate personality, temperament can't necessarily be changed, but being aware that a child tends to be irritable or sensitive can help parents anticipate problems with relatively mild teasing incidents. On the other hand, preteens and teenagers are notoriously moody during those years; they are likely to react strongly to teasing, but this tendency should pass.

Is the Child Ill or Under Stress?

Children who are sick, overtired, or emotionally distressed may react more strongly to teasing than they would at other times. Overreact- ing should be a passing response unless the condition is chronic.

Is the Child Younger or Less Mature Than Classmates or Friends?

A lack of maturity compared to their peers is another factor that may make children more psychologically vulnerable to teasing. As chil- dren grow, they develop a huge repertoire of coping skills whereby they nurture their own self-image and protect themselves from all the potential ego blows of the world around them. Kids whose devel- opmental age—or actual age—is a little younger than that of their classmates or neighborhood friends may be more prone to be hurt by teasing than others.

Is the Child an "Only"?

I've observed that many children who do not have siblings have a harder time with put-downs or insults in school because they haven't become inured to them at home. (Exposure to teasing at home doesn't always have a positive effect on children, though; see Chap- ters 4 and 11.)

How Teasing Evolves with Age

As I said earlier, before they start school, most kids are used to being the apple of their parents' eyes, perfect in every way. Entering school (especially if they don't have older brothers or sisters) can be a rude awakening, and they will automatically become upset when called a name or ridiculed in any way. Innocent of even the "having fun with" kind of teasing, they may react with hurt to any critical or negative words. Some children quickly jump to the conclusion that "no one likes me" because they simply don't get what was intended to be a joke.

Unfortunately, their anger and tears may provoke more teasing, this time with more intent to hurt. Although there are no clear-cut timetables that define the ages when kids engage in teasing behaviors, many kids are cruel at a very early age. Some experts believe intentionally hurtful teasing begins in the toddler stage, while others claim that it does not begin until kids are cognitively mature enough to understand the feelings of others. Preschoolers say funny and absurd things that are not necessarily targeted at anyone. They are often experimenting with words they have recently learned. Dr. Dorothea Ross states that this kind of teasing is actually important and constructive because it provides practice in enduring the name-calling experiences that will undoubtedly occur in kindergarten.

When children enter elementary school, they engage in playful and hurtful teasing. They learn that school offers many opportunities to tease. Many young children don't know the meaning of the words they use to tease or ridicule, and they don't often realize the impact of what they say. They think it is funny to rhyme a word with someone's name, as in the case of the second-grader who was called "Fartin' Martin." A third-grader received a note that said, "Roses are red, Violets are blue, No one wants to sit next to you . . . because you have dog breath." Many young kids also think it's funny to spread the rumor that someone has cooties or germs.

Teasing becomes sharper and more biting as kids' cognitive and verbal skills mature and their vocabulary expands. As boys get older, their teasing often includes challenges about masculinity. Boys who are small and not athletic are likely targets, as are boys who are more creative and artistic. Girls and boys who are "just friends" are often teased. Laura and Bradley had been very best friends since they met in second grade. But when they played together at recess and took gymnastics classes together in fourth grade, they were treated to a lot of ridicule, including the age-old ditty:

Laura and Bradley sitting in a tree
K-I-S-S-I-N-G
First comes love, then comes marriage
Then comes Laura with a baby carriage.

Fortunately for Laura and Bradley, their friendship survived, but it doesn't always go that way.

As kids reach middle school or junior high, teasing may take the form of flirting between girls and boys. It's usually intended as playful teasing but can be felt as annoying. Even in fourth and fifth grades, boys and girls tease each other for attention. Interestingly, the recipients often feel ambivalent. They usually complain about it, yet they often appreciate the attention.

According to Frank Vitro at Texas Woman's University, kids experience the most severe level of self-consciousness in fourth and fifth grades. They compare themselves to their peers in terms of appearance, athletic and intellectual abilities, and popularity. Dr. Vitro states that the sharp focus on their self-consciousness can result in insensitivity to others. I've also observed that it can result in oversensitivity toward being teased by others.

As kids mature, empathy continues to develop, and middle school and junior high students are less likely to ridicule characteristics that are not within one's control. They usually demonstrate more empathy toward those who are physically or mentally challenged. Yet the teasing that continues in the adolescent years is likely to become increasingly hurtful. The teenage teaser becomes expert at pushing the buttons that reach the specific vulnerability of her victim. This can be excruciating for the teasee, who at this stage is certainly more sensitive and vulnerable to negative comments from peers because of the dominant and overpowering need to "fit in" and be accepted.

Parents should also be aware that junior high often brings sexual language and behavior into teasing. This is not only inappropriate but also can constitute sexual harassment. Twelve- and thirteen-year-old boys often focus their teasing and comments on developed girls their age. The same boys can be cruel to boys who are smaller than those of the same age or who lag behind the others in reaching puberty. For kids on the cusp of puberty, such treatment by the opposite sex can be quite damaging.

The Hurt of Prolonged Teasing

As we'll discuss in Chapter 3, children generally tease for the anger or tears they can provoke, not because they really care about the teased child's weight, unusual name, or new hairstyle and not because they sincerely believe that having an accent or wearing a leg brace makes a child inferior. So when victims of teasing have strong emotional reactions, they are adding fuel to the fire: the teasing not only continues but also often escalates. This is not intended to blame the victim for the abuse suffered. My point is that teasees can be taught that they have more power than they may believe. Sometimes all they need to do to put an end to teasing is to refuse to give the teaser what he or she wants most (the goal of most of the strategies in Chapter 6). Other times it's more complicated than that: some teasers are particularly persistent, or the child hasn't learned coping skills before the teasing has had a chance to become entrenched.

Mild effects resulting from occasional teasing can become severe when a child is a victim of prolonged taunting and verbal abuse. Physical complaints can develop into physical illness. Sporadic academic difficulties can evolve into more ongoing learning problems. Occasional nervousness and worry due to teasing can lead to acute anxiety and chronic stress. Mild and moderate anger can increase to rage and violence. Persistent and chronic taunting, harassment, and verbal bullying can lead to emotional despair and depression. Feelings of helplessness can evolve into hopelessness and sometimes result in suicide.

Over time, what started as verbal taunting can evolve into exclusion, rejection, and spreading of rumors, especially among girls. It's heartbreaking to hear a child say, "No one ever wants to be my partner in gym class," or "As soon as I sat down at the lunch table, the kids moved to the other end." Collective rejection of this kind can be devastating and can leave lasting emotional scars.

When kids are ridiculed and teased on an ongoing basis, it is typical and predictable that they do not want to go to school. How would *we* feel about going to work day after day if someone at the office was ridiculing and belittling us? Trying to avoid or escape a stressful situation is understandable when you hear kids describe their anguish.

Kevin, a second-grader, was teased about the way he handled a ball in a game of kick ball during recess and was excluded from playing by some bossy classmates. School officials found Kevin leaving school on his bicycle before recess was over. He said that he just wanted to go home because he hated recess.

Nine-year-old Sally was told by a classmate that she sang off-key in a music program. The classmate suggested that Sally just move her lips and not sing out loud. All of a sudden, she made excuses for not going to school on the days that she had music.

Other children go to school but react to teasing with behaviors that are both worrisome and troublesome. Eight-year-old Daniel is a very bright boy who has attention deficit hyperactivity disorder (ADHD). He is an easy target for teasing because he usually reacts impulsively and emotionally. It's very hard for him to stop and think before he acts. Daniel's reactions contributed to his frustration and isolation. He began paying other kids to play with him.

Jonathan, age eleven, was teased about going to the nurse for the medication he needed for his attention deficit disorder (ADD). He tried to avoid taking his medication at school to prevent the possibility of embarrassing comments from some of his classmates.

When eight-year-old Paula was ridiculed about her glasses, she took them off and refused to wear them at school.

Dawn, age thirteen, had many friends and never experienced social difficulties until she became a victim of teasing and verbal harassment in seventh grade. The teasing intensified as the year continued. Her resulting depression required medication and psychotherapy.

It is believed that Eric Harris and Dylan Klebold, the teen gunmen who killed twelve students and one teacher at Columbine High School in Littleton, Colorado, in April 1999, were seeking revenge for the ridicule, teasing, and insults they experienced. Witnesses reported that as the gunmen opened fire with their semiautomatic weapons, they said, "This is for all the people who made fun of us all these years" (abcnews.com). On March 25, 1994, fifteen-year-old Brian Head cried out in his classroom, "I can't take this anymore!" He killed himself with a single gunshot. His parents learned that Brian was a victim of harassment, humiliation, and bullying at school. Nathan Faris, who was an excellent student and slightly overweight, experienced extensive teasing, harassment, and humiliation at his elementary school in DeKalb, Missouri. Kids called him names such as "Walking Dictionary" and "Fatso" on the playground and school bus. The taunting and peer abuse increased in junior high school. When Nathan was twelve years old, he sought revenge when he took a gun to school. He killed a fellow student and then himself in his history class.

These extreme examples illustrate the despair, distress, and excruciating pain experienced by some kids who are teased, harassed, ridiculed, and verbally bullied over a long period of time. Tragically, many parents never know that their children are suffering in this way. Many kids who endure taunting and ridicule don't want to tell anyone. Some are embarrassed at being in this predicament and find it difficult to admit what is happening. Other kids think that telling someone is tattling, which will only make the situation worse. But when they tell you what's happening, you are in a position to help.

So as hard as it is to hear about these hurtful experiences, be thankful that your kids are sharing them, because this knowledge gives you the opportunity to help your child develop essential coping skills, such as those in this book.

As I said at the beginning of this chapter, it's hard to tell what's really going on when your child comes home complaining of having been teased. It's important to look at the child's mood, the situation, the child's temperament, and other factors to assess what types of interactions might be occurring out there beyond the sanctuary of your own home. Don't overreact or react reflexively. Nor should you shrug off a complaint that sounds "silly" to you. The range of things for which children are teased is surprisingly huge, and just because what your child is being taunted about sounds like nonsense to you doesn't make it hurt any less. The next chapter will help you understand what your child is going through by exploring what children are teased about.

2

---◆---

What Are Children
Teased About?

"They teased you because you like egg salad sandwiches for lunch? What do you mean you haven't eaten your favorite sandwich since then? That's silly!"

"You don't want to wear your Michael Jordan jersey anymore because it's too long? But you *love* that jersey more than anything else in your closet—you go ahead and wear what you like and never mind what anyone else says."

"Of course you have curly hair—so does your grandmother and your mother and all of your aunts. You should be proud of your heritage, and you may say that to those rude children!"

Too tall, too small; too smart, not smart enough; too quiet, too loud—there probably isn't an adult alive who escaped being teased for some physical attribute or unconscious behavior at some point in childhood. But many adults, including me, are amazed by the huge range of other things about which children are teased.

Kids are teased about anything and everything. No trait, characteristic, or situation is spared. If your child is being teased, you may find comfort in realizing that other kids are being teased about the same things that your child is tormented for—or about something very similar. You and your child are hardly alone. Read through the quotes from kids in this chapter and you'll see how pervasive teasing on all subjects really is.

You might also be reading this book because your child has a difference that you fear he or she might be teased about. Experts agree that differences invite comments and teasing from peers, and you may very well find your child's unique or unusual quality in the pages that follow. It's important to know, however, that *kids with a difference are not necessarily teased.* Whether your child will be targeted depends on many factors, some of which were introduced in Chapter 1, others are discussed in Chapter 4. The thought to hold on to is that you and your child can do a lot to protect him or her, whether it is using the types of coping skills offered in Chapter 6 or taking steps to enlighten the children and adults with whom your child has daily interactions.

The following are my observations about what kids are teased about, along with quotes from the kids themselves about their experiences. If you're a parent, knowing that nothing is sacred will probably help you listen to a child's complaints about teasing with an open and empathetic mind. If you're an educator, I hope this list will help you stay alert to the many instances of teasing in our schools and inspire additional efforts to address the problem.

My experience with elementary school–age children confirms what the experts say: being different is the basis of most remarks, opinions, and judgments that are intended or taken as teasing. Beyond that, however, it's hard to quantify which differences are most likely to be targeted. Since no scientific studies have been done to come up with data, I decided to compile a "Top Ten" list of the differences in characteristics, attributes, and abilities that I've found children are most likely to be teased about. Unfortunately, I didn't know how to rank them, so I decided to go directly to my most reliable resource—kids. I conducted a survey of third-, fourth-, and fifth-graders at my school to find out what they thought were the most common objects of teasing. A colleague at another school surveyed a class of thirty eighth-graders. The results of both surveys follow, and my comments on the results are incorporated into the discussion of each of the Top Ten.

Before I distributed the surveys, I specifically clarified what each item on the list meant. I then asked the students to rank the Top Ten in descending order, from what they think kids are teased about most to the least. Because the resulting order is based on their perceptions, it may not be accurate at all. It could reflect instead what kids are most sensitive to; we all tend to remember the incidents that hurt the most. Or it could reflect what attributes elementary school kids consider most important. Ask your own children how they would rank these items and you might get a completely different answer—and some interesting insights about those unique individuals in your family.

The Teasing Top Ten

1. Appearance
2. Abilities—physical and intellectual
3. Identity—gender, race, religion, culture
4. Behavior
5. Family circumstances
6. Possessions
7. Opinions
8. Names
9. Feelings
10. Friends

The question was "What do you think kids (in general) are teased about the most?"

Third-Grade Girls

1. Appearance
2. Names (a close second)
3. Behavior
4. Feelings
5. Abilities
6. Identity
7. Opinions
8. Friends
9. Possessions
10. Family circumstances

Third-Grade Boys

1. Appearance
2. Behavior
3. Names
4. Feelings
5. Abilities
6. Possessions
7. Friends
8. Opinions
9. Identity
10. Family circumstances

Fourth-Grade Girls

1. Appearance
2. Feelings
3. Abilities
4. Behavior
5. Names
6. Identity
7. Friends
8. Opinions
9. Family circumstances
10. Possessions

Fifth-Grade Girls

1. Appearance
2. Abilities
3. Behavior
4. Identity
5. Friends
6. Feelings
7. Possessions
8. Opinions
9. Names
10. Family circumstances

Eighth-Grade Girls

1. Appearance
2. Abilities
3. Opinions
4/5. Feelings/Friends (tie)

6. Possessions
7. Identity
8. Names
9. Behavior
10. Family circumstances

Fourth-Grade Boys

1. Appearance
2/3. Feelings/Behavior (tie)

4. Names
5. Abilities
6. Identity
7. Friends
8. Possessions
9. Opinions
10. Family circumstances

Fifth-Grade Boys

1. Appearance
2. Abilities
3. Behavior
4. Identity
5. Friends
6. Possessions
7. Feelings
8. Opinions
9. Names
10. Family circumstances

Eighth-Grade Boys

1. Abilities
2. Behavior
3. Appearance
4. Opinions
5. Feelings
6. Friends
7. Possessions
8. Identity
9. Names
10. Family circumstances

Appearance

Children's powers of observation are critical to their ability to learn. Discerning differences and noticing similarities help them make sense of the world around them. Unfortunately, this facility also means that kids' acuity is razor sharp when it comes to visible differences in appearance among their peers. Whether it's about weight, glasses, freckles, or a physical disability, kids are frequently ridiculed about appearance. In fact, for every group surveyed except the eighth-grade boys, appearance was ranked number one among objects of teasing. Teasing is aimed at both innate characteristics that can't be changed, such as height, and appearance factors that can be controlled, such as clothing.

Interestingly, I had always gotten the impression from classroom discussions that boys felt more attention was paid to their abilities (or lack thereof) than to their appearance, but on these surveys it became clear that appearance is a big concern to them. Perhaps they simply feel more comfortable talking about abilities, but when they can express themselves confidentially, in writing, they feel freer to acknowledge being teased about appearance. Because this is a small sampling, it's difficult to draw any reliable conclusions. Girls, not surprisingly, said on the survey what they say out loud as well: they are teased most often about their appearance.

One thing you can't see on the surveys (though you'll undoubtedly notice it in your children) is that the focus on appearance sharpens in fourth and fifth grades, when looking "cool" is more important than ever before. In fact, the numbers from the surveys, which I haven't supplied here, showed that more kids ranked appearance number one in fourth and fifth grades than in third grade. According to this one very limited survey, appearance continues to get a lot of attention for girls, but less so for boys, by eighth grade. Kids compare their appearance to others on an ongoing basis. Hairstyles and clothing fads, from designer jeans and shoes to trendy jewelry, are top priority and often elicit a direct remark or a whisper about an apparent difference.

Kids of all ages talk about being made fun of about their size—their weight or height. Children in fourth and fifth grades begin to focus and make comments on whether their peers have started to develop physically. It's always difficult to be the first girl in class to start wearing a bra. Women who had this dubious honor have told me they were sure "everyone" was staring at them, which only made them more sensitive to any comments from others. The late bloomers have similar stories, of course. If you're the parent of a middle-schooler, you should probably be prepared for your "perfectly normal" daughter to feel anything but. As the following comments illustrate, however, kids are teased about their size at every age:

- "I'm six years old, and I'm bigger than most kids in my class. Two boys in third grade call me 'Fat Girl' on the bus. I wish I weren't fat. I hate riding the bus."
- A ten-year-old girl acknowledged, "I know that I'm overweight. I can't help it. Kids always tease me . . . even kids who don't know me. Why do kids have to keep teasing me about it?"
- "I'm very short—probably the shortest kid in my class. Kids call me 'Shrimp' and 'Midget.' I wish they would leave me alone."
- "I'm tired of being called the 'Jolly Green Giant.'"
- "I hate having to walk by the boys on my way to gym class. They all stare at my chest as I go by, and then I hear them laughing hysterically once I'm past them. It makes me feel really bad."

Other obvious differences about appearance that kids are often teased about are glasses, freckles, ears, hair, and teeth. Some children receive stinging insults about their crooked teeth or overbites, while others are ridiculed about their braces. These comments from kids are very typical:

- "When I was in third grade, someone made fun of my glasses. I decided not to wear them anymore because I didn't want to be teased."

- "I have a lot of freckles on my face. A girl in my neighborhood said that I have so many freckles and asked if we could play dot-to-dot."
- "I have to wear a patch on one of my eyes. A boy in my [first-grade] class teased me about it."
- "Kids make fun of my ears, which stick out. Someone said they look like wings."
- "Just because I have long hair, kids say I look like a girl."
- "Kids tease me about my buck teeth and call me 'Chipmunk.' "
- "When I got my braces, someone called me 'Metal Mouth.' Other kids laughed. Someone else called me 'Brace Face.' "

Dr. Dorothea Ross, a psychologist who has done extensive research on teasing and bullying, asked a group of children with leukemia to talk about the worst pain they experienced. Instead of describing pain related to their treatment, they explained that the worst pain was going back to school and being teased about their appearance—their baldness and extreme paleness.

Differences in appearance are usually obvious and hard to deny or refute. Kids who have not comfortably accepted their physical difference will be more sensitive about the trait or characteristic and, therefore, experience more hurt from heartless remarks. Conversely, kids who have learned to live with their difference more comfortably will deal with a teasing situation more confidently.

In the summer of 1999, I presented a workshop for children who are burn survivors at an annual camp sponsored by the Illinois Fire and Safety Alliance. The camp staff refers to the children as burn survivors, not victims. Yet many of these children have extensive scars and disfigurement and are victims of pointing, double takes, and stares, in addition to cruel and insensitive comments. One of the counselors told me that when he was growing up, many kids were merciless in their ridicule, and he remembers even many adults keeping their distance because of his extensive scars. The counselor felt gratified that he could help the kids who might be going through what he did. As for me, I hope that the Easing the Teasing strategies will empower such kids. I feel bad when any child is teased about anything, but my heart goes out to kids who are ridiculed about a chronic disability, deformity, disfigurement, or illness that they are coping with on a day-to-day basis. Fortunately, these children can lessen the hurt they feel, even if they can't always expect compassionate treatment from those around them.

Abilities or Disabilities

Children with differences in their physical and intellectual abilities are also prime targets for needling and belittling comments.

Physical

Because it has always been my impression that boys are teased more about what they do rather than how they look, I was surprised to see what my first attempt at measuring this turned up. Boys who are small, shy, or weak or who don't fit the "macho" image are common victims of teasers and bullies in all grades. Nicknames such as "gay," "sissy," or "girl" are used for boys who don't fit the male stereotype, whether it relates to physical image or physical abilities. But, as the survey affirms, it may be that as they get older boys are more and more likely to be teased about their abilities and less and less about their appearance. This may have to do with low tolerance for a lack of athletic prowess once boys have participated in organized team sports for a number of years, but again, it's hard to draw solid conclusions from this small sampling of children. See what your children think of these comparisons.

I've heard the following complaints, among many others, about kids making fun of other kids' physical abilities on the playground, the baseball field, in the gym, as well as in the neighborhood.

- "I struck out with the bases loaded. A kid on my team said I was a loser because I caused the team to lose the game."
- "No one throws the ball to me when we play football at recess."
- "My next-door neighbor made fun of me because my bike has training wheels."

- "At my school, if you're no good at basketball, you're nobody."
- "A mean kid at my school called me a 'sissy' because I'm not that good at sports."

Fine motor skills also draw attention, as in the case of Brian, a first-grader, who was sad and distracted when kids at his table laughed when he wrote some of his letters backwards. Second-grade classmates made fun of Bianca and her Velcro shoes and she was embarrassed that she could not tie them.

Intellectual

Some kids are mocked about their weak intellectual or cognitive abilities, whether they demonstrate academic difficulty on a day-to-day basis or whether they make a glaring mistake in front of the class. Students who receive special education for learning disabilities or speech and language problems might be teased because of their differences. Other kids are put down about their academic achievements. Again, any deviation from the norm draws attention from peers.

- "My brother always brags that his grades are better than mine."
- A first-grader complained, "Most of the kids in my class read better than me. A few kids laugh at me when I read."
- "Kids call me 'Brain' because I'm smart and like to answer my teacher's questions."
- "Sometimes when I get nervous, I stutter. Kids begin to laugh, which makes me more nervous."

Identity

Many children are teased about who they are in regard to their gender, race, religion, or culture. Boys who don't conform to the masculine stereotype or girls who don't exhibit feminine characteristics will be the topic of discussion for some teasers, especially in middle school and junior high. Gay bashing, whether based on accurate knowledge of a person's sexual orientation or mere supposition, is an unfortunate fact of even elementary school life. Differences in skin color, religious practices and traditions, and cultural beliefs can elicit caustic comments and vicious slurs. I know kids who have been teased because they speak two languages or because they have accents. This may vary, however, depending on the setting. In the two schools where the surveys were done, identity was ranked fairly low as an object of teasing. This could be because both schools are fairly homogeneous in many ways, or it could be that there is just enough diversity for the children to be more comfortable with these differences. There is no way to tell.

Sadly, though, teasing about these differences in the school setting is a reflection of our society in general. Prejudices, stereotyping, and stigmas regarding cultural, racial, religious, and sexual differences should alert us all. As parents and teachers, we must continue to celebrate diversity and to model appreciation and respect for these differences (see Chapters 9 and 11 for more on positive modeling). And if your children are potential targets for teasing or slurs aimed at their identity, you should prepare them. Do what you can to make sure their self-esteem and self-confidence remain high (see Chapter 4). Also teach them the strategies in Chapter 6 as prevention. A parent of two adopted Chinese children explained that the Easing the Teasing strategies helped her children nip in the bud some teasing about their heritage before it had a chance to evolve into anything truly hurtful.

Behavior

Behavioral differences, from being extremely shy and timid to being very loud and boisterous, invite needling and jeers. Nose picking, loud belching, incessant talking, slurping, and being a poor sport are just a few behaviors that draw peer criticism and ridicule from elementary school–age children. When kids can no longer tolerate the offensive behaviors of peers, they often make unkind remarks or exclude them. In many cases, they do so out of frustration. I know of several kids who tried to approach classmates about their behaviors. When their attempts were unsuccessful, their unkind comments or rejection increased. In fact I've found it much more difficult for peers to accept behavioral differences of classmates than differences in appearance, abilities, or identity. Kids feel these differences are largely controllable and don't understand why kids continue to exhibit offensive behaviors.

In many cases they are right: kids *can* decide to stop picking their nose or to start cleaning up their table manners. But sometimes the behavior is unconscious or they don't know any better. In these cases it's up to the parents to help them make a change. See Chapter 4 for suggestions for helping kids overcome correctable behavior problems. Behavior problems can also stem from mental and emotional disorders, which may require a sensitive approach by everyone.

Interestingly, the girls in the eighth-grade class surveyed ranked behavior ninth, while the boys ranked it second. This may have something to do with the fact that by age fourteen many girls' public behavior is more regulated and thus interpreted as more mature than that of boys the same age.

Family Circumstances

Differences in family circumstances or situations are not overlooked by curious and often insensitive peers. Kids who split their time between their divorced parents and others who live with only one parent are sometimes the targets of unkind remarks. Over the years, a few students have told me about their hurt when they were ridiculed about their handicapped siblings. Nine-year-old Maggie was reluctant to invite friends over to play after one of her schoolmates made snide comments about her younger autistic brother.

Melinda, a Vietnamese six-year-old, was questioned about why her mom was white and older than most of the other moms. I have found that children in kindergarten, and first and second grades are often curious and don't know how to react when they encounter a classmate who has a different family circumstance. The typical questions and comments that arise are sometimes taken as hurtful remarks. Young children often feel helpless because they can't change their situation and usually don't know how to respond. It's important to note, though, that family circumstances were ranked a consistent tenth for all four of the grades surveyed. Most children seem to know that making fun of one's family is hitting below the belt. One eighth-grader added a comment to this item on his survey: "It's just *too* mean."

Possessions

In our material world, children are teased about what they have and what they don't have, whether it's the deluxe box of crayons or the latest gym shoes. Until teachers got wind of the plan and put a stop to it, one class of middle school girls had hatched a scheme to ostracize any girl who didn't wear Guess? jeans to school the next day. Younger children label certain possessions as "babyish." Second-grader Paul loved his Power Rangers lunch box, but a few of his classmates thought it was for kindergartners. Carrie liked to bring her favorite stuffed bear with her in her backpack. When her locker partner saw it, she laughed hysterically and whispered to everyone that Carrie was a baby. Jo was excited when her parents bought her a scooter. Her excitement over riding it to school for the first time was suddenly squashed when two of her neighbors said in a condescending way that her scooter was not like theirs. To make it worse, they made fun of Jo's helmet.

As previously mentioned, fourth- and fifth-graders, especially girls, become more focused on what their peers wear. This focus magnifies in middle school. Catty statements are made about styles of clothing, types of fashion jewelry, and stores in which their peers shop. Kids may be teased about not having the same style or brand of clothes as everyone else or for being "posers" and wearing the same clothes or hairstyles as the cool kids. The unusual outfit that makes one girl a trendsetter would make another a "dork." Teasing can be direct or behind the victim's back.

I recently heard a wonderful statement in the video *I Was Just Kidding* that sparked a lively discussion in a fifth-grade class: "When you are concerned with labels, you are really labeling yourself."

These are just a few of the statements I've heard from children who were made to feel different and inferior because they did not have what most other kids did.

- "I don't have cool gym shoes. Kids say that my shoes suck."
- "My neighbor told me that my bike is weird because it doesn't have hand breaks. I wish I could get a new bike, but I can't."
- "A few girls told me that I couldn't play with them because I didn't wear the right kind of jeans."

Opinions

Other children are teased about what they like and what they don't like. Kids often criticize peers who like books or television programs that are geared toward younger children. Other kids will put down peers for their opinions about games, what they like to play at recess, or what they like to eat. Middle school and junior high kids might tease each other for liking music that's not considered cool at the moment. When Jason was teased about his egg salad sandwich, he refused to bring it for lunch again. Being criticized for their unique likes and dislikes can stifle kids' individuality and discourage their personal growth. Notice how opinions jumped up higher in the rankings in eighth grade: a comment about the growing importance of peer connections that is seen in junior high.

Names

Many adults remember to this day how they were teased about their names. Rhymes or jokes about names can stay with you in your mind long after your path parts with the teaser. One of my best friends, Myrna Lynch, remembers chants of classmates in junior high school, "Let's lynch Lynch." I know a teacher named Helen who recalls, "Go to HELLin." My friend Chris remembers becoming worried about whether she was fat in third grade when a classmate started calling her "Crisco—fat in the can," even though she was of average size.

Kids are still often ridiculed about their names. Lily was upset when a boy on the bus asked, "Hey, Lily, do you smell like a flower?" I think she felt worse about it because she's named after her grandmother. Matt, who is overweight, is referred to as "Fat Matt." "Rob the Slob," "Odd Todd," and "Harry the Fairy" are just a few derogatory nicknames that can stay in kids' minds for a long time.

Mocking someone's name is a fairly immature form of teasing, however. Notice that it drops down to number nine for both boys and girls in the eighth-grade class surveyed.

Feelings

"Crybaby" and "Scaredy Cat" are common names kids are called to make fun of their feelings. If a young child is teased about something and begins to cry, the first tease is usually followed by "Crybaby." Jake is a third-grader who has a short fuse. He explodes easily, especially when things don't go his way. Kids began calling him "Volcano Boy," which made him more upset. When children exhibit a fear of something, they're often referred to as a "Scaredy Cat" or "Chicken." Kids of all ages are teased about "liking" someone of the opposite sex. Now that society has begun to value emotional as well as mental intelligence, teasing about feelings is clearly destructive. Kids who are taunted about their emotions may begin to deny their authentic feelings about many events.

Feelings were very close to the top of the list in the fourth-grade class surveyed, perhaps because fourth grade is a time of transition. It's the first year when crushes develop among many groups. Fourth grade is a year when, many teachers report, the cooperative, congenial third-graders of last year seem to explode in a frenzy of emotion and energy. In fifth grade, feelings were ranked sixth and seventh, but by eighth grade they were back up to fourth and fifth.

Friends

Some children are criticized about their friends. They are mocked for talking to or playing with classmates whom the teasers either don't like or regard as weird or unusual. "How can you be friends with that geek?" In these situations, the teasees may feel torn. Do they stand up for their friendship, or do they decide to give up the friendship to avoid the teasing? This is a real dilemma for some when there is such a powerful need to be accepted and fit in. And it only gets worse as kids mature and begin to form boy-girl relationships. Kids

who feel pressured to "dump" a young crush because he or she isn't "cool" or "hot" get the message that it's not their own feelings about people that matter and that the criteria for affection are superficial. As we know, peers become more and more influential and more and more important to children's daily lives as they mature. This fact is reflected in the way friends crept upward on the list toward eighth grade, though they remained in about the middle.

Let's hope kids who are teased about their friends will stand up for their friendships confidently and assertively. See Chapter 9 for advice on helping kids support each other despite peer pressure from teasers.

It doesn't take much imagination to look through the Top Ten list and see that each item is an area of great importance to growing children. How they look and what they can do or achieve, what their heritage is and who their family is, how they act, what they own, what they think, what they are called, how they feel, and who their friends are—these are the cornerstones of a child's world. Mock them, debase them, belittle them, and you tear down everything the child knows and values and threaten the child's very sense of self. Why do children do this to other children? There are many possible reasons—we'll consider them in Chapter 3.

3

---◆---

Why Do Children Tease?

When Louis came home angry because Josh had razzed him all day about his new gym shoes, it wasn't too difficult for either Louis or his father to figure out why Josh had started the teasing. Josh had gotten a new pair of gym shoes the week before and had been making the most of the attention the other kids gave him for having the latest Nikes. Now their attention had turned to Louis, whose Air Jordans were proclaimed even cooler. Josh was angry and envious and used teasing to try to put Louis back in his place.

When eight-year-old Jamie suddenly started picking on Alicia—she was too slow in gym, she chewed her sandwich with her mouth open, she looked like a toad—Alicia tearfully told her mother she couldn't understand why Jamie would say things like that to her, especially because none of them were true. Alicia's mother wisely asked if Jamie had anything to be angry at Alicia about. After some prodding, Alicia said that Jamie had been one of the few girls in the class that Alicia had not invited to her birthday party, but she had been very careful to pass out the invitations when those not invited weren't around, so she was sure Jamie didn't even know. Jamie did know, and she reacted to her hurt and anger by attacking Alicia in any way she could think of.

For both Louis and Alicia, understanding why they were being teased helped ease the pain. When attacked by a teaser, many kids have a hard time distancing themselves from their own pain and the injustice of the attack. But their maturing minds have a great capacity to grasp logic, and when they can see that *A* led to *B*, their outrage and hurt often dissipate.

Understanding why they were teased also gave both kids the impetus for problem solving. Alicia took Jamie aside on the playground and privately told her she was sorry she couldn't invite her to her party but her mother would let her have only a certain number of guests. That was enough to satisfy Jamie, it turned out, and the teasing ceased.

Louis had to exercise a little more creativity and subtlety. First he tried responding to Josh's teasing with "You're just jealous, dude, 'cause my shoes are better." But that only seemed to make Josh's teasing more vicious. So Louis thought about how Josh's pride had been hurt by his shoes being compared to Louis's. The next time Josh pushed him aside in the lunch line and said, "Your ugly feet are in the *way*, man," Louis said, "I didn't even hear you coming, man, those shoes are so fast and quiet." "That's *right*," said Josh, and he left with a high five and a conspiratorial smile.

Alicia and Louis had it relatively easy. They were teased in response to an easily identifiable event and could take action to resolve the problem pretty quickly. Children often tease each other to get revenge, to express anger, because they're envious, or because they've been hurt by something or someone. But not all teasing can be traced to such obvious and immediate causes. Children tease for a multitude of reasons.

Teasing to Gain Personal Rewards

To put it simply, some children tease others because doing so makes them feel good—or because they think it will.

"Look at Me!"

The desire to get attention is an enormously powerful force behind all kinds of childhood behavior, as any child therapist or social worker will tell you. Kids have been known to turn themselves into the class clown, perform reckless physical feats, and risk punishment at school or at home just to put themselves in the spotlight for a moment. All of these actions seem foolish at best to adults, but to kids the laughter and applause of their peers is a coveted reward. As they grow, all children struggle to find a comfortable niche in their social world, one that makes them feel good about themselves. It can take a while for them to find ways to maintain positive self-worth that isn't inextricably tied to the acceptance and approval of others. In the meantime, getting attention is often translated as being well liked, and being well liked means having worth.

To adults there is, of course, a difference between making faces behind a teacher's back to elicit the giggles of classmates and tormenting another child about some perceived flaw. In the teaser's mind, however, there's always a chance that teasing another child will evoke admiration from others, who will see that the teaser is tough and apparently self-confident enough to take whatever response the teasee delivers. Unfortunately, that belief is often borne out and will continue to be until we teach our children the importance of being supportive and compassionate toward each other, which is the subject of Chapter 9.

Many adults are baffled by the cases when teasing brings the teaser nothing but negative attention—disciplinary action from teachers and other supervising adults, avoidance by many children who are afraid of becoming the next victim, and active dislike by those who are more self-assured. Why would a teaser who gets only this kind of reaction continue to tease? The simple answer is that, unfortunately, for many children, negative attention is better than no attention. Children tend not to simply shun someone who is behaving in ways they don't like; they are usually very verbal and even physical in demonstrating their disapproval. To a teaser, being called names may very well be preferable to being treated as if he or she is nonexistent—any spotlight is better than the shadows. This is why a basic strategy like ignoring the teaser (see Chapter 6) can be so effective in stopping a child from teasing altogether.

A child might resort to teasing and might settle for negative attention for several reasons. He or she might have been taught that this type of attention is desirable, either by society or at home, both of which I'll discuss a little later in the chapter. In my experience, though, the most likely reason for the teasing is that the child has weak social skills and therefore has been unable to relate or connect with peers in a positive manner. Numerous factors contribute to the development of social skills, from temperament to intelligence to the examples set by parents and other role models to mental health problems. Some methods for helping the teaser replace negative attention seeking with social competency are in Chapters 7 and 11, but parents and teachers should always be alert to the possibility that help from a social worker or psychologist might be warranted.

"I'm Better Than You"

Some kids just seem to need a lot more attention than others. As a casual observer, you'll probably find it difficult to determine why. Some children simply seem to have a more fragile self-esteem. Maybe they are timid by nature and not so sure of themselves or their standing in their social world. They might have suffered some kind of damage to their self-esteem that you can't see on their faces or in their behaviors. Whatever is at its root, the need for attention can be translated into a need to feel not just worthy but superior.

Many teasers simply feel superior when they put others down. They often feel better about themselves when they can make others look worse. Teasers feel powerful when kids react emotionally or physically to their teasing. It is as if some teasers have a remote control. They know where to point the control and which buttons to push. Their emotional payoff is provoking tears, anger, fear, or distress, which contributes to awesome feelings of power and superiority. What an ego boost for the teaser!

Evidence in schools and in research indicates that being aggressive is "cool," and that kids who put others down and tease often receive admiration and gain popularity because of their hurtful behaviors. It is very difficult for us to explain to our children that "popular" children are not always nice children. In Chapter 8, I discuss ways to help your child form good friendships, where mutual affection and companionship are based not on the compulsion to belong and to be popular but on shared interests and caring for each other. It's disheartening that some children engage in teasing behavior because they perceive it as being the "cool" thing to do. We can work with our schools to change this perception. See Chapter 7 for ideas.

"I Was Only Kidding!"

Many kids who tease, ridicule, or name-call will try to excuse themselves and escape the consequences of their actions by claiming that the whole incident was a joke. They were only kidding, they didn't really mean it, it was all just good fun. They might try to turn the tables on the teasee and express indignation at any offense that is taken. "Chill out—can't you take a joke?" seems to be the stock escape route for junior high students who realize they've gone too far and want to save face and retain their "cool" image. Needless to say, most of the time teasers are not "just" kidding. Teasing is often a passive-aggressive way of getting to someone—cloaking an insult in a joke so that the teaser doesn't have to take the consequences for meanness. The best way I know to make it clear to the teaser that the teasee is not being fooled is for him or her to bypass accusations about intent and simply state how the teasing made him or her feel. See Chapter 6 for more about "I" messages.

In a way, though, many teasers are engaging in these behaviors simply for the fun of it. This is related to the idea that teasing makes them feel superior and powerful. Teasing someone and getting the expected emotional reaction is like being a puppeteer pulling someone else's strings. It's not one of our most admirable human instincts, but it's one we sometimes have to own: watching the puppet dance is entertaining and fun. Children who claim with wide-eyed innocence that they tease only to have fun can learn that manipulation of others, especially hurtful manipulation, should be avoided. Empathy is the key. See Chapter 9.

"Don't Get Mad—Get Even!"

I'm sorry to say that I have met many parents who don't care if their kids get in trouble for teasing in response to being teased. In fact, they want their children to get even. Research and current events indicate that many kids resort to violent behavior because of the longing and need for revenge against peers who have ridiculed and tormented them.

In these cases, children don't initiate the teasing but react with hurtful behavior to get even or seek revenge. "I called him names, but he called me names first. I just want to get even." Kids often feel that teasing is justified as long as they didn't start it. Any parent or teacher can tell us that kids use this excuse to absolve themselves of responsibility for all kinds of misbehavior, from hitting to stealing to gossiping. Sometimes the fact that they get in trouble themselves teaches them that "He started it!" is never an acceptable excuse for their own misdemeanors. If not, it's up to us to teach them this tough lesson. See Chapters 7 and 11.

As the story of Jamie and Alicia illustrates, kids also initiate teasing sometimes because they are hurt or angry about some slight or other perceived offense. If they are indirect, as Jamie was, the victim may have no idea why the teasing has begun because it seems unrelated to any harm the teasee might have inflicted on the teaser. To Jamie, being excluded from Alicia's party merely confirmed the message that she felt she received often from her peers—she wasn't very popular because she wasn't very likable. In truth, many kids liked Jamie but found her "moody." When Jamie felt she was being slighted by the other girls, she tended to act surly, and then naturally her fear about being unlikable became a self-fulfilling prophecy. Her social skills definitely needed some work. But being excluded from a party that *everyone* was whispering excitedly about seemed like an especially hurtful offense to Jamie, so instead of withdrawing, she attacked. Alicia, unfortunately, had no idea what was going on—until she got some help in figuring it out from her parents. The entire episode might have been avoided had Jamie been able to tell Alicia how she felt about being excluded, an important skill that is introduced in Chapter 6.

"You Make Me So Mad!"

Many kids, unfortunately, don't know how to express their anger in appropriate or constructive ways, and so, as Jamie did, they resort to name-calling and ridicule when they have been hurt. Poor anger control is a common problem among children, and teasing and taunting are common ways that kids act out their angry feelings. Many of us are familiar with adults who have never learned to control their anger, and the repercussions for their inappropriate expressions can be very damaging in the grown-up world. Poor anger control should be spotted and addressed quickly by teachers and parents because it tends to get children stuck in a vicious circle that is hard to break. Many kids need to unlearn certain behaviors that have become bad habits. When Jamie was particularly hurt by some affront by her classmates, she struck out as she did with Alicia, and this behavior only further isolated Jamie from many of her peers. The more isolated she felt, the angrier she got . . . you can see where this will lead unless someone who can help intervenes. Tips for helping your child with anger control are in Chapters 4 and 11.

Sometimes children are angry about something that has nothing to do with the children they are teasing. When ten-year-old Max suddenly started lashing out at school—picking on the first-graders he passed in the hall, harassing boys for missing a pass or an easy basket, calling the girls "ugly witches"—the kids didn't know how to react. Max had always been easygoing and friendly. At first the teachers tried the usual stern admonishments, but Max just seemed oblivious. Fortunately, his teacher realized something must be wrong and investigated. It turned out that Max's parents were going through a difficult divorce, and he was having a hard time adjusting to the major family change. Max's life had been turned upside down. He was very angry that his parents no longer loved each other. Max was not able to tell his parents about his angry feelings because he thought they would get mad at him. His aggressive behaviors at school were symptomatic of his anger about the divorce.

What could Max's teachers do? His teacher referred him to me, and I talked to Max about the divorce, encouraging him to talk about the situation, how it had affected him, and how he was feeling about it. I conveyed an understanding of his feelings and assured him that they were normal under these circumstances. Although we can't change a situation for a child, actively listening to his feelings and conveying empathy can be very comforting. Because Max was relatively mature and intelligent, I encouraged him to talk to his parents about his feelings. I then met with Max and his parents to further discuss the importance of recognizing and understanding his feelings. I also suggested that Max participate in a divorce support group that I facilitated at school. It took time, but Max began to feel a little better, and as he did, he eased up on teasing the younger kids. In fact, by the next year he had become something of a champion for younger kids who he thought were having emotional difficulties of their own, passing on what he had learned in the support group.

As a parent, you can use an opportunity such as this one to instill empathy in your children while you try to resolve the teasing dilemma. If your child tells you that someone who "used to be nice" is suddenly not, suggest that the child might be going through some kind of troubles. Give the child the coping skills included in Chapter 6, but also see if there's an opening for your child to ask the schoolmate what's wrong. Whether this idea will be received well by your son or daughter depends to a great extent on the history of his or her relationship with the teaser. Unless he or she feels some connection to the teaser, your child may not feel comfortable reaching out in this way. Whether this approach will end up working also depends on a number of factors, such as how old the kids are and how open the teaser is or can be about what is going on. Some children are told by their parents not to discuss their family problems with anyone else, and other kids just are not comfortable talking about personal matters at school. They should not, of course, be pushed to do so.

How Society Sanctions Teasing

Children also tease because society tells them it's OK to do so—or at least fails to tell them it's wrong.

The Low Value We Place on Self-Control

Where do kids learn how to express their anger appropriately? Unfortunately, in our society today, rage is all the rage. Road rage is an alarming element on rush-hour highways. Air travel seems riskier now that passenger rage seems to be on the rise. Our entire society reflects poor anger control. Many outraged people resort to violence to get rid of their intense anger. The anger and violence are all around our kids and ourselves in the daily news, movies, television, and video games. Models for appropriate conflict resolution are few and far between. No wonder kids are aggressive toward each other. What we need to do is to supply them with the models that unfortunately seem so scarce today. Try making a news story or a neighborhood event into a teachable moment. Talk with them about what happened and what might have caused the person to feel so angry. Then discuss what the person could have done instead of acting out that anger in a negative way.

A Model of Meanness: Cultural Messages on TV, in the Movies, and Elsewhere

We hear and see all the time how violence in the media influences our kids' behavior. So many television programs geared toward children are riddled with teasing, put-downs, insults, disrespect, and other forms of so-called cleverness that are reinforced by bursts of canned laughter and applause. Our kids couldn't receive a louder message that they're supposed to applaud too. Cartoons are filled with mean remarks and actions. Children often copy the offensive humor that they see and hear on television or in movies. In fact, kids perceive it to be acceptable because of its frequent occurrence. Often no clear boundary exists between what is funny and what is disrespectful. Adults are exposed to this belittling humor very frequently on late-night talk shows. Cruel ridicule of people is supposedly humorous. Candidates who are participating in national elections are primary bait for comedians. Political campaigns filled with name-calling and put-downs toward opponents serve as poor examples for our children. Chapter 9 contains some ideas for monitoring your children's media influences and making them aware of the negativity of some of the messages they are getting.

Our Failure to Celebrate Diversity

Many children don't encounter or understand cultural, ethnic, or physical differences, and when they do, their uneasiness sometimes leads to a negative judgment. Some kids alienate, exclude, or avoid children who exhibit a difference, while others ridicule them or make insulting or abusive remarks. Discriminating and hurtful remarks often result from fear and insecurity.

Parents need to promote a healthy curiosity about differences, which should enhance understanding and diminish children's fear of the unknown. Chapter 7 suggests reading selections that parents can use as a great springboard for discussion about differences, as well as ideas for teachers to promote an appreciation of diversity among their students. Chapter 9 also includes advice on fostering empathy in children. The most effective device, however, as always, is the parents' own example. If you treat others with an innate respect for their differences, your children are likely to do the same.

The Examples We Set at Home and in the Neighborhood

Some children treat classmates or neighbors the same way they are treated at home. They imitate what is happening to them. These are children who may be taunted by their siblings or perhaps put down by parents. Jessica, age nine, was quite critical of her classmates and frequently called them names. She ridiculed them in- and outside of the classroom. She was quick to exclude the girls and talk about them behind their backs. I learned from Jessica's parents that she was frequently the target of teasing and verbal abuse by her two teenage sisters. Apparently she was engaging in the same behaviors and patterns that were occurring in the relationships with her sisters. Jessica felt powerful when she imitated her sisters at school.

Some children enjoy teasing their younger siblings and treat their classmates the same way. Seven-year-old Alex was the oldest of three boys. His parents said he often was quite bossy with his younger brothers. He liked to call them names and tease them. Alex continued these verbally aggressive behaviors with his peers on the playground and on the bus.

Children who experience harsh or abusive parenting may exhibit aggressive behaviors at school. Joey, age nine, frequently fought, verbally and physically, on the playground. I met with him to try to explore the possible causes of his aggressive behavior. At first he was very quiet, and then he broke down in tears when he shared that his stepdad was mean and criticized everything he did. Joey said that his stepfather constantly made fun of him. He felt humiliated, helpless, and depressed. His aggressive behaviors at school were imitating his stepdad's behaviors and were the result of his underlying feelings about what was happening at home.

Do you criticize others with biting words or dirty looks either directly or behind their backs? Is this behavior a pattern in your personality? Kids not only model how their parents treat them but also how their parents talk about other people. Some parents habitually criticize or comment negatively about other people's appearance, habits, or behavior. They make rude, offensive, and insulting remarks about friends, acquaintances, or strangers. Kids tend to model the judgmental behavior they live with and observe from day to day.

As parents, we try hard to set a good example for our children, and it can be painful to turn a harsh light on ourselves and see if we are inadvertently setting a pro-teasing example for our children. More help for parents of teasers can be found in Chapter 11.

A Word About Young Teasers

Children tease each other for many reasons, in infinite variations. But keep in mind the age of the teaser if you're trying to determine why someone may be teasing your child. In my experience, very young children, say first grade and younger, often tease for no reason—at least that they are aware of or that anyone else could pinpoint with certainty. In fact, many don't realize the power of their words or actions. Their teasing is usually not meant to be intentionally hurtful. In some situations, young children don't even know the words they're using. They often repeat what they hear others say without fully understanding what the words mean. I've seen this happen even with older kids. I encountered a fourth-grader who was calling another girl a "slut," and it turned out she had meant little harm—she thought a slut was simply someone who kissed boys.

In my opinion this is most likely another case of children following the poor examples that are being set, emphasizing the importance of setting a zero-tolerance policy for harmful teasing in our own behavior. But, when you're talking to your child who has been teased, you might tell him or her that it's entirely possible that, if very young, the teaser truly does not mean any harm, in which case the "I" message can be the perfect response; see Chapter 6.

In summary, it's often helpful to discuss with your son or daughter why a particular child might be behaving in this hurtful way. Although this does not condone or excuse the behavior, an understanding of the teaser's motivation often helps the teasee see the situation differently. Helping your kids understand the motivation of teasers reassures them they are not to blame.

4

Exploring the Teasing

Why Is Your Child Being Teased?

Dear Judy:

My children are going through a really tough time. My son is in sixth grade and my daughter is in fifth. They both had many wonderful friends up until fifth grade. We are in a Catholic school, so they are still with the same group of kids through eighth grade. I felt so happy for them to have such good friendships. The problem seemed to start as each child reached fifth grade. The kids they were so close to for six years all of a sudden have turned on them. My son suffered humiliation as his friends left him out of games and teased him about everything from his clothes to missing homework assignments. At times it even got physical with kicking him when he was down during recess football and stabbing him with a pencil.

Now my daughter is in fifth grade, and three of her closest friends have told her they can't be her friend anymore because she is not a popular kid. I had to pick her up from school the other day because she was so upset by the third blow. My kids are good kids. My husband and I give them lots of love, nice clothes. They participate in sports, music, and any other activity they want to try. Yet I feel we are somehow letting them down. We did not give them what they needed.

I have taken a lot of psychology courses in college and I have told them things such as ignoring the teasers, or say "so what" and not let anyone see it is getting to them. I also talked about the benefits of a positive attitude and that they don't need friends who treat people like that. I don't think anything is helping. We are about to pull them out of the school and start over. But isn't that just teaching them to run away from their problems? I am overcome by a terrible sadness. I was not popular as a child and teased all the time, and although I think it made me stronger in some ways, I also feel bitter. I don't want my kids to grow up with that pain. How can I help them?

Sincerely,

Tanya

This letter, like so many others I've received over the years, poignantly expresses the pain and helplessness that parents feel when their child is being hurt by teasing. It also illustrates how memories of having been teased themselves can heighten parents' negative reactions to their child's predicament—as well as the parents' desire to intervene effectively.

If your child is being teased, whether or not the teasing has reopened old wounds of your own, you want to "kiss it and make it better." Unfortunately, a simple kiss usually won't do the trick because the teasing might occur again. You need to find out exactly what's happening and why.

Preliminary Detective Work

Obviously, your very first source of information will be the child who has come home complaining about being picked on. Chapter 5 tells you how to communicate productively with your child about teasing, from what's happening and why, to what the two of you can do about it. But in many cases conversations with your son or daughter won't give you all the information you need.

Brianna, a sixth-grader whose mother was being called a drunk by the girls in the class, wouldn't hurt her mother's feelings for the world. It was up to her mother to find out that Brianna's recent sullen gloominess was due to vicious teasing by her peers—and this she discovered only after persistent probing. She had to ask her older niece, who was a close confidante of Brianna's, to find out why her daughter seemed so down. From her niece she learned that the story being passed around among the girls was that Brianna's mother was constantly being seen going in and out of the town's bars during the day. Brianna's mother was the sales rep for one of the major soft drink manufacturers that supplied all the area's taverns, and the ringleader of Brianna's tormentors, a girl who had competed unsuccessfully against Brianna in the student council election, had gotten this story from her older brother. If Brianna's mother hadn't gone to her niece, she never would have found out what was happening to her daughter and what the source of the rumor had been.

Nguyen, age six, came home crying one day and complaining that everyone on the playground was "mean" to him and called him names. But that's all he would say, even when his father pressed him for more information "so I can help you solve the problem." Finally Nguyen's father called his teacher to ask her if she'd noticed anything unusual going on. The teacher wasn't aware of the abuse Nguyen was suffering on the playground, but she was able to tell Nguyen's father that he had a bad habit of picking his nose, which the kids had noticed. I've known several kids who have been ridiculed for nose picking, a behavior that turns off kids of all ages. Obviously Nguyen knew why he was being called names but was embarrassed to tell his dad.

Danielle was a fountain of information when her parents asked her to tell them all about the teasing that had been bothering her for the last week. They now knew exactly what the teasers had said to Danielle, who the offenders were, when the teasing occurred, who witnessed it, and how Danielle had responded, in words and actions. What they didn't know was that the little girl they thought they had taught so well to stand up for herself was languishing in the shadow of her older sister, who was in all honors classes in high school, a champion figure skater, and, as Danielle put it, "prettier than Britney Spears." Every time Danielle compared herself to her older sister, she found she was falling short. Now she was carrying this feeling into her relationships with her peers. Everyone else, she believed, was "cool" while she was a "dork." It didn't take long for her classmates to agree with her, and now one of them had begun preying on the weakness that Danielle perceived in herself.

In each of these cases, what the child told the parents was incomplete. Nguyen told his father he was being teased but wouldn't tell him what he was being teased about. Danielle told her parents everything about the teasing but couldn't reveal how she was making herself vulnerable to it because she didn't understand it herself. Brianna couldn't even tell her mother how she was being treated; she only demonstrated a big change in mood and attitude. If Nguyen's father hadn't talked to the teacher, he wouldn't have been able to help him stop picking his nose. If Brianna's mother hadn't asked her niece for input, she would never have known that her daughter was being taunted. If Danielle's parents hadn't taken the time to observe her behavior in a variety of settings, they never would have enlisted their older daughter's help in boosting Danielle's self-esteem.

Sometimes parents need to do some detective work to get the full story and solve the problem. If you think you know as much as you need to to help your child, you may wish to turn to Chapter 6 and start on the coping skills that can help ease the teasing for your child. If these strategies don't end the teasing or help your child cope with it, you can step back and investigate why your child has been chosen as a target. Here are various avenues for exploration.

Talking to the Teacher (or Scoutmaster, or Coach . . .)

When is it appropriate to call your child's teacher (or whatever adult is in charge where the teasing is happening)? Contacting the teacher may be the first thing you consider or the last, depending on the personalities involved and a host of other variables. Generally, parents will confer with others when a child frequently complains about being teased and when they sense that the child is feeling more and more helpless or stressed. If your child is exhibiting the symptoms described earlier in the book—trying to avoid going to school, making physical complaints, demonstrating a change in mood or the desire to do things—you will want to take action of some kind, and for many people the teacher or other adult in charge is the obvious place to start to gather information.

Before you try this tactic, however, consider your child's feelings. Older children are often loath to have their parents contact the teacher about any problem. They may hate the prospect of drawing more attention to themselves than they are already getting. Or, they may fear that the news of a parent's call to the teacher will get back to the teaser and only make matters worse. They might view this as tattling and fear that it will make them look even more contemptible. If you plan only to ask the teacher for understanding of the situation, and not intervention, you may be able to talk to the teacher without letting your child know; only you can decide. But some parents are reluctant to bring the situation to school officials' attention because their children have already begged them not to tell anyone what they are going through. If you feel you must talk to school personnel and must let your child know you are doing so, emphasize—as I do—that this is reporting, not tattling. You can also ask that the principal or teacher preserve your son or daughter's anonymity.

Before contacting the school, consider what you know about the teacher's attitude, the school's philosophy, and your current relationship with both. Have you established a rapport with the teacher? Did the teacher invite parents to come to her with concerns at the beginning of the year? How responsive was he when you asked for help or information in the past? Is the school heavily involved in issues of socialization? Does the administration seem interested in and current on various social concerns? Does it take a proactive approach to establishing a nurturing, accepting, and positive atmosphere?

If the answer is "no" to any or most of these questions, you may not get the response you are hoping for when you contact the teacher. Even in the best of circumstances, there is no guarantee that any adult you talk to will take the problem seriously. Many adults, including teachers and school administrators, believe teasing falls into the category "kids will be kids" and that it is just part of growing up. They might believe that kids need to work these situations out without adult help. Others might simply respond that they haven't observed what you are describing. What do you do if you run into a brick wall like this? Obviously you'll have to resort to other sources of information, such as those described in the sections following this one.

Ideally, however, the teacher or other adult will welcome your communication, explore the situation with other school personnel, and talk to the children involved in a discreet way. To set out on the right foot, start by calling your child's teacher at a time you know is convenient or by leaving a message asking the teacher to call you when he or she is free. Many schools are now online, and leaving an E-mail message gives the teacher a chance to prepare to talk to you on the phone at a later time.

Basically, you want to know if the teacher has observed any of the incidents your child has described. So it's very important that you avoid any suggestion that you are calling to blame the adult in charge for what may be happening. Approach him or her with the attitude that you would like to work together to resolve the problem. You might say something like this: "I'm concerned about a situation that Jackie shared with me yesterday, in which a classmate apparently made comments to her about her learning disability. I hope you can help me understand what might be going on." By asking for help, you avoid any suggestion that you might believe the adult is at fault for not addressing the problem. By saying you're interested in understanding the situation, rather than starting out by insisting that it be stopped, you give the adult a chance to offer insight you might not otherwise gain.

Mrs. Graziano was very concerned about a situation that her eight-year-old son had recently shared with her. Carlo visits the nurse every school day right before lunch to receive his medication for ADHD. Carlo told his mom that a boy in his class had been making fun of him during lunch because he had to take medicine every day. Mrs. Graziano called Carlo's teacher to share her concerns and asked for her help in understanding the situation. Carlo's teacher said that she would bring this to the attention of the lunchroom supervisors, so they could closely observe Carlo and this classmate. She also said that she would share this with the school nurse, who could talk to Carlo about the situation. She thanked Mrs. Graziano for calling her and asked her to call again if Carlo continued to complain about being teased.

Although it's important not to put the teacher or other adult on the defensive, state in no uncertain terms that you are investigating the situation because the teasing makes your child feel emotionally or physically unsafe. If the child is afraid to ride the school bus in the morning, say so. If he is coming home starving because he throws out most of his lunch so that he can escape the cafeteria, be sure to state that. If she says she's being shoved around, tell the teacher.

Teasing most often occurs outside the classroom, so remember that some teachers may be completely unaware of taunting that your child reports is occurring "at school." In this case you can ask the teacher if she will confer with lunchroom and playground supervisors or monitors to get a better picture of what is going on in these settings. If they are not initially aware of specific teasing behaviors, the teacher should ask them to observe the child's peer interactions, very inconspicuously. Teasing may occur in gym class when class activities are not as structured. (Older kids may be teased in the locker rooms.) Usually the gym teacher can be a valuable source of information. You can ask the teacher if she would talk to the gym teacher or ask if you should call. You can also enlist the help of the school social worker or counselor, who may be better able to tell the teacher what to watch for.

Be open to whatever you might hear back from the teacher and other school personnel. Although this is unusual, you might just find out that your child isn't being teased at all. Annie, a third-grader, came home from school every day complaining about various classmates excluding her and making comments about her weight and about her limp. She complained that she was alone during lunch and recess. Understandably, Annie's mother felt helpless and was quite upset. She repeatedly called the teacher or me to talk about her daughter's situation. After much exploration and monitoring at school, we determined that Annie was fabricating and greatly exaggerating this situation. Why did she do this? It seemed to be a great way to get her mother's attention. Annie's mother was quite busy with work and volunteer responsibilities that required some evening commitments. Annie missed her mom, and she felt somewhat "neglected." She found that complaining about her social situation elicited focus and attention from her mom.

Annie's mom got very upset when she heard her daughter's complaints, insisted on pursuing them, and then was somewhat reluctant to let them go even after we had amply demonstrated that we had investigated thoroughly and that the child really was not being teased. Why? Because she had painful memories of being excluded when she was in elementary school. So, when you decide to approach a teacher or other adult, remind yourself that what you find out might make you uncomfortable in some way. Surprising news might be easier to take if you remember that your number-one priority is to help your child. Annie's mom swallowed her embarrassment by telling herself she was only trying to be a good mother and by resolving to see what she could do to make Annie feel she was paying attention to her.

Heading for the Scene of the "Crime"

There's nothing like seeing things for yourself. Some parents take this precept to heart and decide to observe their child's interactions directly, in the setting where the child reports the teasing occurs. It's not unheard of for parents to show up at school during recess to see for themselves whether and how their children are being teased. Whether the parent is behind the fence or in the center of the playground, this will most likely bring unwanted attention to your child. "Does your mom want to play with you at recess?" other kids are likely to ask. In almost every case this only makes the problem worse.

In contrast, one parent, extremely frustrated by the passive approach the school was taking with a teasing problem her kindergarten son was experiencing on the school bus, finally decided to ride the bus for a few days with her son. She confronted the older student who was making the bus ride miserable for her son. Her approach was firm and authoritative, not angry. The teasing stopped. This situation had a happy ending, but it could easily have made the situation worse for her child. This kind of intervention may work as a last resort, but I advise you to try other avenues first, as this mother did.

Observing the Child in Other Settings

Danielle's parents thought they had done everything right. They had taught their younger daughter to stand up for her rights and to reject cruelty. She knew and seemed to use the golden rule in her interactions with other kids, and she knew when and how to ask adults for help. That's why she was so forthcoming when she experienced teasing. What baffled them was why Danielle was being victimized. The teacher couldn't explain it, and it had never happened before. When I asked them if anything had changed at home that might affect the way Danielle was acting around others, they said no. So I suggested that they take a little time to observe their daughter unobtrusively. When they did, they noticed that Danielle had started to put herself down in ways they hadn't seen before: "I can't do that turn on the ice—only Beverly can do that one." "I'm sorry I got a B in science. I guess I'll never get straight A's like Bev." "Why don't they ask Beverly to do the reading in church? After all, she's the smart one."

Danielle had expressed interest in taking a baby-sitting class offered after school. Her parents thought this might be a good idea. They thought that the responsibility of baby-sitting for younger children would help Danielle feel better about herself. They also bought Danielle a journal, so she could make daily entries about something she thought she had accomplished or done well that day. Many kids begin feeling better about themselves when they see over a period of time what they have achieved. (I've recommended this technique for younger children too, having the list posted on the refrigerator as a visual reminder and reinforcement.) Danielle's parents also encouraged her to do something she really enjoyed for fifteen minutes a day.

Observing how your child behaves in settings other than the one in which the teasing occurs might give you some valuable clues about why your child is being teased. Watch how your child behaves with other children. Is he self-confident and outgoing? Shy and timid? Assertive or overly deferential? Accepting or aggressive? Kind or mean? We all hold a bias in favor of our own children, so you'll have to keep reminding yourself to let go of your preconceived notions and try to view your child objectively—no easy feat for any parent. If, in fact, you're not sure your view is accurate, try asking a friend or relative how your child seems to interact with others, making it as clear as you can that you want an honest answer because you're trying to help your child with a difficult problem.

How does your child get along with siblings or other members of the household? Is there a comfortable balance of power or a constant struggle? Open communication or silent hostility? Is your child teased at home? Does your child tease brothers or sisters?

Does your child have any bad behavior habits that he seems to adopt without conscious awareness? Are his table manners appropriate? Does he pass gas, burp, or pick his nose in front of others? Do you have to remind him of proper hygiene, or does he take responsibility for this on his own?

Does your child express herself appropriately for her age and for the setting? Or is she prone to interrupt, laugh too loudly, make odd noises, or tell bad jokes over and over?

Does your child act the same with all kids, or do you notice any difference in his behavior depending on the age or gender of the other kids? Does your child treat all kids the same way, whether they are old friends, new acquaintances, or total strangers? Is he as comfortable in these situations as at home, with family?

When you drop your child off for soccer practice or Scouts, does he rush in eagerly to join the others or hang back? Do kids gather around him or leave him standing by himself? At home, do kids seek him out, coming over to play or calling on the phone, or does your child always seem to be making the overtures?

How does your child behave in the car pool with other kids? On the athletic field? While sitting on the bench during a game? When other kids are at your house?

You may not come up with any revelations based on your observations, but many parents begin to see their children in a new light when they make a concerted effort to observe the child's behavior rather than taking it for granted. You may see something you haven't seen before, or you may notice a change from the behavior you've been used to seeing. Any change in the child's habits or daily functioning could indicate stress. And it may give you an idea as to your child's possible role in the teasing that he or she has been complaining about.

Talking to Relatives and Friends

Sometimes grandparents, aunts, uncles, and cousins can give you a fresh perspective on your child's behavior. On the other hand, they may be almost as close to your child as you are and therefore find it difficult to see the child objectively. But if you have an open and honest relationship with any of these people, it can be helpful to ask them what they see in your child—whether the child does anything that he might be teased about or whether they've noticed any recent change in his behavior. As Brianna's mother did, you can seek out a person who has a close relationship with your child to find out if anything seems to be bothering her. Or you can talk to the person who sees the child in settings where other kids are present. Maybe your mother-in-law picks your daughter up from school and takes her to the skating rink twice a week. Or your father baby-sits on Saturday afternoons and can watch your son playing with the other kids in the neighborhood. Ask what these people see and you might get some additional insights.

Talking to the Child's Peers

I've had parents ask me whether they should ask their child's friends about any possible reasons for their child being teased. I usually advise them not to do this. An exception might be a longtime family friend whose loyalty can be relied on and who knows your child well. But in other cases you could be subjecting your child to further humiliation. Your child might very well view this as a type of betrayal of the trust between the two of you as well. Because they are so self-conscious and their self-esteem is often so precarious, this tactic seems particularly risky with middle school–age children.

Approaching the Teaser's Parents

Sometimes parents of teasees want to go directly to the source, that is, the parents of the child who is allegedly doing the teasing. I must stress that this can be risky because many parents of kids who tease and taunt are often very verbally aggressive themselves. Parents of teasers tend to deny the problem. They will often project blame onto the teasee. The teaser's parent might say, "It is your child who is making my son's life miserable. He is the one who is acting like a bully. Why doesn't your kid stay away from mine?"

You may get this kind of response even if you do your best to avoid being confrontational when you call the teaser's parents. Naturally, parents don't like to hear that their child may have committed some act of cruelty toward another child, and some people are instinctively defensive. Therefore it is crucial that you begin the conversation by saying, "I am very concerned about a situation my child is experiencing, and I need your help to deal with it." Then begin as you would with the teacher—not by making an accusation and demanding an explanation or a resolution but by asking if the parent is aware of the situation and might be able to shed some light on it. You might get nothing but a denial, and if the parent doesn't offer any additional help, your conversation may very well be over. But if you already have a good or at least cordial relationship with these parents, there's a chance that you can not only find out what's going on but end up serving as successful mediators for your children. There are even parents who will thank you for letting them know about their kids' behavior.

One mother told me that her fourth-grade daughter, Hannah, who has speech and language disabilities including word retrieval difficulties, was ridiculed for several days by Jeremy, a new boy in the class. He would come up to her and say, "umm, umm, umm. . . ." Hannah felt quite upset but did not have the verbal skills or confidence to deal with this effectively. Hannah's mother called Jeremy's mother asking for her help so that her daughter could go to school without the dread that had developed. She tried to convey her feelings as a mom, hoping that Jeremy's mother would understand and empathize. Jeremy's mother appreciated the call and said that she would talk to her son about the situation. Later that day Jeremy and his mom came by with some ice cream treats as a way to say, "I'm sorry."

When Your Child's Behavior Is the Cause of the Teasing

Let me reiterate that in no case do I consider intentionally hurtful teasing excusable. Cruelty is never acceptable no matter what your child is doing to provoke the teasing. However, sometimes children's behavior does bring on the teasing, and the behavior can be changed. Here are some of the most common examples that I encounter—with some suggestions for what you might do about them.

Socially Unacceptable Behavior

Your detective work may uncover some behaviors that invite teasing. Kids who look dirty or sloppy, have body odor or poor table manners, or who are prone to temper tantrums and emotional meltdowns are regular targets of teasing. So are kids who behave in ways typical of much younger children, such as a third-grader who sucks her thumb. I have known several kids who were ridiculed about their nose picking. An eleven-year-old boy's obsessive nose picking resulted in alienation, exclusion, and negative remarks.

I knew a seven-year-old boy who wore red nail polish to school one day. A few of his classmates made rude remarks that upset him greatly. Should he conform to the general peer group norm that boys don't wear red nail polish to school, or should he continue the particular expression of his individuality? The answer has to be based on how he feels about the comments and remarks made and how much he likes his fingernails.

Eleven-year-old Danny brought his five-year-old sister's lunch box to school because he had lost his. Although I am not aware that he was teased about this, I think that a picture of Barbie on a pink lunch box might invite some comments from fellow fifth-graders.

Eight-year-old Jake was extremely competitive and lost his temper every time he lost a game or did not get his way. He was ridiculed and called "Volcano Boy."

I strongly encourage individuality and the appreciation of differences, and I advocate not giving in to peer pressure. However, it is important to assess whether your child's behavior is inappropriate or out of the realm of "normal" expectations. Is your child bothered by comments about the difference? Most young kids want to feel like they belong to the larger peer group. Although they may have individual differences, they want to feel they are similar to their peers in many ways. Conforming to peer norms becomes more important as kids get older. Children often suppress some individual traits when certain qualities or trends are valued by the peer group. There is a delicate balance between fitting in and maintaining one's individuality and uniqueness.

Eight-year-old Lev stood out among his classmates. He usually wore sweatpants and T-shirts that looked like he had outgrown them last year. His clothes contributed to his classmates' perceptions that he was "different." Lev's English-as-a-second-language teacher was able to tell the parents, in a nonjudgmental way, that perhaps wearing jeans and some bigger T-shirts would help Lev feel more like one of the kids. I have found that many parents from other cultural backgrounds are not often aware of the "styles" of their children's peer group. Some parents welcome such helpful hints, while others dismiss the issue as unimportant.

Seven-year-old Charlie's nonverbal learning disability makes it difficult for him to read social cues of his classmates. In fact, he thought it was funny when a few kids called him "Dog Breath." Charlie's mom was concerned because he said that he played by himself at recess, and his classmates never invited him over. When social concerns were discussed at a parent-teacher conference, Charlie's teacher mentioned to his mom that she didn't think Charlie was brushing his teeth in the morning. She had noticed his bad breath, which apparently precipitated the chant of "Dog Breath." Following the conference, Charlie's mom made sure he brushed his teeth and used mouthwash before he left for school. In Charlie's case, he probably enjoyed the attention when the kids called him "Dog Breath," but it would undoubtedly serve him better in the long run if he brushed his teeth before going to school.

What Parents Can Do to Help Children Change Problematic Behavior

Helping a child cease behavior for which he or she is teased can be tricky and involves at least two steps:

1. Telling the child that the behavior is the cause of the teasing and it could be stopped.
2. Finding a way to help the child remember not to repeat the behavior.

The first requires a little diplomacy, and Chapter 5 offers some guidelines. As to the second, here is a place where the teacher might be able to help, although that depends on the age of the child and his or her comfort level with the teacher. Some kids who are trying to change some behaviors will want to be very discreet about it and not involve the teacher. Even if willing, some kids will respond to a teacher's cues to stop the offensive behavior, while others won't. Visual reminders on a child's desk may be helpful for some kids.

Other behaviors may be more readily correctable at home. For problems like poor table manners—chewing with their mouth open, eating with their hands rather than using proper utensils, slurping—practice can be the key. Make sure that everyone at the dinner table uses good table manners, and reward your child for doing the same. For very young children, you might make a game of it, such as playing Simon Says. Mind Your Manners is a great board game that heightens awareness and reinforces the use of good manners.

When Kids Get Labeled

You can hope that if and when the behavior subsides, the teasing will too. This may not be the case, though, if the child has created this image of himself. It is sometimes hard to change the perception that sticks in the minds of peers. It might be especially hard in smaller schools. I know a school social worker who works in a very small school. She told me that a fifth-grader was still being ribbed about something very embarrassing that he had done in third grade. Unfortunately, kids' reputations are likely to follow them. The child who erupts like a volcano whenever he does not get his way may learn, over time, to handle his anger more appropriately, but kids may continue to exclude him from games because of his prior explosive behavior. If this has happened to your child, look to the strategies in Chapter 6 that can teach the child to prevent slights from hurting too much. This is also a place where self-deprecating humor is particularly helpful. Kids who drop antisocial behavior and then take the extra step of making fun of themselves for past mistakes often gain the admiration of their peers, and the label quickly disappears.

Dr. Jekyll and Mr. Hyde

Sometimes kids behave very differently away from home, and parents therefore have no idea that they are doing something that provokes teasing. In one situation, a mother minimized the concerns about her son's behavior that his teacher repeatedly expressed during conferences and phone calls. The second-grade teacher stated that the boy's aggressive behaviors were causing his classmates to avoid him. His mom repeatedly said that she never saw the behaviors that the teacher described. The teacher decided to invite the mom to chaperone on a field trip. Her son's behavior was glaring as he protested when he did not get his way, insisted on being first in line for the bus, and constantly interrupted others with his attention-seeking comments. His mother saw what the teacher had seen for several months.

In these cases, another perspective might be helpful. If you are inclined not to take the teacher's word for your child's behavior, ask a third party who is in a position to observe objectively.

Disabilities and Differences

Most parents anticipate trouble when their child has a disability or other difference. If you worry that your child might be teased for some such characteristic, be proactive. A mother of a child with Tourette's syndrome was concerned that he would be teased about his facial tics, so she asked his teacher if he could talk to the class about his affliction. His doing so educated his classmates, reduced their uneasiness, and satisfied their curiosity about his tics and throat noises. With the permission of his parents, information was also sent to parents of classmates, so they would be able to answer kids' questions. The same proactive approach was taken in second grade by a child who was born without an arm when he began wearing a prosthesis.

Your Child's Behavior . . . or Yours?

As hard as it can be to see your child clearly, with all her wrinkles, it's even harder to see when your own behavior might be causing a problem for your child. Gerry was constantly mocked by her fourth-grade classmates because she made frequent mention of her own intelligence and yet was always asking her teacher for help and guidance and couldn't seem to do her class work independently. Her parents, it turned out, had read a lot about giftedness and thought that Gerry fit the profile of a gifted child, but they also complied with her pleas for help with her homework. In fact she never did her homework without a parent by her side. Gerry had developed what we call *learned helplessness*. No matter how high Gerry's IQ was, she stood little chance of reaping the true benefits of her intelligence until she developed stronger self-esteem. Without it, she would continue to set herself up for the disdain of her classmates as she proclaimed her brilliance but belied it with her actions.

Julia was in fifth grade, and all of her classmates were allowed to walk home from their neighborhood school on their own. Not Julia. Her mother showed up at the classroom door every day to pick her up and walk her home. She would even appear at school during the middle of the day with a sweater when the weather got colder. If she had a sniffle, Julia's mother would bring her soup at lunch to replace the sandwich she'd packed in the morning. Julia, like Gerry, had become a victim of learned helplessness, typically asking the teacher for lots of academic help and depending on her mother to bring in the homework she'd forgotten. At first, Julia told her mother that the kids didn't like her and she was always by herself during recess. But Julia's mother called the school when she started complaining that the kids were calling her "Preschooler" and asking her at lunch where her bottle was. Julia's mother was chagrined to learn that her overprotectiveness was a big part of her daughter's problem. She felt she couldn't help herself sometimes; Julia was her only child, and she got very worried about her safety and health. We came up with a plan by which Julia's mother would back off gradually, cutting down the number of days she walked her home, until both mother and daughter felt comfortable with Julia walking by herself. She also stopped showing up during the middle of the school day. It took a while, but the other kids began to accept Julia once her mother stayed away and Julia had to take more responsibility for herself.

When Your Child's Low Self-Esteem Encourages Teasing

Part of your detective work, especially if your child is a frequent rather than a one-time target of teasing, may involve assessing how your child generally feels about himself. Kids who feel good about themselves don't make easy targets; kids with low self-esteem often do. Of course you have to address the chicken-and-egg question. If your child seems to have low self-esteem, is it because he has been taunted and ridiculed, or did an existing negative view of himself make him a more likely target?

Find out if your child is suffering from low self-esteem in general, because teasing can do further damage to the child's sense of self. A child who does not feel good about who she is and believes that something is wrong with her may believe everything the teaser is saying. It's as if she is wounded on the inside and hurtful words add salt. Whether you can see that this is happening to your child, of course, is a big question. As parents, it is often difficult to see our children objectively because our lenses are distorted, magnified, or rose-colored. An objective professional can view the situation with clear and focused eyes, providing the necessary insight and direction. Your pediatrician, school social worker, counselor, or psychologist can help you if you don't know how to answer questions like these:

- Can your child take pride in her strengths and successes, or does she constantly put herself down?
- Does your child accept or reject compliments?
- Does your child feel insecure or anxious most of the time?
- How does he handle frustration and anger?
- How does she feel about herself within the family and with her friends?
- Does your child have a negative lens through which life is viewed?

A professional can also help you determine the reasons for low self-esteem if this seems to be a problem for your child.

As with behavioral problems that might be eliciting teasing, however, you can start by doing some investigation of your own. Compare the following descriptions and see which one seems to fit your child better:

Children with High Self-Esteem

- They feel good about who they are.
- They are generally secure with themselves and proud of their accomplishments—not bragging or showing off, being conceited or feeling superior to others, but taking pride in others' accomplishments as well as their own.
- They realize their limitations or weaknesses and have a realistic perception of their abilities and qualities.
- They are able to take responsibility for their actions—positive and negative.
- They can accept successes and failures.
- They have an "I think I can" attitude and are motivated to continue their success.
- They appreciate who they are.

Children with Low Self-Esteem

- They feel and believe that they cannot be successful.
- They have negative feelings and thoughts about themselves: "I'm dumb." "I'm ugly." "I'm a loser." "Nobody likes me." "I can't do anything right." The more negative the feelings, the lower the self-esteem.
- They are often tentative about trying new experiences or tackling new challenges, afraid to take risks, and often have a hard time making mistakes.
- They are generally insecure, doubting themselves, feeling unworthy and inferior to others.
- They may be shy or quite aggressive.
- They have difficulty patting themselves on the back and may have difficulty accepting compliments from others.
- They might put others down so as to feel better about themselves.
- They often compare themselves unfavorably to others.

We all have days when we don't like something about ourselves. A person with low self-esteem has this feeling most of the time. If your child is a preadolescent, however, be aware that kids this age can be very moody, liking themselves one day and feeling insecure and doubtful the next. This may have nothing do with their level of self-esteem.

Your child's teacher may be helpful in determining your child's level of self-esteem. Why not ask, following the guidelines for contacting teachers given earlier in this chapter? Be aware, though, that generally a teacher who has concerns about a child's self-esteem will indicate this on a report card, a progress report, or during a parent-teacher conference. A child who does not feel good about himself will demonstrate symptoms within the school setting: a lack of confidence about academic ability, difficulty making decisions, frequent or chronic difficulties in peer interactions, difficulty with independent work, a need for excessive guidance and direction, a tentative attitude toward risks, and frequent physical complaints.

How to Build Your Child's Self-Esteem

Whole books have been written on this subject, so I will offer only a few suggestions here. Self-esteem can definitely be improved. In fact, parents can be instrumental in shaping a child's view of and feelings about himself. Here are a few well-proven ideas.

• **Teach your children that it is OK not to be the best at everything.** We want to encourage children to do their best, which is not the same as striving for perfection. Praise kids realistically for their accomplishments, talents, achievements, and, most important, their efforts. False praise can lead to an unrealistic view of their own abilities. Accepting your child's weaknesses will help him learn that it is OK not to do everything well. Children should not feel like failures when they make mistakes.

• **Teach your children responsibility.** Although your child may complain about her chores, they do help a child feel capable and productive. Don't forget to show appreciation for a job well done: "I really liked the way you quickly put your laundry away." "Thank you so much for shoveling the snow on the sidewalk."

• **Convey interest in what your children are doing and support the interests they choose.** Ask your child for his opinions and encourage him to express his feelings. Let her know that you value what she thinks and how she feels, even if it differs from what you think or how you feel. (Remember, respect differences.) Accept your child for who he is, including his feelings, opinions, and interests.

• **Provide opportunities for your children to make decisions and choices.** If you make every decision, how will they learn to think for themselves?

• **Don't try to protect your children from all possible discomfort or hurt.** Overprotection can give the child the message that he cannot fend for himself, which contributes to low self-esteem.

• **Help your child express his anger appropriately.** Angry feelings that are kept inside can contribute to low self-esteem.

• **Use the "I" message (see Chapter 6) with your children.** Avoid "you" statements that convey blame and can be accusatory.

• **Teach kids how to self-talk in positive ways.** See Chapter 6.

• **Make sure your expectations for your child are realistic for his age and maturity level.** Some children fall short of parental expectations that are unrealistic, which reinforces negative feelings.

• **Show love and respect to your children.** Sure, it sounds obvious, but it always bears repeating.

• **Model healthy self-esteem for your children.** Review the description of children who have low self-esteem. If it reminds you of yourself, address your own self-esteem problems.

Getting Help from the Experts

If you feel you need assistance, you might start with your pediatrician for referrals to mental health professionals—social workers, psychologists, counselors who are in private practice or work in local community agencies, mental heath centers, or counseling departments in hospitals. Some parents begin with the school mental health professional for guidance and possible referrals to community resources or private practitioners. Still, others are bound to the list produced by their insurance provider. Sometimes just talking to the child's teacher can confirm that outside help would be a good idea. Teachers can often put things in a different perspective. They may very well have had experience with kids with similar problems, and they are more objective than parents in the first place.

Some self-help books on self-esteem in children are quite good. Here are a few suggestions:

- *101 Ways to Make Your Child Feel Special,* by Vicky Lansky
- *Boost Your Child's Self-Esteem—Simple, Effective Ways to Build Children's Self-Respect and Confidence,* by Karen Ireland
- *Bringing Up Kids Without Tearing Them Down—How to Raise Confident and Successful Children,* by Kevin Leman

A terrific book to read with your kids is *Don't Feed the Monster on Tuesdays,* by Adolph Moser.

Reading can help you put your child's problem in perspective— maybe her problem is not as severe or worrisome as you originally thought. It also might give you some solid information and guidance. Self-help books can confirm that you are already on the right track. However, in no way does a self-help book take the place of professional intervention when it is necessary, just as no medical dictionary is a substitute for a doctor. If you are still concerned about your child's self-esteem, seek professional intervention. Your anxiety and worry can further impact your child's self-esteem. One of the greatest gifts parents can give their children is a chance to feel better about themselves. Of course there is also lots of self-help material available on the Internet. The problem, of course, lies in differentiating between authoritative, accurate information and irresponsible, unfounded advice. Your best bet is to look for sites run by major professional associations.

Creative but Simple

Sometimes a child can get a big boost in self-esteem from a small measure offered by parents, teachers, or others. Many years ago, I worked with Teresa, age ten, who was quite sensitive. She frequently complained that her feelings were hurt by peers and that she felt victimized. Teresa was overweight and struggled academically, which contributed to her low self-esteem. It was very difficult for her to say anything positive about herself. I decided to give her homework. I suggested that she ask her mom, dad, teacher, and other relatives to write three positive things about her in a special little book we made in my office. I began the list with three strengths I perceived about Teresa. She returned the next week with her assignment complete. Although she seemed pleased with the wonderful things that were written, I was not convinced that it made a difference in how she felt about herself—until I ran into Teresa four years later. She was very happy to see me and asked if I remembered the little book we had made in my office. She said that she keeps that list in her jewelry box.

When Your Child Has Problems with Anger

Emotional problems of many kinds can make children the target of teasing. Nancy, age eight, was ridiculed unmercifully by her classmates for being a "big baby." In fact Nancy had a mild anxiety disorder, which made her fearful and worried about things the other kids considered unthreatening. While many emotional disorders are treated with medication, a psychotherapist or social worker can be just as important to a child who has one of these disorders. The professional can help the child adjust to daily living in a way that prevents the symptoms from taking over the child's life. If your child's emotional state concerns you, get a referral to a psychologist or psychiatrist who can diagnose the problem—or assure you that nothing is wrong. The school's social worker may be of great help to a child with a difficult temperament.

One of the biggest emotional problems in teasing scenarios is anger control. Chapters 3 and 11 discuss how poor anger control can motivate a child to tease and what parents of a teaser can do to solve the problem. But poor anger control can also make a child the target of teasing. Anger management, like self-esteem, is the subject of many books, so I won't go into detail here. Suffice it to say that many children are ostracized or taunted because they simply can't control themselves when frustrated and angry. Teasers, seeing this lack of control, will often take advantage of the ability to push the child's buttons, just for the fun of seeing his or her reaction. If your child, like the one called "Volcano Boy," shows signs of being unable to control his anger appropriately, try the following ideas:

- **Teach your child that feeling anger is normal, but it's what we do with it that makes it positive or negative.** Everybody feels angry, and it is OK to feel mad, but it is not OK to show anger with hurtful or destructive behavior.

- **Teach your child that he is responsible for what he does with his anger.** Many kids say, "He made me so angry." My response is "I can understand that what he did made you feel really mad, but what you do with those mad feelings is your choice."

- **Encourage your child to express her anger verbally, using the "I" message.** The "I" message (explained in Chapter 6) can help the child identify the reason for the anger. Some kids need "permission" or encouragement to express their angry feelings, especially if they have received the message that "you should not get angry."

- **Set some ground rules for expressions of anger.** Examples might be no yelling, no swearing, and no physical aggression.

- **Convey an understanding of the child's feelings.** This is not the same thing as agreeing with the feelings. Saying, for example, "I understand that you are mad because I won't let you go to the mall with your friends" validates the child's feelings without forcing you to give up your parental authority.

- **Give your child some ways to cool down.** Some kids need help in cooling down before they can talk more calmly about their anger. They can either slowly count to ten, learn and practice relaxation techniques such as taking deep breaths, let off steam by exercising, or take a time-out.

- **Give your child an acceptable nonverbal method for expressing his feelings.** I have found that some children who cannot easily put their feelings into words might be able to draw how they are feeling. I once worked with a young boy who had frequent temper tantrums at home and school. I asked him to draw a picture of what anger looked like to him. He drew a picture of a boy who had a volcano erupting from his head. Drawing helped him calm down to the point where he could more appropriately talk about his feelings and what he does when he gets so mad. Some kids are able to write about their angry feelings.

• **Model appropriate anger control.** The most important lesson in anger management is how you express anger. Can you express yourself calmly, use "I" messages, and give yourself permission for being angry without expressing anger by using hurtful behavior?

• **Discuss expressions of anger that kids see on TV and in movies.** Is it appropriate or violent? Unfortunately, children model much of what they see on television because they assume that is the way to handle their feelings.

Other sources to help with anger control include books, as mentioned. Two of the best I know are Adolph Moser's *Don't Rant and Rave on Wednesdays*, an excellent resource for parents to read with their kids, and *Stick Up for Yourself!*, by Gershen Kaufman, Lev Raphael, and Pamela Espeland, which teaches kids how to express their feelings effectively—how to be assertive, not aggressive. You could also consult your child's teacher or school mental health professional. Perhaps there is an anger-management class at school or at a local mental health agency. If a child has frequent temper tantrums or is chronically explosive, seek professional help.

When Your Child Is Modeling Victim Behavior Learned at Home

Your detective work may include examining your own behavior to see how it might be contributing to the child's victim role. Do you model the behavior of a victim, or do you tease your child inappropriately? Do you consistently put down your son or daughter?

Perhaps you are teasing in a playful or sarcastic way, but it is taken as hurtful.

A child who is a frequent target of teasing and reacts as a helpless victim with peers is sometimes duplicating the role he observes or assumes within his family. He may be the target of older siblings' aggressive behaviors or the victim of harsh or abusive parenting. Kids who have very critical and judgmental parents often feel victimized. It is very easy for these children to easily assume the same role outside of their families because it is so familiar. It is what they are used to.

Susan, age eight, was always complaining that the girls in her class were "mean." I learned from Susan's teacher that she had the tendency to perceive general comments or the slightest criticism in a very negative way. Why? Susan's teenage brother was verbally abusive to her at home. Apparently, this behavior had continued for years without effective parental intervention. I later learned that Susan's dad had a bad temper and would frequently vent his anger toward her. Susan was a daily victim in two relationships in her family. She continued this role at school even when she was not really victimized in her peer relationships. Kids in situations like Susan's will likely perceive an unintentional slight as a major rejection.

The behavior that parents and other adults model is extremely powerful. The old adage "actions speak louder than words" should be the guiding principle for all parents. Our own behaviors speak louder than any speeches or lectures we give. We need to practice what we want our kids to learn.

When Your Child Needs to Balance Fitting In with Being an Individual

Kids like to feel accepted by their peers. Feeling as if they "belong" makes them feel secure and validated. But many kids have a hard time finding that elusive balance between fitting in and retaining their individuality.

Kirsten was ignored, ridiculed, and disliked by the girls in her sixth-grade class because she repeatedly showed up at school wearing the same new shoes, hair accessories, or jewelry that one of the popular girls wore. To Kirsten it was just "the sincerest form of flattery" and a way to fit in. She didn't realize that buying *exactly* the same shoes as a girl she admired looked like an attempt to "steal" the other girl's creative ideas and get credit for them herself. She failed to understand that she had crossed a line and thus erased her individuality—and that no one liked her for it. Kirsten needed help. Her mother confessed to having no knack for fashion, especially twelve-year-old fashion, and I asked if there was anyone else who might help Kirsten. Her fifteen-year-old cousin, it turned out, was coming for a visit. Kirsten's mother took the two girls on a shopping trip after a little private coaching from Kirsten's cousin. Every time Kirsten snatched up an outfit and said something like, "This is just like the one Stacy has!" her cousin steered her to something similar but that suited Kirsten in particular: "Sure, that's cute, but this one is your color. And since you're tall, you can wear this length really well." Kirsten happily reported that Stacy asked her where she'd gotten the cute skirt the following week.

The peer group often has its own norms and values that influence each member's individual choices. When I go into a third- or fourth-grade classroom, it is not uncommon to see two or three girls wearing the same shirt, jeans, and jewelry. In fact, they often call the night before to plan what they will wear. The sameness creates a bond and a connection that helps them feel part of their group. It sometimes identifies them as best friends. In the more general peer group, it is usually easy to observe the current trends in clothing styles, shoes, hairstyles, and fingernail polish. Boys also get into the trends, whether it is wearing cargo jeans or having blond highlights in their hair. In some groups there may be pressure to conform to each other, which then helps many kids feel secure within their clique.

Many kids distance themselves from peers who are different or out of sync with their styles or preferences. Mr. and Mrs. Williams were concerned about their eight-year-old son, Timmy, who was a loner. They perceived that he was not part of the group and so did

Timmy. He was one of the youngest children in his class and was socially less mature than most of his peers. Timmy usually wore sweatpants and tight T-shirts, which contributed to the perception that he looked different and younger than most classmates. I talked to Mr. and Mrs. Williams about how many children like to dress like their peers because it helps them feel more like the others and it sometimes helps in peer acceptance. We also talked about the possibility of my working with Timmy in a small group to help strengthen his social skills. Finally, Mr. and Mrs. Williams asked what I thought about calling their son Tim instead of Timmy, at least when he was around his peers, because it sounded more mature. I suggested they talk to Timmy about this idea. Mr. and Mrs. Williams discussed this issue with Timmy over the summer. He tried this out at camp and decided he really liked "Tim." The "name change" took place at school when he began fourth grade. During that year Tim showed signs of more maturity, especially after we worked on strengthening his social skills.

I've had many similar conversations with parents over the years, and I always stress the importance, when they are helping their child fit in, of encouraging the child to express his or her personal preferences. For some kids, like Timmy, how to dress has never really been a subject of deep thought, but they do have likes and dislikes. When asked, Timmy said he'd like to wear jeans like the other guys. His parents took him to the mall and let him pick out the ones he liked.

Nico was called a "nerd" by his classmates because they saw him carting around his violin case twice a week before his lessons. Classical music wasn't considered cool. But when Nico showed that he could play one of the latest hits on the violin, the kids thought he was cool. Nico never played anything like that again—he really preferred symphonic music—but he had earned the respect of his peers by showing that he could play their music if he wanted to. They now assumed he liked all music—and in time he did.

Eleven-year-old Jasmine was excited that she was invited to a slumber party. She was particularly thrilled because she was new to the school and was eager (but scared) to make new friends. As the evening progressed, Jasmine was feeling uncomfortable with the way the girls were criticizing and ridiculing several girls who were not invited. Her discomfort level increased when the girls decided to watch an X-rated movie that one guest had brought with her. Jasmine did not know what to do. "Should I watch the movie even though the thought of it makes me cringe? I know my parents would have a fit if they found out. Maybe I should go along with the girls because I want them to like me." Jasmine quickly decided that she didn't feel well and told the girls that she wanted to rest for a while. She decided to call her parents to pick her up. Although she felt very bad about being dishonest, she felt too insecure to stick up for what she believed. Fortunately, she was able to talk about the situation with her parents. Her mother helped Jasmine see that her values seem to be quite different from those of the other girls. Jasmine decided to pursue other friendships at her new school while she made extra efforts to keep in touch with her friends from her former school.

Bradley, a third-grader, came home from school pleading with his parents to buy him certain athletic shoes that "everyone" was wearing. Although he had never been teased about his shoes, he really wanted to be like everyone else. Bradley's parents could sense how much this meant to Bradley and decided to go shoe shopping. (Incidentally, *Albert's Old Shoes*, by Stephen and Mary Jane Muir, is a great story about being teased about old shoes.)

In almost all cases of teasing, the key is how different is the difference and how the child feels about the difference. Is she proud of it or does she try to hide it? Like Timmy, LaTanya always wore sweatpants rather than the more popular jeans or overalls, but unlike Timmy, LaTanya never had a problem with this because she exuded self-confidence. She'd laugh along with anyone who made fun of her clothes, shrug and grin, and go back to playing soccer. Fourth-grader Elizabeth has the longest hair in the school, and her classmates are always telling her to cut it to a more current style. She loves her hair the way it is and responds to their comments very appropriately: "I like my hair the way it is." In contrast, nine-year-old Jenna began wearing her very long hair in a braid similar to the one worn by several classmates.

Kids may vary from year to year in how much they want to fit in. Children between fourth and sixth grades are especially self-conscious, and so are many seventh- and eighth-graders. That's why most people assume that the older children get, the more they are ruled by their peers. As kids get older, they also begin separating from their families as they gain more independence. The peer group becomes a place to feel accepted and secure, and feeling secure often means conforming to the group norms. A compliment from a twelve-year-old friend often means a lot more than one from a parent. Peer influence can be very powerful, and peer acceptance is critical. Each preteen has to decide how much individuality he or she will sacrifice or maintain or perhaps go back to later on. Research shows, however, that another turning point looms ahead. If their individuality and self-worth are reinforced by the adults and kids around them as they grow, most kids become very independent and individual sometime during high school. Many junior high cliques lose their power in high school, especially when two or more junior high schools merge into one high school.

Now that you understand what commonly motivates teasers and why your child in particular might have been targeted, you're ready to take action. Chapter 5 will tell you how to talk to your child about the teasing, and Chapter 6 will give you strategies that will help the child avoid being hurt and also discourage the teasing.

5

Talking to Your Child About Being Teased

Talking to your child about being teased can be as delicate as talking about the birds and the bees. A child who has been teased feels hurt and probably humiliated and may be ashamed to talk about it in the first place. He may be angry and confused and primed to take out his frustration on you—even while he's seeking your help and comfort. She may be so wrapped up in hurt that she won't want to hear what *she* could do to improve the situation. She may then become very defensive when your reaction is not simply to ride to the rescue.

Add to that the strong feelings that we parents are likely to bring to talks about teasing, and these conversations can become unpredictable at best and unproductive at worst. In this chapter, I'll tell you what I've learned about talking constructively to children about teasing. When your child first confides, you have an opportunity to establish a supportive and open climate that will help you stay fully informed and help ease the big hurt he or she is feeling right now. This will facilitate the more difficult discussions about who is doing what and why. With those conversations behind you, you can both put all your resources into discussing what can be done about the problem.

How to React to the News That Your Child Is Being Teased

Establishing a positive, empathic, and attentive tone from the start is essential if parents are to help their children deal with being teased. You want your child to feel free to express his feelings and safe about telling you the whole story, including details that he may find humiliating or even condemning. Because you know your child better than anyone else, it's up to you to decide exactly how much to say, in which words, and with what tone of voice and facial expression. You'll be the one who will know, from the subtlest twitch of the lip or the tiniest gesture, when it's time to call a halt, switch tactics, or stop talking and start listening. I can, however, give you some guidelines that parents, teachers, and counselors have found fundamental to successful communication with children who are being teased.

Take What Your Child Says Seriously

When your child tells you she is being teased and feels hurt by it, do not dismiss her with comments like "Forget about it" or "Don't worry about it. He probably didn't mean what he said." First of all, there's a good chance that your child has already been trying to ignore it or brush it off and is now coming to you because these efforts have neither stopped the teasing nor made her feel better. Depending on their age, kids often do try to "fight their own battles." Even if your child tends to bring you every little complaint, you should take reports of teasing seriously, at least until you've had a chance to investigate what might be going on—for all the reasons I've been stating and restating about the damage that persistent teasing can do. The last thing you want is to force your child to internalize and repress emotional harm because when she finally decided to confide in someone and ask for help, you brushed her off.

Sometimes parents shrug off reports of teasing because they're looking at the reported object of the teasing from an adult point of view. Sure, to you, being taunted for having "feet the size of canoes" would be laughingly insignificant. But to your daughter, who's just beginning to go through puberty, this could be a major affront to her feminine self-image—especially with the seventh-grade dance coming up. To you, accusing your son of being "the stupidest kid in the class" because he was the only one who got a B on a test that everyone else aced is negligible, because you know he gets straight A's on his report cards. But to your son, who isn't much of an athlete and takes great pride in his intellectual abilities, this is an outright challenge to his self-esteem.

It's natural to want to teach our kids not to "sweat the small stuff" and to use their brains to sort through nonsensical criticisms. But remember that children haven't developed adult perspectives yet. Even if you can ultimately bring them to the point of understanding that a tease was inaccurate and ludicrous—and you should definitely do so—this moment is not the time to try. First you need to acknowledge how seriously they have taken the hurt. You can work on revealing how unfounded the tease was later. What seems insignificant to parents can be a major stressor for kids.

You need to try to see the situation from your child's point of view before imposing yours on the conversation. Look straight at your child, stop what you're doing, and listen—hard. How upset is your son or daughter? What signs do you see that would indicate how big a deal this is relative to other problems in the child's life? How comfortable does he or she seem talking about being teased? Is your child looking you in the eye or looking down at the ground while talking? Is she evasive when she's usually effusive? Is he laying it on thick and playing up the drama of the situation?

At least for now, you should take the situation as seriously as your child seems to be taking it. This does not mean, however, that you should get emotional when your child is being emotional. Rather, stay calm, but acknowledge right away how your child seems to be feeling:

- "It sounds like what Cindy said really hurt you."
- "You seem really upset by this."
- "That must have made you really mad."

Delivered calmly, these statements not only tell your child that he or she is being heard but as a result tend to tone down the expressions of anger and hurt and pave the way for more productive communication between you. They are also part of what therapists call "active listening," a technique I'll be advocating throughout this chapter.

Give Your Child Your Undivided Attention

Before you begin to talk about the teasing with your child, I suggest that you sit down with him in a quiet place. In our hurried routines, parents often talk with their kids as they are preparing dinner, emptying the dishwasher, or doing laundry. The more you can focus on the conversation without distractions, the more your child will feel that you are really listening. Sometimes driving in the car with your child is a good place to talk. A mother recently told me that she and her daughter have their best talks when they walk the dog together. There are no interruptions; she leaves her cellular phone at home. The important prerequisite is that your child has your undivided attention as you listen and try to understand the hurtful situation.

Again, however, be sensitive to your child's comfort level with the topic. Many children bring up difficult subjects sideways or offhandedly. If your child is trying to ease into a conversation about being teased because she is ashamed in some way or afraid of how you might react, she might not respond positively to your being overly attentive. You'll have to be the judge. After years of encouraging eye contact, a friend of mine realized that these kinds of conversations are best held in the car or in the kitchen while she is working at the counter or while her son is working at the table. He is more comfortable when there is not direct eye contact. So while your attention should be undivided, you may need to *look* as if you're not focusing on the topic or the child too intently.

Encourage Your Child to Tell You About the Teasing

"I really want to know what happened at school today; please tell me all about it" is a simple and direct way to ask the child to open up. In most cases, children will be happy to give you the blow-by-blow details of the teasing. But some might be reticent despite your invitation.

Some children need gentle encouragement to open up. It may help for you to acknowledge how difficult it is to talk about situations that are embarrassing or uncomfortable. "I know it's hard to talk about this. You might feel embarrassed, or maybe you're afraid I'll think less of you. I'm hear to listen and help." Sharing that it was hard for you to talk about a teasing experience in your childhood may help your child open up. In fact, just sharing the story of one of your teasing experiences normalizes it and also tells your child that you may have some proven advice to offer.

But when kids do not and will not talk about what has happened, it is better to respect their wishes. After all, we can't make them talk. Kids often become more resistant when parents become more insistent. Perhaps another time will be better. Many younger children tend to open up more before bedtime. Other kids might not talk about it until it happens again.

Some children are more comfortable talking about teasing in more general ways that are less personal. For example, you might ask, "Are kids in your class ever teased?" or "Do kids tease other kids on the bus?" This might open the door for your child to talk about his teasing experience. Reading stories or books about kids being teased is a great way to engage in valuable discussion about how kids feel when they're teased and what they can do. Kids can often identify with characters in a story, which may help them realize that other children also experience teasing. For recommended literature see Chapter 7 and "Recommended Books for Children."

I know a mother who became quite concerned when she sensed that something was bothering her ten-year-old son, David. He was more irritable than usual. She realized that David was no longer hanging out with one of his neighbor friends, Michael. When she asked David about Michael, he quickly changed the subject or said, "I don't know." Her continued efforts to encourage him to express his feelings were futile. One night she decided to E-mail David. She wrote that she was concerned that he did not seem as happy as he usually is. She asked if his friendship with Michael had changed. She encouraged him to write to her about what was bothering him. David shared in his reply E-mail that Michael had been avoiding him at school and on the bus for a couple of weeks and had made fun of him when they played basketball in gym. He wrote that Michael was hanging out with another classmate. The E-mail communication continued for several days. She explained to David that friendships often change in fourth and fifth grades, and she conveyed an understanding of how he must be feeling because he had been friends with Michael for several years. David's mom asked him if he felt comfortable talking to Michael about the situation. He said no. She encouraged him to make plans with a couple of other boys in his class and a camp friend who attended another school.

When the child does talk, listen patiently and attentively. It's OK to ask for clarification if you get confused about what seems like an important point—"Do you mean he actually pushed you with his hands or that you felt like he was trying to make you do something you didn't want to do?"—but it's best to hear the child out without interruption. Try to save your questions for the end of the story.

If your child doesn't seem to be able to tell you the story of the teasing, in a calm and reassuring way ask questions to get a clear picture of what he or she has experienced. Ask your child to describe the teasing. The following questions are examples of the types of queries that might elicit details. (Just don't ask them in list form, one after the other, as printed here. Your child might feel as if you're holding an inquisition and clam up.)

- Who is the teaser?
- Is the teaser a classmate, a friend, a neighbor, or a passenger on the school bus?
- Is the teaser older, younger, or the same age as your child?
- What is your child being teased about?
- Is your child being teased about a physical trait or difference or about something he does or doesn't do in the classroom or on the playground?
- Where is the teasing occurring?
- Is your child being picked on or harassed on the playground or while riding on the bus?

- Is ridicule occurring in the classroom?
- How long has it been happening?
- Is it a fairly recent occurrence, or has it been going on for a while?

Here is an actual dialogue that took place between a mother and her eleven-year-old son:

Mother: When I was talking to my friend this morning, she mentioned that there were some problems on the bus. Her daughters told her about it and said they really feel bad.

Son: Yeah? So?

Mother: Is that true?

Son: Yeah. [Tears are now filling his eyes.]

Mother: I'm wondering why you haven't told us or an adult at school.

Son: I don't want to talk about it because it hurts too much to think about it.

Mother: I'm sure it does, but it sounds like you need to talk about it so that we can get adults involved who can work on the situation with you. You shouldn't have to deal with that every day.

Son: Why?

Mother: Well, I think this may be part of the reason you miss the bus so often. I would dread getting on the bus every day knowing that kids might bother me when I got on.

Son: Yeah, it's pretty awful. [Now he's crying.]

Mother: Why don't you talk to Mr. S., the assistant principal? He is always very helpful in these situations.

Son: It won't make any difference, and besides, if the kids find out, they'll just be mad and tease me worse. The bus driver is the only adult on the bus, and she can't do anything.

Mother: Let's think of how you might avoid dealing with these kids.

Son: OK.

Mother: Where do these kids sit on the bus?

Son: In the back.

Mother: Why don't you sit in the front?

Son: Because my friends are already sitting in the back when I get on the bus.

Mother: Can you ask them to sit in the front?

Son: I'll try.

Mother: Do your friends get teased too?

Son: Yeah.

Mother: How do they deal with it?

Son: They try not to pay attention to them. They continue talking to each other.

Mother: What do you do when you get teased?

Son: I usually get mad at them and tell them to shut up.

As this mother explained, the two of them proceeded to discuss what the boy could do or say that might be more effective. They talked about how anger can make the teasing get worse. The boy was not comfortable telling the assistant principal but agreed that his mother should make the call. The assistant principal and the boy talked later that day. It seemed to help her son, she said, that adults in his life were aware and supportive. He did report the next incident to the assistant principal, who later spoke to the boy and the teaser. There have been no more incidents.

Don't Give Premature Advice

Parents tend to interrupt before they hear the whole story, sometimes because they want to "fix" the situation so quickly that they can't hear their child out. If you find yourself interjecting comments and advice before your child has finished talking, it may be a sign that the whole incident is very disturbing to you. In that case, your child may very well clam up or cut the conversation short, and you should ask yourself what is making you so anxious before you try to pick up where the two of you left off.

• **Are you reliving old hurts of your own?** Some parents can't separate themselves from their child's pain because the report of being teased opens their old wounds. They not only put themselves in their child's shoes but start walking around in them. They may feel desperate to solve the problem right away to reclose their own old wounds as much as to soothe their child's new one.

• **Has your child been hurt often in the past?** If your child has suffered teasing before, you may feel a familiar dread come over you when he or she comes to you with a new complaint. You know how much pain teasing has caused the child, and you don't want her to go through that again. Before you jump in with questions about whether the child has tried all the advice you've given in the past, consider a couple of possibilities. If the child is a repeated victim of teasing, maybe what you have suggested before just isn't working. Stop, listen, and then tell your child you're going to help her find some new ways to deal with teasing. See Chapter 6. Or maybe something different is happening this time. Don't jump to conclusions. Listen to the whole story and then ask your child if she thinks this is the same kind of thing that has happened to her before.

• **Do you feel your child's being teased somehow reflects on you?** All parents want their children to be liked and appreciated for who they are. But sometimes parents forget where the child ends and the parent begins. It's normal to feel pain when your child is hurt and to feel sad when your child is humiliated. But if your child's humiliation humiliates *you*, you are crossing that line and will tend to feel compelled to take action when you should instead help your child take action. Sit back and listen.

Don't Overreact

As you begin to hear the details of the cruel and hurtful behavior, you will probably feel appalled and enraged. You might feel like calling the teaser and telling him or her exactly how you feel. Or, you might immediately threaten to call the teaser's parents. It's crucial that you not overreact. A parent's overreaction will often result in the child's overreacting. Or, with older children who may have hesitated to come to you in the first place, your overreaction may drive them back into their shell.

If you were teased severely as a child, you may have to exercise great restraint to avoid getting hysterical. Remind yourself that you haven't learned everything that you need to know. Even if you've heard your child's story in full, you still have to investigate to make sure you understand exactly what's happening. (See Chapter 4.)

Paraphrase What Your Child Has Said to Make Sure You Understand

Much of what you just read could be an instruction manual for active listening. We call it *active* listening because it requires a lot more effort than just sitting back and letting sounds pour through your ears and into your brain. You actively pay close attention to your child, making eye contact, nodding, or using other gestures to show you understand what your child is trying to convey; acknowledge the feelings the child seems to be expressing; and ask clarifying questions. Paraphrase what your child has told you to make sure that you understand and to assure him of this. In the case of teasing, it makes sense to do this after your child has told you the whole story. You might say, "So you feel really angry that Kenny, who you thought was your friend, has started calling you names because you have to wear a back brace and can't play baseball after school for a few months? And that makes you sad too, because you'll probably feel kind of lonely being on the outskirts, I guess. You want the name-calling to stop, and you also want to find a way to be with your friends again after school." At this point your son will either confirm that you've gotten it right or correct your perception. Now you need to assure him that together you'll find a way to deal with the problem.

Validate Your Child's Feelings

This may seem repetitive, and in a sense it is. Validating your child's feelings at various points during this conversation keeps the talk flowing and your child's trust in you complete. Now that you've gotten the child's story, take one more opportunity to communicate that you understand her feelings and convey empathy. "I really understand that you feel so upset." "I know how sad you must feel." "You must feel so angry that you feel like exploding." "It's perfectly normal to feel so upset when this happens." "I imagine you felt totally embarrassed when that happened." "It is really hard when someone says such mean words." Validation of her feelings can't stop the teasing, but it is very comforting and consoling. Conveying an understanding of your child's feelings helps her feel safe while talking about this difficult situation. Praise and compliment your child for sharing his or her feelings with you.

How to Talk to Your Child About What's Going On

Once you've listened to your child tell you about being teased, you're undoubtedly going to want to investigate further, following the guidelines suggested in Chapter 4. When you have as much information as you think you're going to get, you'll want to talk to your child about who is doing what and why.

Talking About Your Child's Role in the Teasing

Part of your investigation includes exploring how your child has handled the teasing. Gently ask how he usually reacts. By fighting physically or by exchanging insults with the teaser? By crying in front of the teaser or instead trying hard to hide her tears? By getting so angry he feels like exploding? You will need to assess whether your child's reactions encourage more teasing. A teacher's insight might help you get a clearer picture of the situation if your child holds back in answering these questions. Instead of criticizing him for the way or ways he dealt with the teasing, try to be positive and say, "We are going to think of some other things that you could say or do that might help you feel better." It is important for you to reassure your child that you will help him.

What if some habit or other behavior of your child's is the cause of the teasing? We talked about all kinds of behavior that elicit teasing in Chapter 4. If your daughter is being teased because she picks her nose or your son is being teased because he likes to dress differently from the other boys, you'll need to find a way to talk to the child—without humiliating him or her—about possibly changing the behavior. Of course, sometimes a little shame or guilt motivates a child to change, especially with behaviors such as nose picking, thumb sucking, bad table manners, poor hygiene, or inappropriate classroom behaviors. Please don't read this as permission to talk to the child punitively or harshly about these behaviors. I am advocating a serious conversation about the consequences of offensive behaviors. The last thing you want to do is start a power struggle. Your child should recognize that you are on his side, not on his back.

Is Your Child Motivated to Change?

It is logical to begin by exploring how your child feels about the behavior and how she thinks her peers feel about it. "What do you think about your thumb sucking?" "How do you think your classmates feel about your thumb sucking?" A big first step in changing a behavior is for the child to want to change it. If the motivation isn't there, the behavior is likely to continue. If the child has the tendency to be stubborn and resistant to parental suggestions and guidance, parents may feel increasingly frustrated and helpless. Many preteens are oppositional just because they are preteens.

Whatever the behavior, the best chance for a change is to involve the child in the brainstorming process. Kids who play a part in the problem-solving process are often more successful. Lorie was the only student in second grade who sucked her thumb during the school day. After repeated pleas from her parents and hints from her teacher, the behavior continued. Occasional comments from peers didn't seem to bother her until she reached third grade. Negative remarks from her peers upset her enough to talk about the habit with her mother. Her mother consulted with the dentist, who suggested placing an appliance on the roof of her mouth that would interfere with her thumb sucking. Lorie's motivation to fit in and not do something so "babyish" in third grade was the key to her success in kicking the habit.

Nine-year-old Jacob, who goofed off in class on a regular basis, was perceived by his classmates as the "class clown." In fact, his behavior often resulted in negative consequences for the entire class. Needless to say, he was the target of much criticism and offensive remarks from his peers. Apparently, Jacob liked the negative attention because it was better than none at all. Jacob's parents' efforts to talk about his behavior were futile because he had no motivation to change. He enjoyed being the center of attention. In fact, his behavior resulted in a lot of his parents' attention. Again, negative attention feels better to many kids than what they might perceive as no attention.

Jacob's teacher, Ms. Marks, decided to implement a behavior-modification plan that would positively reinforce behaviors. She began an incentive program for the entire class by giving the class a "class point" each day they behaved appropriately. She outlined what behaving appropriately meant. This included no outbursts from students and no put-downs of classmates. When a certain number of class points were earned, they could have a popcorn party and an extra recess. At the same time, Ms. Marks gave Jacob a tally mark for each half day that Jacob did not disrupt the class. (Sometimes a full day is too long and a child may not be successful, especially at the beginning.) The chart was kept in a private place on the teacher's desk, out of sight of other classmates. Jacob took the chart home at the end of each week. When he earned a certain number of tally marks, his parents allowed him special privileges that were agreed upon at the beginning of the plan.

Kids often respond well to a progressive "menu of rewards" as an incentive to change behaviors. For example, five tally marks could mean an extra or special dessert. Ten tally marks could earn a later bedtime over the weekend or playing a game with Mom or Dad. Fifteen could mean a visit to the video store or inviting a friend to sleep over. Or, perhaps the child wants to wait until twenty-five marks are earned for a special outing to the video arcade. The specific rewards depend on the age of the child and what would serve as effective incentives. This plan is most successful when parents discuss with their child what he would like to work toward. I don't believe in or advocate any incentives that cost a lot of money! In addition to the behavior-modification plan, Jacob's parents sought professional guidance at a local mental health agency. They learned ways to deal with his negative attention-seeking behaviors within the family and enrolled Jacob in a social skills group at the agency to help him learn ways to connect with classmates in a positive way.

The behavior-modification plan and the outside intervention made a significant difference. Jacob's classmates actually complimented him on his change of behavior. He was able to gain positive attention from his classmates and his parents. The class enjoyed their popcorn party and extra recess. Ms. Marks told the class that if they earned a significant number of additional class points, they could have a pizza party.

Dion, age seven, had frequent meltdowns when he did not get his way. This had been a problem for him since preschool. His parents thought this behavior was due to immaturity and that he would outgrow it. They repeatedly explained to their son that his behavior was not appropriate and that he was going to lose his friends. Although Dion seemed to understand the possible consequences of his meltdowns, they continued. Dion's parents felt increasingly helpless and frustrated. They decided to seek professional guidance to help their son. I admired how they conveyed hope to Dion that they were going to find ways to help him.

Do You Need to Talk to Your Child About His or Her Self-Worth?

Ten-year-old Nicki is very pretty and achieves academic success in school. She has been the victim of ongoing comments and "looks" from many of her classmates about her clothes and her grades. She was accused of "taking away" the boyfriend of a classmate, which was not the case. When Nicki returned home from school, she frequently called her mom at work and cried about the put-downs and meanness she had endured during the day. Nicki's mom listened, knowing that her daughter often felt better after she could vent to her mother. However, Nicki's mom could tell that the cumulative effects of the put-downs were tearing down her self-esteem. She consistently told Nicki that she was a wonderful girl with so many special qualities—she was loving, thoughtful, smart, and gentle. She reminded Nicki of her musical talents and her achievements in gymnastics and dance. "I love you very much and you are the light of my life. I know that it hurts to hear those girls make fun of you and not accept you, but it is more about them, not you." She proceeded to talk to Nicki about how the girls were rude and ill-mannered and most likely envious of her.

Even though Nicki agreed with her mom, it was hard to experience the negative perceptions and comments from kids she encountered on a daily basis. Repeated affirmations from Nicki's mom and grandparents were necessary to help her deal with the repeated verbal aggression and exclusion at school. Nicki's mom talked to her daughter about the visualization strategy (see Chapter 6). She explained to Nicki that she needed to pretend there was a thick shield protecting her from the hurtful comments and put-downs. She also emphasized the importance of self-talk—reminding herself of her mom's words, not the words of her classmates. Nicki's mom plans to talk to the school headmaster about class placement for next year and she wants to actively pursue getting Nicki together with girls from camp and her dance and gymnastic classes.

Nicki never hesitated to tell her mother how she felt about how she was being treated at school, but many children are more reticent.

If your child is being teased, encourage her to express how she feels about herself. And always remember that you may not know what would help her feel better. *Ask.*

Does Your Child Feel Comfortable Being Who He Is?

It's not easy to find out whether children are actually ashamed of who they are or what they might feel embarrassed about in themselves. If a child is being teased about a difference or a physical trait that cannot be changed, ask him how he feels about that characteristic. Chances are, if your child is comfortable with his difference, he is not likely to be bothered by comments or teasing about it. On the other hand, if he feels sorry for himself or wishes he were "just like everyone else," he will be more vulnerable to what other kids say. Some kids may be comfortable with a difference until they reach third or fourth grade, at which time they begin to compare themselves more to their peers. Brandon complained to his mom about a few boys commenting on his slow running in a game at recess. "I know you wish you didn't walk with a limp," his mother would say. "I realize how much you want to run like the other boys." As mentioned previously, acknowledging your child's feelings is the first important message. You can be hopeful that your child will talk about how he feels, as painful as it is for you to hear about his hurt. In this case, Brandon started to cry and poured out his feelings, saying how unfair it was that he had been born with this condition. His mom felt his pain and more—she felt guilty about his deformity. (Sometimes parents' guilt about the child's difference can interfere with helping the child. Professional help can be a positive alternative for assisting your child in coming to terms with the difference.) She said to him, "It does seem unfair, and I understand how you feel, but it's not the end of the world. Think of the kids who can't run or walk at all." She continued to talk to Brandon about making the most of who he is and the importance of doing his best. She reminded him of Jim Abbott, the major-league pitcher who was born without a right hand.

Praising your child's efforts is the next important message. "I was so proud of the way you did your best as you ran to first base. You really hit the ball hard." It is also important to encourage your child to give himself credit for his accomplishment and efforts.

In some instances, parents might want to talk to kids about the lack of understanding other kids have of the difference. "I am wondering if some of the kids in your class don't understand what it's like to have a physical disability. Perhaps we can talk to your teacher about explaining to your classmates what your limp and slow running mean." This intervention can be quite successful in heightening kids' awareness and sensitivity to a child's difference.

Luis came home from school looking like the world was on his shoulders. He carried his doom and gloom into his room as he slammed the door. After a while, he came downstairs ranting and raving about how he hated school and didn't want to go back. When his mom asked why he was feeling so angry, he said that he wanted to return to his previous school. His mom told Luis that it is often hard to get used to new situations. She assured him that in a few weeks he would feel much better. These words didn't console Luis. He continued to complain about the school and how he didn't like the kids. When his mom asked why, he reluctantly said that a few kids wouldn't let him play a game at recess. She responded with understanding and empathy: "I understand that you felt upset when the kids wouldn't let you play. Most kids would feel the same way. I know it must be hard to be a new kid in fifth grade." Luis just said, "I hate those kids." His mom again acknowledged his anger. She asked, "Did anything else happen?" As his eyes filled with tears, he said, "They told me that spicks aren't allowed." His mom's heart sank as she felt the hurt her son had experienced. "No wonder you don't want to go back to school."

Luis's mother told him that she was so sorry that this had happened but that she was glad he could share his feelings with her. She continued to show empathy for his emotions: "I understand that you don't feel like going back to school tomorrow to face those kids who are so mean and hurtful. Unfortunately, it is a very sad part of life that some people have such ugly words to call people who are different from them." Luis appeared to listen intently, so she continued to say, "We are proud of our heritage and of who we are. Even though it hurts to hear such terrible words, we must remain proud of who we are. I can understand why you don't want to go back to school and why you are so angry at those kids. I feel angry too when I hear people make remarks like that. Let's think about some ways you could seek out other kids." Later, when Luis's dad came home from work, the family had a discussion about prejudice and discrimination.

Alicia, an overweight eight-year-old, was frequently teased about her size. The taunting usually took place on the school bus, where there was no adult supervision. The cumulative effect of the ridicule took its toll. She was extremely irritable, tried not to eat much at mealtime, and lost interest in playing with her friends. It took many attempts by her parents to get her to open up. Finally, she could not hold it in anymore. She sobbed and sobbed about how she hated herself and the way she looked. Her mom held Alicia in her arms as she cried. Then she acknowledged how Alicia must be feeling. "I know exactly how you feel, Alicia. Some boys in my class in fourth grade made fun of my weight when I was about your age. It is an awful feeling. You feel like you want to run and hide." Alicia's dad shared his experience of being teased about being the tallest boy in the grade and wearing the thickest glasses.

Alicia's mother explained that kids are teased a lot about the way they look—kids are teased if they are overweight, and others are teased if they are very thin. Tall kids are teased as well as short kids. Alicia said she would give anything to be very thin—that she would not mind that teasing. Alicia's mom talked about how kids are teased about anything that is different and that everybody is different in some way. She asked Alicia to think about how each of her friends might be unique in some way—in appearance, abilities, culture, or family situation. In fact, they began making a list, which helped Alicia feel that she was not alone in being different in some way.

Alicia's dad told her that he was extremely proud of the kind and sweet person she was. Her mom praised Alicia's good grades, her willingness to help with chores, and her help with her younger brother. Alicia's parents reminded her that her friends liked her for the good friend that she was. The discussion did not help Alicia shed pounds, but it surely lightened her "heavy" heart. Alicia's dad asked how she felt about his talking to the principal about the situation. Alicia said that would be a good idea.

Talking About the Teaser

In most cases, it's just as important to talk about the teaser's possible internal motivation as it is to discuss your child's role in the teasing. Especially if the teaser has been considered a friend or perceived as a generally nice boy or girl, your child may issue a plaintive "Why is he [she] being so mean?" You probably won't be able to answer this question with certainty, but it gives you an important opportunity to help your child see that the reasons might have nothing to do with him. Sometimes you might know that the teaser is experiencing family changes, such as divorce or death of a family member. Although this does not condone or excuse the behavior, an understanding of the teaser's motivation often helps the teasee see the situation differently. If you tell your son or daughter that the teaser might be saying or doing these things to receive attention, your child may be able to think of ways to give him or her positive attention.

Ask your child if *he* has any idea why the teaser is giving him such a hard time. "Why do you think Jimmy is acting so mean?" "Is he acting this way to other kids?" "I just found out that Jimmy's dad is in the hospital. I wonder if his worry about his dad is causing him to act this way." Children often have more insight than we think. Nicki's mom asked her daughter, "Why do you think one of the girls accused you of taking away her boyfriend?" Nicki quickly answered that her assigned seat was next to his in class and he often talked to her. Whether your child has ideas or you offer your own, it's important to convey, "I don't think that any of these reasons gives him a right to hurt your feelings."

Nicki's mom thought this "circumstantial evidence" sounded pretty flimsy and said, "Then I wonder what they would say if you asked them why they comment about your clothes and grades so much." Nicki's mom warned her that she might hear more negative things from them, but Nicki decided to ask them. When she did ask them, she caught them off guard and they could not respond. After this, the "looks" and comments seemed to decrease.

At times, we simply cannot understand why a person is so cruel and hurtful. It's very difficult to explain something to a child that we don't understand ourselves.

How to Talk to Your Child About What Can Be Done

You've listened to your child tell you about being teased and how much it hurt. You've talked to your child about herself and her role and about the teaser and his possible motivation. Now it's time to talk about action.

• **Express confidence in your child's ability to handle the situation.** Saying "I know you don't like it when someone teases you, but I know that you can handle it" conveys that you have confidence that your child can handle this hurtful behavior. Dealing with a situation that is difficult or adverse is the essence of coping. (Remember, however, that if the situation is chronic and repeated and if your child feels unsafe, he or she may be the victim of bullying. Adult assistance and intervention are necessary in bullying situations.)

• **Ask what your child wants you to do.** Ask your child what action she wants you to take. Don't ask a leading question, such as "Should I talk to the teacher about this?" or "Do you want me to come to the playground with you tomorrow?" First, see if your child has something in mind. If so, promise to think about it and come back to the child with a proposed plan. But make it soon, such as after dinner, after you've had a chance to talk to your spouse about it, or just once you've had a chance to review it in your own mind. If not, or your child just says something like "I want you to make him stop!" calmly assure your child that you will help her find ways to deal with the hurt and at the same time see if you can stop the teasing. For many children, this reassuring, confident statement of intent is enough to soothe the hurt while you investigate the situation further.

- **Be realistic.** Tell the child that it might not be possible to control what the teaser does. I tell kids all the time that they cannot control what other kids say. I tell young kids that I wish I had a magic wand so that children would use only kind words. Kids need to learn that other kids might say unkind and hurtful things. We cannot do anything to completely prevent that. How kids respond to the teases is what's important. I sound like a broken record (is there such a thing anymore?) when I say that kids cannot control the words and actions of the teaser but they can control their reactions. I talk to kids of all ages about accepting responsibility for their own behavior. They can't make other kids behave certain ways—they are only responsible for their own words and actions.

- **. . . But it *is* possible to control how your child feels about being teased.** Kids often "automatically" feel upset, hurt, sad, or angry when someone teases them. The whole point of the Easing the Teasing strategies is to help kids learn ways to control the expression of their feelings. Consistent practice can help children reduce their anger, fear, sadness, and helplessness. They may not like it, but they can learn to handle it.

I tell kids that what hurts one person's feelings may not be hurtful to someone else. If a child feels helpless, teasing will bother him. If a child feels empowered (prepared to respond effectively), he will not be afraid. Neither child will like hearing ridicule or hurtful comments, but it is less likely to bother the child who demonstrates coping skills, which after all, reduce stress. I have found that kids who have practiced and role-played the strategies are less fearful of being teased. Perhaps it is similar to kids taking tests. Those who have studied and prepared are ready and feel confident that they will do well. Children who are not prepared will most likely feel anxious and nervous about the test.

I believe that kids need to believe their self-talk. They need to say: "Just because someone calls me names or makes fun of me doesn't mean something is wrong with me." "I may not like what some people say, but I can decide to believe them or not. I can decide if I am going to act angry or sad."

We call this *positive self-talk*, and it's just one of the coping skills that helps children ease the teasing. Chapter 6 contains ten of them, so read on.

6

Teaching Your Child Strategies That Work

We send kids to school with new shoes, a new backpack, and all the supplies they need to succeed academically. But when it comes to coping skills that can help them avoid being hurt by teasing, an almost inevitable part of children's social lives, we pack them off empty-handed. True bullying (defined in Chapter 1) requires adult intervention. But my research and experience have shown that, when armed with the coping skills in this chapter, most children can ease the teasing on their own.

A child who comes to you complaining of teasing will probably want you to "fix" the problem and "get Steven to stop it" (especially if the child is relatively young). However, you're not likely to be there when Steven harasses your child on the school bus, taunts her on the playground, or bugs her in the classroom. As we've discussed, calling Steven's parents or talking to the teacher may or may not resolve the problem. So your child needs tools that she can use on the spot, whenever and wherever the teasing occurs.

I call the strategies in this chapter *coping skills* because they focus on changing the reactions and feelings of helplessness of the teasee. A principle that underlies the strategies is that it's simply not realistic to expect any child to change another's verbally aggressive behavior. Modern psychology tells us, in fact, that no matter what our age, we can't expect to control anyone but ourselves. This principle certainly applies to children. When they learn to control their own responses to teasing, they reduce the amount of hurt they feel. This alone can be a boon, especially to children who tend to be very sensitive to anything perceived as criticism from their peers or when teasees mistake affectionate kidding or other benign behavior for malicious teasing.

Thanks to the nature of teasing, however, the teasee's controlling his or her behavior does often have an effect on the teaser *at the time of the teasing incident.* As I've said before, many teasers are looking for an emotional response from their victim. When they don't get it, they are likely to move on, in search of another victim who is not so self-controlled. My strategies may not, therefore, get the teaser to change his stripes, but they should at least force him to seek different prey.

The strategies in this chapter may prevent a particular teaser from returning to torment your child again, which means they serve as both intervention and prevention. I've also found that children who use these coping skills effectively tend not to become the victims of bullying. Easing the teasing means nipping in the bud any impression that your child is easy prey, which is exactly what bullies seek.

Without scientific data to back it up, I can't claim that the Easing the Teasing strategies have a more global dampening effect on teasing. But, I have seen the atmosphere change in classrooms where I have proactively taught kids to be prepared when they encounter name-calling, ridicule, or put-downs. Many kids become desensitized to being teased after a lot of practice in it and dialogue about it. Teasing is no longer a big deal for them. Theoretically, discussing teasing in each classroom on a routine basis should create a schoolwide norm that teasing is not respectful or appropriate behavior. Recently, one fifth-grade class confirmed that for me. The students said they believed teasing had decreased around the school, a perception echoed by one girl, who emphatically stated that no one would tease her now because everyone should know that it would not bother her or, if it did, she would not show it. I firmly believe that a group attitude of zero tolerance for teasing tends to discourage it before it begins. It's my fondest hope that if all kids learn these strategies, teasing will eventually become simply socially unacceptable.

I teach the strategies to children in the following order. It has always seemed sensible to start with self-talk since kids need to tell themselves ahead of time what they are going to say and do when teasing occurs. Ignoring is a natural second choice because so many parents advise their children to do this but fail to tell them how. And the "I" message is a good strategy to add to a child's repertoire early on because in many situations it's important for the child just to express his or her feelings. Except for the last one, asking for help, the remaining strategies can be learned in any order. You might review them with your child and follow the first three with the ones that the child is most eager to try.

A word on the ages appropriate for these strategies. In the sections that follow, I've tried to indicate at what ages children are ready to learn each strategy, which ones work best for certain ages, or how the strategies can be adapted to meet the needs of different age children. But so much depends upon the child's cognitive and social development and maturity. What works for one six-year-old may be difficult for another. You will have to judge the usefulness of a particular strategy based on all your intimate knowledge of your child's strengths and personality traits. I don't want to suggest that your child *should* be able to use a certain strategy at a certain age—and that if she can't, there's something wrong. (Remember those developmental charts in the baby books? I always used to get nervous when one of my kids didn't reach a milestone at the predicted age. The point of this book and these strategies is to make you and your children *less*, not more, nervous.)

Self-Talk

Six-year-old Joy loved first grade. That's what she told her teacher, Ms. Burke, and anyone who observed her in class would have said she was a happy child, enthusiastically engaged in learning. But when she got off the school bus every day, her mother could see that Joy had been fighting back tears. The kids on the bus, it turned out, relentlessly teased Joy, calling her "Fat Girl," pointing and laughing.

Andy hadn't gotten off to a good start in third grade. Once again, his grades were dreadful right from the beginning of the school year. That didn't bother him too much. Andy was used to struggling academically. Andy, you see, had ADHD and just sitting still long enough to complete his schoolwork was a triumph for him. What he wasn't used to was the teasing. Even though he knew it was coming, Andy found himself losing his temper and yelling back at the kids who taunted him whenever the teacher passed their graded papers back to the class. It was Andy who inevitably got in trouble with the teacher for his outbursts.

Levon loved egg salad sandwiches. All through first grade that was what he'd find in the lunch box his mother had packed. But on the first day of second grade, Syed, who was a good six inches taller than Levon, sneered at lunchtime, "What's *that* gunk? Are you really gonna *eat* that? Hey, everybody, Levon's got a puke sandwich for lunch!" Levon was mortified. Unbeknown to his mother, he started throwing out his sandwich before he even got to the cafeteria. When he came home starving every afternoon, she chalked it up to a growth spurt. Levon knew differently.

Kids who are teased often react automatically with tears or temper. The younger they are, the less likely they are to stop for a minute and ask themselves whether the tease was even true. Yet when *I* ask them that question and the answer is "no," they immediately realize there isn't much to get upset about. This realization can help teasees let go of feelings of hurt, sadness, or anger a lot more quickly than they are used to doing.

This mental exchange is just one example of what I consider one of the most important coping strategies that kids can use when they are teased. It's called *self-talk*, and it reminds them first that they don't need to let teasing upset them and second that the tease may very well be total nonsense and not even worth listening to.

• **Is the teasing true?** Self-talk can take many different forms, depending on the circumstances of the teasing and the age of the child. The internal Q&A I just described is the most fundamental form of self-talk and should probably be any child's first reaction to being teased.

- **Whose opinion counts?** A second type involves the child reclaiming self-respect when the answer to the question "Is the tease true?" is not such an obvious "no." Levon, for example, can't say that his egg salad is either definitely delicious or definitely disgusting because egg salad is a matter of taste. Syed's tease was an opinion. In this case Levon should ask himself, "Whose opinion is more important, mine or Syed's?" It's not Syed's lunch, and Levon's lunch is none of Syed's business. The answer is clear: Levon's opinion in this case is the only one that counts. When we polled Levon's classmates about this, they all agreed. Following some role-playing about what he could do if Syed teased him again, Levon ate his egg salad for lunch the very next day. This message that he received from his classmates became a very powerful self-talk for him.

- **Think lovely thoughts . . . about yourself.** A third type of self-talk calls for children to remind themselves about some of their positive qualities while they are being teased. Joy *is* overweight, but when the kids started calling her "Fat Girl" on the bus, she tried hard not to cry, tried to ignore the teasers, and as she looked out the window thought about something special about herself. When I asked her what that was, she replied with a big smile, "I said to myself that I am a great friend." And she is—Joy has dozens of friends, and when she told this story in front of her class she got a big round of applause! Thinking lovely thoughts may not help kids fly as it did for Wendy in *Peter Pan*, but it sure lifts the spirits and bolsters the courage of the kids I teach.

- **STOP: Stop, *think* about your options, and *plan* what you can do.** Some children are quick-tempered, impulsive, and generally less self-controlled than others. This puts them at risk for ill-considered aggressive reactions to teasing, as in the case of Andy. I teach these kids to anticipate certain situations that might cause them to feel and act upset, to role-play these situations, and to repeat the acronym STOP to themselves the instant they are teased. Many kids with ADHD have found this method especially helpful after much practice and repetition.

When to Teach This Strategy

As I said, self-talk is one of the most fundamental strategies that children can use to cope with teasing. I teach it to the youngest ones I work with (although one kindergarten teacher described it as "too tough" for her students, saying they needed constant reminders not to react with anger or tears). You will have to judge whether your very young child can handle this, probably through trial and error. The older kids get, the more sophisticated and complex their self-talk can become, but many four- or five-year-olds can in fact start to make use of this strategy. Merely saying to themselves, "I am not going to get mad or cry" is a powerful tool that helps prevent the "automatic" feelings of hurt that most young children feel. A seven-year-old child said to himself, "This mean boy is trying to get me upset. I'm not going to give him what he wants." A sixth-grader said to himself that he was not going to give the teaser the power he wanted.

Where Children Can Use This Strategy

Self-talk, as I hope I've already shown, is applicable in just about any teasing situation. In fact, the question "What can I say or do?" is important for kids of all ages to ask themselves as step one the moment they are teased or ridiculed. The second step is to say or do it.

The most important self-talk for kids to use is "I don't like when kids say mean things to me. I hate it when kids make fun of me, but I'm going to handle it. This is not the end of the world." This is what coping with teasing is all about: dealing effectively with an adverse situation.

How to Teach Your Child Self-Talk

I've found the following to be foolproof in illustrating to children how important it is to ask themselves whether teasing is true, and you can use it to the same effect at home. Pretend you're a teaser and say to your child, "Your face is so green. Why do you have such a green face?" If your child is like all the ones I've worked with, he or she will laugh because this statement is so clearly untrue—and silly too. Now say to your child, "You're a total dork." Before you have a chance to feel like a brute for putting the hurt look on your child's face, quickly ask, "Is this true?" Your child will undoubtedly say something like, "No! Of course not!" Now say, "The next time someone teases you, ask yourself whether the tease is true, and then ask yourself this question: 'If the tease is not true, why am I so upset?' " Most likely the child will find the feelings of hurt, sadness, or anger fading a lot more quickly than he or she is used to.

For this and the other forms of self-talk, practice and repetition are important so that the child's *first* instinctive response to teasing is self-talk rather than hurt or anger. I suggest that parents come up with teasing scenarios to role-play with their children. Pretend that your child is teasing you. Respond with self-talk. Reverse the roles so that your child can practice. You can practice this in the car, at the dinner table, before bedtime, or just before your child leaves for school for a quick rehearsal. If your child is frequently teased about being short, you could ask, "What would you think to yourself if someone came up to you and teased you about being short?" Appropriate self-talk would be "I really am tired of being teased about being short, but I'm not going to get mad. I'm going to use one of the strategies I've practiced." Some kids need more practice than others. You'll know when your child is feeling confident and empowered.

At times, kids' hurt overwhelms them and they don't self-talk quickly enough. In these situations, you can always practice after the fact to prepare for the next time the teasing happens. Bobby was badgered by a player on his soccer team because he missed scoring a goal that would have won the game for his team. He felt bad that he had missed the goal, but the hurtful words of his teammates made him feel worse. Bobby reacted with tears, which embarrassed him more. Later that night his parents asked Bobby what he could say to himself if the same situation were to occur again. He practiced his self-talk out loud: "I'm going to try to stay cool and decide what I can do or say. I can also remind myself that I had the game-winning hit in a baseball game, which felt awesome. Nobody's perfect."

Ignoring

If someone makes a rude or insulting remark to you as you're walking down the street, do you stop, make eye contact, look hurt or angry, or toss out a retort? Probably not. Instinctively we adults know not to give someone who insults us unprovoked the satisfaction of a response. We understand that giving the offender the reaction he was hoping for only empowers him and may invite another comment.

Your child may not know this yet, depending on her emotional and cognitive maturity and the types of experiences she has had so far. Simply ignoring a tease and walking away from the situation can be one of the most powerful tools a child can learn to withstand *and* discourage teasing.

Eight-year-old Sam had been sent to the principal's office three times in the last month because he kept giving Jared exactly what he wanted. Jared would taunt Sam about his little sister, who wore thick-lens eyeglasses to compensate for severe nearsightedness. Without fail, Sam's face would turn a deep red and he'd start to sputter, "You . . . you." This only made Jared laugh louder and louder. It had gotten to the point where Jared could turn Sam into a fuming volcano just by whispering his sister's name in his ear as they stood in line to go to the cafeteria for lunch. When Sam started shoving and hitting Jared, the trips to the principal's office began.

Sam had no way of understanding that his strongest weapon was silence combined with distance—ignoring Jared—because, according to him, "I didn't want the guys to think I was chicken." Many children believe that they will lose the respect of their peers if they don't stand up to those who torment them, and that often means expressing themselves loudly and aggressively. Naturally, it's the victim who usually gets in trouble in these cases.

Ignoring a tease gives children a powerful alternative that reduces their feelings of helplessness and empowers them to exercise self-control and cut off their automatic emotional response. Sam didn't want to ignore Jared; he wanted to "get him." But his teacher and I persuaded him to just try walking away the next time Jared began his attack—otherwise he risked being suspended from school. Eventually Jared got bored and stopped bothering Sam about his sister.

I believe that ignoring not only empowers the teasee and deters the teaser but also protects the teasee from potentially harmful situations. Just as I would quickly walk away from a sidewalk harangue to make sure that I am not encouraging interaction with someone who may turn out to be deranged and dangerous, I teach kids to ignore a teaser, who may take advantage of getting a reaction to turn into a full-blown bully. I firmly believe that children should remove themselves from situations in which they feel afraid or unsafe—physically or emotionally. That just seems like common sense. But I'm also attempting to protect the teasee's self-esteem and potential for developing confidence in his or her own competence. When subject to sudden, unprovoked verbal attacks, most kids, not surprisingly, are caught off guard. They don't know what to say or do, and staying in the situation usually means the teasing will continue or escalate. The victim of the teasing just ends up feeling more and more helpless, and often he or she feels ashamed of this helplessness as well.

As strongly as I feel that ignoring is an effective strategy, not everyone agrees. Some experts concur that ignoring removes the teaser's "payoff" and therefore will deter the teaser, but others say that ignoring is a reaction that lets the teaser know that the teasee is upset and is trying to "escape." He might even be called a "chicken" as he leaves the situation. I think the difference lies in whether the teasing is an isolated event or part of a long pattern. In my experience, ignoring works quite well in isolated incidents. A few experts emphasize that parents should prepare kids for the fact that ignoring will not discourage or deter teasing immediately, especially for kids who have reacted emotionally in recurring teasing situations. In fact, teasing may intensify when a child first begins to ignore the teaser. If the teaser is used to getting a reaction and all of a sudden he doesn't, he is likely to feel more challenged and try even harder to provoke his victim. It may take weeks for the teaser to give up. Consistency is the key in these cases.

When Is Ignoring Not Ignoring?

It's a familiar picture: Kyle is dancing around Sara, cackling and even poking her a little while he taunts, "You smell like garbage! You live in a garbage can!" Sara is standing stock-still, arms crossed tightly over her chest, her nose in the air, her eyes closed. Sara is not ignoring Kyle in the way that I mean. She *is*, in fact, reacting emotionally, in a sense daring Kyle to break through the rigid barrier she has erected with her body language. Of course he obliges her.

What I mean by ignoring consists largely of the child's removing himself from the situation, if not physically, then emotionally. Ignoring entails not looking at or responding to the teaser. Teasees should pretend that the teaser is invisible. Whenever possible, the child should walk away from the teaser and join other children. The teaser is not likely to continue his taunting in a crowd. Some kids pretend that they are interested in something else that is happening elsewhere.

When to Teach This Strategy

Ignoring is a great strategy for younger children, though it will not come naturally to them. (After all, one of the biggest lessons we try to teach a kindergartner is to listen to the teacher!) The younger a child is, the more important ignoring a tease may be because young children will not yet have many skills for handling situations in which they are being ridiculed or taunted. Removing themselves from the situation so that they are not subjected to verbal abuse protects their self-esteem from being damaged.

Children of all ages can learn how to ignore a tease or taunt. The key word is *learn*. It is not a skill that they automatically know how to use, although many of you may say that your kids do a great job of ignoring you, especially when you ask them to clean their room or do their homework.

Where Children Can Use This Strategy

Ignoring a tease or put-down can be used anytime and anywhere. Whether the teasing takes place in the classroom, on the playground, or at home, children can decide to ignore the teaser. It is generally a useful strategy when kids encounter name-calling on a sporadic basis or the occasional needling by a classmate. Sam found ignoring effective with Jared but only because he hung in there. Jared had already established a teasing routine with his classmate, and at first when he was ignored, Jared tried to push all of Sam's buttons, calling him "Chicken," saying he was as wimpy as his weird sister, and so forth. It was only after Sam continued to ignore him no matter what he pulled out of his hat that Jared finally gave in.

Ignoring may not deter the teasers who are persistent in their efforts to upset their targets. In fact, in these situations, ignoring may result in harsher or more intense teasing. It is often difficult to ignore taunts like "Why aren't you listening to me—are you deaf? Why don't you get a hearing aid?" and "Cat got your tongue? Can't you talk?"

Students have reported to me that it is harder to ignore teasers on the school bus because they cannot get away from them. Nevertheless, they work hard at not looking at or responding to anything the teaser says.

You might want to talk to your child about how some teases are low blows and ignoring should always be the first response. Some teasing is so demeaning that any other strategy would only acknowledge something that deserves no recognition at all. Try putting it this way to your child: "When you just don't know what to say or do because what the teaser is saying is so insulting or cruel, that's when you should always try ignoring."

How to Teach Your Child Ignoring

"Oh, just ignore it."

How often have we said that to our kids when they've complained of some annoyance or injustice? Telling kids to ignore teasing is stock advice, but it's easier said than done. We must specifically teach kids what ignoring means and looks like. As illustrated by Kyle and Sara, ignoring does not mean making a display of not responding; it means truly not reacting.

To demonstrate, role-play ignoring with your kids. Young children can learn the concept of body language and how they can communicate without using words. Begin by asking your child to show you (without using words) how he looks when he feels happy, sad, and mad. It's like playing a game of charades. Point out the differences in his body posture and his facial expressions, including his eyes and mouth. It is helpful for you to demonstrate these variations. Ask him to describe how your body and face appear when you are happy, sad, and mad.

Ask your child to show you "what ignoring looks like." Stress the importance of not showing how sad, hurt, or angry he might feel inside. Some children act as if they are emphatically walking away, while others appear nonchalant. The child should walk away from the teaser with his head held high and upright posture. Pretend that you are the teaser and insist your child ignore you, then that your child is the teaser and you ignore him. At some point during your practice, change your body language so that your child can see the difference between looking confident and looking scared, sad, or angry. A mother of a second-grader told me that she exaggerated the different body language to emphasize the nuances to her daughter.

Ignoring requires practice and repetition, especially with young children. When I begin to role-play ignoring with young children, they initially think it's very funny. In fact, more times than not, kindergartners and first-graders laugh as they act it out. Ignoring is a new and different situation for them. After a few tries, they usually get the hang of it and can ignore my teasing without the giggles. In fact, almost everyone wants the chance to demonstrate ignoring.

As mentioned earlier, you will have to remind children that ignoring usually works but may not stop the teaser who is determined to get a reaction from them. Some children do a great job of ignoring on several occasions and then all of a sudden blow up when they can't take it anymore. If your child is likely to encounter that situation, it may be helpful for her to use self-talk (see page 103) as a reminder to stay cool, such as "I can outlast the teaser. I will not lose my cool." When Sam tried to ignore Jared when he made fun of his little sister, Jared got louder, put his face in Sam's face, and acted more and more menacing. Walking away really felt like running away to Sam, but he persisted by saying to himself, "Controlling myself is the bravest thing I can do." It wasn't an easy couple of weeks, but by the end of that period Jared was finally convinced that Sam wasn't going to react anymore and he moved on.

The "I" Message

For almost forty years, "I" messages have been a favored tool for facilitating communication between two people. This technique, originated by Dr. Thomas Gordon, is a proven method for preventing conflict when one person wants to resolve a problem involving the other. It's also effective in helping people resolve an already smoldering conflict. The theory behind the technique is that when we are hurt or angry we tend to accuse or blame the person that we view as the cause of our distress: "*You* make me so mad!" "Why do *you* always do that?" Naturally this puts the other person on the defensive, making a mutually agreeable resolution pretty unlikely. When we deliver "I" messages instead—"*I* feel very angry when . . ." or "*I* don't understand . . ."—we invite the other person to empathize and consider our feelings, without making any accusations about his or her behavior or intentions.

Another important element of "I" messages is the trust that self-disclosure elicits. The more people reveal about their feelings, it turns out, the more others are inclined to trust and even like them.

The "I" message empowers kids who are being teased by giving them a way to express their feelings assertively without feeding the flames ignited by the teaser. Saying "I feel sad when you say nasty things about my sister" focuses the teasee's efforts on articulating the emotion that the teasing evokes. In this way it cuts off the automatic response, which in the case of most children is to act out those feelings. Using an "I" message can bring a half-hearted teaser over to the teasee's camp, though it won't necessarily deter one who will welcome news that the teasee is upset.

The "I" message may, however, have a positive effect on the teaser. "I" messages as I teach them have three parts.

The "I" message conveys how the teased child feels: "I feel sad . . ." The second part states why the child has these feelings: ". . . when you say nasty things about my sister." In the third part, the child expresses what he would like the teaser to do: "I would like you to stop talking about her." Sometimes the simple statement encased in the first two parts makes the third seem undeniably logical. In many cases (though certainly not all, as I'll discuss a little later), this is enough to make the teaser stop and think and then, well, *stop* (the teasing).

Here are a few examples of what "I" messages might sound like:

- A child who is teased about his glasses could say, "I feel upset when you make fun of my glasses. I would like you to stop."
- A physically challenged child once said to a child who ridiculed him because of the way he runs, "I don't like when you make fun of the way I run. This is the only way I can run. Please stop teasing me."
- Another child was upset because his classmates would often laugh when he gave the wrong answer in class. His "I" message was "I feel embarrassed when you laugh when I say the wrong answer."

When to Teach This Strategy

I routinely teach and review the "I" message strategy to students at all elementary grade levels, including kindergarten. Students seem eager to learn this simple technique to help them deal with stressful or uncomfortable situations. Perhaps that's because young children feel so frustrated and helpless when they first encounter hostility or criticism like teasing. If they're lucky, all they have learned at home is kindness, understanding, and empathy, and they tend to be thrown by anything else. Instinctively, because they learn so much by imitating, they will respond to teasing in kind. So in a sense the youngest kids already have to unlearn unproductive responses to teasing, and the "I" message gives them an alternative that they welcome.

Because they have to unlearn the automatic emotional response, it's critical that teachers and parents remember to encourage children to use this tool. Mrs. Barron, a kindergarten teacher, saw that Will became very upset when Tony knocked down the tower he was building with wooden blocks. She could see Will's anger quickly building. After finding out what had happened from both boys, she asked Will how he felt when Tony knocked down his tower. He said he was very mad. She reminded him of the "I" message and encouraged him to tell Tony how he felt. Will said, "I feel mad when you knock down the tower I'm building. Please don't do that again." With prompting from Mrs. Barron, Tony said that he was sorry. After this exchange, Will and Tony began building another tower together.

Kindergartners and first-graders often become upset when classmates budge in line or invade their space. Our teachers consistently remind them to use the "I" message in these situations. "I feel upset when you budge in line. Please stay in your space." These assertive words can replace the typically aggressive verbal and physical responses from young children. One first-grader shared in class, "I feel proud when I use the 'I' message. I'm going to use it a lot."

I know a kindergarten teacher who has a very big letter *I* hanging in her classroom as a visual reminder of the "I" message. When a child wants to use the "I" message with another student, he or she takes the *I* and holds it while saying the words. Holding the big *I* imparts more emphasis and importance to the words and seems to empower the child even more. I know a parent who applied the same kind of idea at home by putting the letter *I* on the refrigerator as a reminder to her kids to use the "I" message.

You may have noticed that the "I" messages I've given as examples seem a little formal in wording, fairly different from the natural speaking style of most children today. When I teach "I" messages to kids as young as kindergarten, I encourage them to use simple, direct language whose meaning is unquestionably clear. Their goal is to articulate their feelings about what the teaser has done and what they want the teaser to do instead. So, I tell very young children to say, "I feel . . . when you. . . . I would like you to. . . ." It may seem overly polite and formal, but its meaning is crystal clear. Using the word *feel* keeps children focused on reporting their emotional response to being teased. Giving kids a relatively strict prescription for the wording of their "I" messages keeps them from accidentally deviating from "I" messages and drifting back into "you" messages or into acting out their hurt and anger.

When these scripted "I" messages have become ingrained in children at a young age, they will develop their own, more natural wording as they get older. Older kids who are learning "I" messages for the first time can usually adopt their own unique phrasing successfully because they understand the subtle nuances of language and which words comprise an "I" message. A nine-year-old boy once said to his rude and offensive neighbor, "I get really upset when you tease me. I wish you would cut it out." One eight-year-old girl said, "I don't like it when you make fun of me. I wish you would leave me alone."

One junior high girl said, "I get so ticked off when you keep mocking me. Why don't you chill?" A thirteen-year-old said to his father, "I hate it when you don't let me go to the mall with my friends. I wish I had parents who weren't so strict." Gary, a sixth-grader with a learning disability, also has the tendency to be clumsy and, at times, physically awkward. Although he intended to place his lunch tray on the table, it spilled all over the floor. A classmate who was considered "cool" shouted, "Can't you see where to put your lunch?" Gary replied calmly but assertively, "I have a learning disability that sometimes makes it hard for me to know where I place things. I have a hard time judging space. I don't think it's anything to make fun of." The teaser said no more.

Where Children Can Use This Strategy

"I" messages have one weakness that can determine how effective they are. If they are to have the optimal effect, they require the teaser to stop and listen for a second. Teasers are usually so wrapped up in their own script that they are not too inclined to be good listeners. So "I" messages seem to work best in structured settings such as the classroom or at home when an adult is present. In unstructured or less supervised settings, such as at recess or on the school bus, the teaser may simply respond to an "I" message the same way she would respond to any verbal response from the victim—with more teasing. When the teaser's goal is to upset the teasee, hearing that the teasee is in fact upset may lead to further taunting. When I was very young, my brother used to have his dog chase me around the house. I hated it. I hated when the dog jumped on me and licked and accidentally scratched me. Of course the more I screamed, the more Harry told his dog to go after me. I'm sure this is why I've never had a dog and never will. If I had tried to stop screaming and said, "I feel scared when you make your dog jump on me and I want you to stop it," I think my brother would have laughed and sent his dog after me again. I may have felt empowered by coming up with a calmer response than running into my room screaming, but I'm sure my brother would have felt some satisfaction from continuing to know that I was upset.

Kids should understand that "I" messages are not just for teasing situations. Learning to express their hurt or anger in the form of "I" messages is a great way to head off tiffs before they start because the person on the receiving end is not made defensive by an accusation. Kids of all ages (and adults too) vary in their speaking and listening skills, and it's not uncommon for a statement intended to be friendly or neutral to be interpreted as hurtful. In such cases, the "I" message can convey the hurt feelings in a calm way. When Cynthia returned to school from the orthodontist with her mouth full of braces, she felt very self-conscious. As they were quietly working on an assignment, Annie began to giggle. Cynthia immediately felt hurt and humiliated, and the more she thought about her good friend laughing at her braces, the more upset she felt. After school, Cynthia used the "I" message to tell Annie that she was upset that her friend had laughed at her braces. Annie quickly clarified that she was laughing at a funny note that another classmate had passed to her. If Cynthia had confronted her friend with an angry accusation, Annie may very well have responded with instinctive anger of her own. Instead, Cynthia immediately felt better and a potential falling-out was avoided.

"I" messages can also help break negative patterns of interaction at home. Family members learn to expect certain behavior and responses in their interactions with each other, and it can be difficult to break out of those dynamics when a change is desirable. Children may hesitate to express certain feelings to their parents because what they say will be interpreted as "talking back." Siblings can end up avoiding each other because a pattern of harassment has backed them into a corner and they don't know how to get out. In these cases "I" messages can open a door to new communication and perspective on each other. When I asked students if they had a chance to use the "I" message during the preceding week, one second-grader reported that she had said to her father, "I feel so scared when you lose your temper. Please calm down." Her dad apparently looked stunned and apologized, saying he'd had no idea he was frightening his daughter.

How to Teach Your Child the "I" Message

The first step in teaching your child the "I" message is explaining the three components:

1. I feel . . .
2. when. . . .
3. I would like. . . .

Second, encourage your child to speak clearly and politely and to maintain eye contact with the teaser. Initially, many young children confuse the "I" message and "eye contact." So be sure to show your child what it means to look directly at the teaser. Just as body language is a crucial part of ignoring, kids should be aware of how they look while they are using the "I" message. Are they standing up straight or are they slouched over? When kids are slouched over, they tend to look at the ground rather than at the person they are talking to. Erect posture conveys confidence. What is their facial expression? Do they look like they are worried or self-assured?

After kids are aware of how they are supposed to look, you can focus on how they should sound. What is their tone of voice? Are they speaking clearly and politely or are they mumbling, shouting, or whining? As with the other strategies described so far, practicing and role-playing are the keys to success. The best mode of instruction is modeling. Parents who demonstrate the "I" message technique on a daily basis—communicating their feelings, why they have these feelings, and what they would like their children to do—find the children picking up the strategy very quickly.

- "I felt disappointed that you did not pick up your toys when I asked you to. I would like you to put them away now."
- "I was very worried when you did not call to tell me that you would be home later than we expected. Please call us if the situation happens again."
- "I feel disappointed when you are not honest with me. I would appreciate knowing what really happened."

Once children are accustomed to hearing these "I" messages from you, you can take advantage of the strategy to reinforce desirable behavior. Remember, what children want more than almost anything else is their parents' approval. Hearing how great their behavior has made you feel packs a lot more positive punch than merely thanking them or calling them "good."

- "I feel happy that you put your toys away when I asked you."
- "I'm so excited about your terrific grades. Keep up the great work!"

One final note: In an interesting twist on the "I" message, an eight-year-old boy recently told me that he said to his taunting next-door neighbor, "I know you're trying to upset me, but it's not working." His neighbor backed off.

Visualization

"You don't have to take it, you know."

"Well, then what do I do with it?"

Good question. We tell kids not to give a teaser what he wants. We tell them what to do and not do, say and not say, instead. But when we tell kids they don't have to take this harassment from a teaser, we better be prepared to tell them what to do with it instead of "taking it."

Fortunately, children have an abundant imagination. The same technique that has been used to help adults reach their highest goals can help kids fend off teasing aimed at them. Visualizing provides children with a "mental picture" of not having to accept or believe what the teaser has said. Through visualization, children can picture themselves protected in infinite ways from the words that are attacking them. Just as playing house and other pretend games helps young children prepare for and learn the skills for real-life demands on them, visualizing taunting words bouncing off them or a protective shield helps children practice mental self-protection.

One visualization that I've found kids respond to very well is the idea that teases and put-downs can "bounce off" them, like harmless soft balls. Another effective visualization is for a child to pretend that he has a protective shield around his body that deflects the teases and bad words. The following are examples of visualizations first-, second-, and third-grade students created.

- "I will hit the teases away with a baseball bat."
- "I am going to power kick the teases away."
- "I'm going to throw the bad words down the field for a touchdown."

- "I will just step on the teases."
- "When I ice skate, I will 'spin' the teases away."
- "I will play basketball and dribble the words away."
- "I am going to dive into the pool and splash the words away."
- "I'm an artist, and I will erase the teases."
- "I am a singer. I'm trying to sing the teasing away."
- "I will hit the teases away with my tennis racket."

- "I want to flip the teases away when I practice gymnastics."
- "When I garden, I'm going to dig the teases away."
- "I will vacuum the teases away."
- "I will pretend that I am a magician and make the teases disappear."
- "I will cook the teases away."
- "I can always flush the teases down the toilet."

When to Teach This Strategy

Here's one that the very youngest children, so adept at make-believe and so open to suggestion, can use with alacrity. In fact, you can turn this into a game in which the child is invited to come up with her own ideas for visualization. The more creative and the sillier, the better.

When you do this, be sure to emphasize that the mental pictures should not include any violence, even when you're talking to a really young child. When I initially asked first-graders to draw their own visualization, one student drew a picture of a gun shooting the teaser. I had to stress that the mental image or picture should be what you want to do with the *teases*, not the *teaser*.

As children get older, their visualizations often get more complex, especially if they've been using this strategy for a number of years. Many fifth-graders recall the visualizations they created when they were in first and second grades. Still others remember the analogy of the shield. Recently a social worker who was teaching a class of sixth-graders the Easing the Teasing strategies told me that one student said that he pictured himself ignoring the ridicule. This is adding a visual component to self-talk. Not only was he using self-talk to call in the ignoring strategy, but he was going to imagine himself doing it. Another sixth-grader said that she visualized her mother holding her back from reacting in an angry way. A few sixth-graders said that they imagined what the consequences would be if they retaliated. Although this is not visualizing what they would do with the teases, it is visualizing the outcome based on ineffective and inappropriate reactions. What a great visualization!

Where Children Can Use This Strategy

This strategy, because it's passive and internal, can be used in all teasing situations. Anytime a child is called a name, insulted, or teased, he can immediately visualize the words bouncing off him or being repelled by a shield he is wearing. As kids become more familiar and skilled with the strategies, they might want to visualize what is happening to the teases while they are ignoring the teaser. A seventh-grader combined self-talk with a visualization that helped her "chill" and calm down. As she reminded herself not to show her anger, she visualized that she was relaxing on the beach, feeling the warm sunshine while she was listening to her favorite Backstreet Boys CD.

How to Teach Your Child Visualization

Teaching your children visualization should be fun. As I mentioned, it calls into play all of the child's powers of imagination. The best way to start may be to plant a couple of suggestions. Explain to your child that teasing doesn't have to get to her. Mention the other strategies in this chapter that can help her keep teasing from hurting her, such as self-talk and ignoring. Then say that another great technique involves creating a picture in her head of how she wants to fend off the hurtful words hurled at her.

- **Letting teasing bounce off.** Tell your child to imagine that the teasing words are soft balls like Nerf balls and they will just bounce off when thrown at her. I once advised a mother to write the put-downs and insults on the Nerf balls and throw them at her son. This concrete demonstration helped him understand that the balls (and the words) bounced off, and he did not have "to take" what the teaser said.

- **Putting up a shield.** Young children are able to understand this concept. I use the analogy of bulletproof vests that police wear to protect them from gunshots. The children's imaginary shield can protect them from hurtful words just as the vests protect the police. Tell your child to imagine putting on this vest when any teasing begins.

• **Creating your own visualization.** Young children like to draw what they could pretend to do with the teases and hurtful words. The visualization may be related to an interest such as baseball, ice-skating, soccer, or gardening. Remember to focus on what your child will do with the teases, not the teaser. One seven-year-old girl who adores ice-skating drew a picture of her "spinning" the teaser away. She later changed it to "spinning" the put-downs away. Important pieces of work like these should be hung on the refrigerator as a reminder.

Turning the Tease Around: Reframing and Accepting the Tease as Positive

When I was a young teenager, my sister, who was nine years younger than I, was terrified of cows. I'm not sure why, but it may have had something to do with the cutouts of the cow jumping over the moon that hung from the wall beside her crib. I do know that I took every opportunity I could to point out cows to Lesley, and the more she screamed when she saw one, the more I laughed and teased her some more. I would point out cows in pictures, I pointed out every cow in a pasture that we passed on our regular trips to visit friends who lived about an hour away, and I mooed when my parents weren't listening. But the worst thing I ever did to my sister was to open "Volume C" of the *World Book Encyclopedia* to the "cow" entry and slip the book under her pillow. I couldn't wait for her to get into bed so I could listen to her scream, and she fulfilled my fondest wish, screaming bloody murder. My reaction? To laugh and taunt her with the picture of the cow. What if Lesley had had the wherewithal to respond to my teasing by thanking me for putting the encyclopedia under her pillow because she could learn so much while she slept?

I'm sure that response would have stopped me in my tracks. After all, the fun of my teasing lay in hearing her react with such upset. Without that, I quickly would have gotten bored.

Reframing a tease, turning it around so that it is taken as a positive comment, is a powerful way to defuse a tease and deflate a teaser.

I usually call this "turning the tease into a compliment," but I know a first-grader who put it best when she expressed the effect of this strategy: reframing "kind of takes the tease out of it."

Reframing is a strategy that involves changing one's perception about a situation or experience. I often use the analogy of a painting that you might have stored in your basement or attic. You think that the painting is so ugly. You decide to select a different frame or reframe the painting. When you do, it has a completely different look. In fact, you love the picture so much that you hang it over your fireplace in your living room. "Reframing" the painting altered your perception.

In its simplest form, taking a tease as a compliment, a child simply responds to any tease with this kind of statement:

- "What a great put-down!"
- "Thanks for your opinion."
- "I appreciate your attention."
- "You haven't paid me this much attention in a long time."
- "How nice of you to notice."

The idea is simply not to take the tease as an insult. A girl who was teased about her glasses—"Four eyes, four eyes, you have four eyes!"—politely replied, "Thanks for noticing my glasses." Nine-year-old Lisa was a convenient target of her classmate Melanie, who liked to make comments about what she was wearing or doing. When Melanie made a rude comment about Lisa's shirt, she responded by saying, "It is amazing to me that you always notice what I am wearing or doing." Melanie did not respond as Lisa raised her hand to ask her teacher a question. Lisa's consistent use of reframing began to discourage Melanie's belittling remarks.

These types of responses usually surprise and discourage the teaser, who (as we discussed in Chapter 3) will often be motivated by the desire for an emotional reaction from the teaser—as I was with my sister.

Reframing and accepting the tease as positive can take forms other than just thanking the teaser for noticing the teasee, as the examples later in this section illustrate. More important than the form of the reframing, however, is its effect. This strategy is certainly aimed at stopping the teasing by discouraging or catching the teaser off guard. But it is not intended to humiliate the other child, even though a teased child may want to see the teaser feel the same pain that he or she inflicted. First and foremost, the strategy, like all others in this book, is aimed at empowering the teasee.

When to Teach This Strategy

Depending on a child's verbal skills, many five-year-olds are able to catch on to reframing. Older kids often demonstrate a lot of creativity as they brainstorm what they can say to reframe the tease. It takes a quick mind—or, more realistically, lots of practice and advance role-playing—to come out with a reframing statement spontaneously when teased.

Still, there are possibilities. A five-year-old could be taught to just say, "Thanks for noticing." These simple words empower many young children. Eleven-year-old Michelle, who was extremely smart, was called a "walking dictionary" and "teacher's pet." She replied to these accusations very confidently when she said, "I take that as a compliment." What more can the teaser say? Kelly, age twelve, was ridiculed sarcastically by an envious former friend about having so many friends who are boys. Kelly responded by saying, "I am so happy and proud to have so many friends who are boys."

Where Children Can Use This Strategy

Reframing can be used in response to teases that are either true statements or opinions. Here are some examples:

Teaser: "Your lunch looks like vomit. How can you eat that?"
Teasee: "I see that you are really interested in what I am eating."

Teaser: "Shorty! Midget!"
Teasee: "I'm glad I'm so short because I can look up to you."

Teaser: "You are really a shrimp."
Teasee: "How did you know that shrimp is my favorite food?"

One boy told me, "Kids call me 'Brain' because I'm smart and like to answer my teacher's questions. I tell them that I'm proud to be smart." A girl described how she reframed a tease: "I have red hair that is really curly. A kid on the bus said that my hair reminded him of spaghetti. I told him that I love spaghetti."

Here's a great example of catching a teaser off guard. In a degrading way, a classmate said to the girl seated next to him, "I see that you got a bad grade on the test." She replied, "I see that you are really concerned about my grade." It's doubtful that the boy wanted to be perceived as concerned, which is likely why he immediately turned back to his own work.

As I was reviewing the strategies with a second-grade class, one of the students asked that I tease him about being short. (He is one of the shortest kids in his class.) When I complied with his request, he responded with a big smile, "I feel happy when you tease me about being short. Please keep it up." He was very proud that he had combined the "I" message and reframing.

How to Teach Your Child to Reframe Teasing

Reframing takes a great deal of practice and rehearsal because very few children instinctively can make these comebacks. You can help your child brainstorm to prepare for teasing situations, however. Explore reframing comments at the dinner table, for example, making a list and adding to it as more comments are suggested at a later date. Which comment does your child like best? The support that kids feel when their family joins in on strategizing in this way is comforting and meaningful.

Parents should practice and rehearse reframing with their kids, but the process should stay fluid and responsive to the child's unique personality, strengths, and weaknesses. As parents, you'll soon learn what particular strategy your kids are most comfortable with. I find that continued review and practice seem to desensitize and alleviate some initial and automatic anxiety about teasing. Review and practice build confidence. It may be necessary to periodically review as social challenges increase as kids get older.

Once you've practiced this strategy, you might try surprising the child with teases to give the child practice in the quick response. (But always keep it pretty bland, so you don't unintentionally hurt the child's feelings while role-playing!) You can make this a very funny—and fun—game between the two of you. You can pop your head into the bathroom while your son is brushing his teeth and say, "You have huge teeth." See how long it takes before he can reframe this tease as a compliment. Also see how creative his responses get over time. He might start out with just "Thanks for noticing my teeth" and progress to "Thanks—choppers like these make great smiles."

Agreeing with the Teaser

"Tell him he's right."

"*WHAT?*"

When I tell kids to agree with a teaser in those cryptic terms, I always get the same response: disbelief. I've been giving them strategies that empower them and deter the teaser, and now I'm telling them to become passive and to tell the teaser that whatever he says is accurate. Naturally they can't believe I mean it—until I demonstrate what the result usually is.

- The teaser says, "You have so many freckles." The teasee then replies, "Yes, I have a lot of freckles."
- The teaser ridicules a child for crying: "You're a crybaby."
  The child who is crying can answer, "I know that I cry easily."

Agreeing with the facts usually eliminates the defensive and embarrassing feelings of wanting to hide the freckles and tears. This strategy usually takes away the reason for the particular tease.

It is amazing to me that many children find this to be such a revelation. They are so used to automatically feeling defensive that they often don't realize they can easily say, "Yes, you're right," or "I know." I have seen so many children look relieved when they realize how easy it is to agree with the facts. A seven-year-old girl, who learned this strategy in first grade, recently told me that a classmate commented that she reads so slowly. She responded by saying, "I am not a fast reader." The teaser never said another word about her reading. When I practiced this with second-graders, a boy who is quite short always wanted to volunteer for role-playing. He pleaded with me to tease him about being short. Each time he role-played he gained more confidence in his response. With wonderful eye contact, a confident tone of voice, and a smile, he said, "Yes, I am short. In fact I think that I am the shortest person in my grade and in my family."

When to Teach This Strategy

Kids of all ages can catch on to this strategy very quickly, but not all kindergartners will appreciate it as much as older children. Some young kids just won't feel right about agreeing with someone who is insulting them. They won't be able to distance themselves enough from being called "short," for example, to remember there's nothing wrong with being short. Sometimes these children are too hurt to understand why someone would mock them for a characteristic they can't do anything about and why something that more directly increases their own empowerment, such as self-talk, would be a more effective first choice.

Older children can have lots of fun with this strategy. In fact I've known some witty middle school and junior high students who were able to turn the entire teasing episode to their advantage by not only agreeing with the teasing but then taking it to hilarious extremes making fun of themselves. I probably don't have to tell you how a teaser feels about the audience shifting their admiring attention away from the teaser to the teasee.

Where Children Can Use This Strategy

This strategy works best in situations where the teasing is about some physical or other innate characteristic. There's nothing more disarming than a simple, succinct "Yes, I do have pretty poor vision," or "I know—math is my worst subject," or "Yeah, I am definitely the crummiest basketball player on this team." This kind of response often renders teasers speechless—which can be the teasee's cue to just walk away. Many teasers will stand there for a minute, waiting for the teasee to say something inflammatory or emotional that will give him a chance to come back with another put-down. If others are watching, the teaser in this case may feel embarrassed and give up on this victim.

I do not advocate agreeing with the teaser if the tease is not true. However, agreeing with a false accusation seemed to work for nine-year-old Andy. When someone told him that his jacket was "dorky," he said simply, "I don't like it either." The teaser never mentioned the jacket again. Although Andy liked his jacket, he thought he would agree with the teaser rather than continue the conversation. He felt in control of the situation. However, I would be concerned about any child who was hesitant to stand up for what he believes or likes on a consistent basis because of the fear of losing friends.

- Samantha was called "Scaredy Cat" during a frightening movie. She replied to the teaser that she was afraid.
- A seven-year-old girl who was teased about being short said, "I'm probably the shortest kid in our grade. Would you like to know how short I am?"
- When nine-year-old Laura was called "Metal Mouth," she answered, "I do have a lot of metal in my mouth."
- When eight-year-old Tracy was called "Four Eyes," she humorously said, "My vision is so bad I *wish* I had four eyes."

How to Teach Your Child to Agree with the Teaser

This is one of the easiest strategies to teach your child. Most children who are teased about a trait, quality, or difference often feel relieved that they can just say, "I do," or "That's right." It's a great idea to involve kids in the process of brainstorming responses that agree with the facts. Perhaps your children will come up with some of the following:

- "You've got that right."
- "People tell me that a lot."
- "That's right."
- "I do that a lot."
- "Yes, I am."
- "That is true."
- "You are exactly right."
- "That is totally accurate."

As with the other strategies, practicing and role-playing ensure success. Don't forget to remind your kids about standing up straight, making eye contact, and speaking with a confident tone of voice.

A child who is not comfortable with the particular trait or behavior that the tease is about may find it difficult to agree with the facts. You may have to help your child develop self-acceptance of the attribute or condition. This will lead to a comfort level that will enable him to agree with the facts without feeling totally embarrassed or humiliated. If your child cannot reach a comfort level with the particular trait or condition, this strategy should not be encouraged. Eight-year-old Amanda was quite overweight and was very self-conscious about it. Occasionally, she would receive comments about her size. She said that she was more comfortable ignoring the teaser than agreeing. She thought that if she agreed with the facts, she would probably feel worse. In contrast, when eleven-year-old Thomas was ridiculed about his weight, he calmly replied, "I know I'm a big guy." Recently, at a parent presentation, a mother explained that she thought that agreeing with the teaser is acknowledging that the trait or attribute is negative. If the child believes it is a negative, this strategy should not be used. Agreeing with the facts is acknowledging agreement with the *reality* of the trait or situation.

Eric, who is in third grade, has difficulty with most academic tasks because of a learning disability. One classmate called him "stupid." Although Eric admitted to his parents that he feels "stupid" sometimes, agreeing with this specific accusation would not be appropriate or advisable. He could use other strategies or just acknowledge that some schoolwork is hard for him.

Perhaps if my sister had said to me calmly, "Yes, I am afraid of cows," my taunting her about the cows would have ceased.

"So?"

When Peter was ridiculed during recess about wearing his Chicago Bears jersey, considering that at the time the Bears were so pathetic, he responded with "So?" His tone was calm and casual, and he appeared unruffled. He did not get defensive of his jersey or the Chicago Bears. The response of "So?" communicates to the teaser that the tease or put-down really does not matter. It is like shrugging your shoulders. This often defuses the tease. It should be said in an indifferent tone, not sarcastically. Teasers often do not know how to respond to "So?" Other responses that convey indifference are "Your point being?" "Really?" "Who cares?" Children find this strategy to be simple, very effective, and fun.

When to Teach This Strategy

Kids of all ages are able to successfully say "So?" This is one of the easiest for younger children because it is simple to remember. Responding with "So?" can be viewed as falling in between ignoring and agreeing with the teaser. The teaser is expressing disinterest but also tacit agreement. So, while it's easy for young kids to remember, it may also be more appealing to older kids than either ignoring or agreeing because it incorporates both reactions.

When Alex, a third-grader, received the results of his state achievement testing, his older brother boasted, "My scores were better than yours." Alex shrugged his shoulders and said, "So what?" His brother was disappointed that Alex did not get mad.

Gary recalls the first day of his first Little League game. He was so excited to wear his uniform. His baseball cap made his curly hair look longer than it really was. Frank, a player on Gary's team, remarked, "Oh man, you look like a girl." Gary answered, "So, I have long hair. Big wup."

Where Children Can Use This Strategy

Kids can say "So?" to any tease, comment, or put-down in any setting. This easy and effective strategy can be used in the classroom, on the playground or campground, on the bus, as well as in the neighborhood. I always emphasize to kids that this strategy is not to be used when their parents point out to them that they have not done their homework or cleaned their room!

How to Teach Your Children to Say "So?"

Most parents find this easy to teach because kids find this easy to learn and use. This strategy is fun to role-play and practice at the dinner table, in the car, or before bedtime. Ask your child what she would like you to tease her about. Generally, you will receive the cheerful response of "So?" Young children love to hear the story *The Meanest Thing to Say*, by Bill Cosby, which humorously addresses this strategy.

If my sister had said "So?" when I accused her of being afraid of cows, I would have been stunned by her indifference. I'm sure it would have taken the wind out of my sails, and the teasing would have stopped being fun for me. I probably would have stopped teasing her.

Complimenting the Teaser

Sometimes Philip was teased about the way he runs. He has a slight physical disability that causes him to run slower than his classmates. When a boy in gym class made a comment to Philip about his slow running, he said, "You're a great runner. I'm glad I'm on your team." Elly, who was teased about her braces, responded to the teaser, "You have beautiful teeth. I hope that my teeth look as nice as yours when I'm finished with my braces." Ten-year-old Martin was an easy target because he was overweight and quite sensitive. He easily overreacted. Kids teased him about many things, including his name. When he was called "Fartin' Martin," he responded by saying (after much practice), "What a clever poet you are!" When eleven-year-old Theresa was teased about being overweight, she answered, "You're lucky you don't have to go on a diet."

Responding to a tease with a compliment catches the teaser off guard in the same way that agreeing does, but it takes agreeing one step further. The agreement is implicit in the compliment. In this case, though, the teasee is not only agreeing with the teaser but turning the focus of attention on the teaser. What really takes the teaser by surprise, however, is that the attention from the teasee is positive! Children who tease often have their own rules—even if they could not articulate them on command—about where the line between teasing and outright cruelty lies. For many of them, continuing to tease a child who has just complimented them after being teased is tantamount to kicking someone when he's down. They just can't go on.

When to Teach This Strategy

Although I have seen kindergartners learn this strategy, it is not one they usually select when we practice. First- and second-graders as well as older kids are able to successfully learn how to respond with a compliment. Most kids need a little clarification that this is responding to the tease with a compliment, which is different from reframing, which is accepting the tease as if it were a compliment. Demonstrating examples of each clarifies the difference.

- A second-grader who was teased about her slow reading said to her classmate, "I am a slow reader. You are a great reader."
- The same girl used the same strategy when someone commented about her soccer skills. She quickly said, "You are a great soccer player."
- A nine-year-old boy who was teased about striking out in the baseball game stated, "I felt bad that I struck out. I wish I could hit the ball as much as you do. You are a great player."

Where Children Can Use This Strategy

Responding with a compliment is a great strategy to use when a child is teased about a trait, attribute, behavior, or condition that is different but is perceived by the teaser as negative or inferior. This strategy, like reframing, can be used in response to teases that are either true statements or opinions. Responding with a compliment can be used with the agreeing strategy.

How to Teach Your Child to Respond with a Compliment

As with reframing, kids often demonstrate a lot of creativity when you brainstorm with them how they can respond with a compliment. Knowing what to say spontaneously when teased requires lots of practice and advance role-playing. This is especially true with this strategy because, initially, the teasee does not often feel like saying something nice to the person who just offended or insulted him. Practicing this will help your child understand how he can pull this off and how this strategy will catch the teaser off guard. While rehearsing, don't forget to remind your child to maintain eye contact and appear confident while expressing the compliment. Don't be concerned if your child appears awkward or uncomfortable at first. Repeated practice and rehearsal will lead to familiarity, comfort, and confidence. Also stress that you don't mean the child should fawn over the teaser or seem obsequious. That will only convey to the teaser that he or she has gained some additional power.

If Lesley had said to me, "You're so lucky because you aren't afraid of cows. Maybe you could help me not be so afraid," I doubt I would have continued my taunts. Realistically, I must admit that I am not sure I would have helped her with her fear. Make sure your child understands that complimenting the teaser is not necessarily going to turn the teaser into the child's best friend or even a helpful acquaintance. Deterring the teasing should be good enough!

Humor

Humor is a great stress-reducer, and it can often ease a teasing situation. Many of the previously discussed strategies can be humorous. The child being teased can either respond by saying something funny, or he can just laugh or smile. The teasee can say, "That's so funny. You make me laugh." The teaser, who is expecting an angry or tearful response, is surprised when the teasee reacts with laughter or humor. I've known a few kids who laugh or smile as they walk away from the teaser. A student told me that she looked in a mirror to decide what kind of smile she was going to use. As with the other strategies, practice and rehearsal are crucial for success.

- A boy's physical disability caused him to run slower than other kids. When kids teased him about his slow running, he answered, "I think I run like a turtle."
- Brian, who was frequently teased about his large nose, began to sniff and wiggle his nose, which defused the situation.
- Angela, who was teased about her freckles, asked the teaser if she wanted to play dot-to-dot.
- When Alyssa was called "Four Eyes" when she wore her glasses to school for the first time, she replied, "These glasses are 'for' my eyes."
- When Jake was ridiculed because he was consistently the last one to finish his work in class, he said, "I come from a family of snails."

When to Teach This Strategy

All children appreciate humor, but not all of them can deliver it, especially under pressure. It can be particularly difficult for younger children to put on a smile or emit a laugh when they are already making a huge effort to appear impassive rather than hurt or angry. I'd save this strategy for a child who already exhibits the aplomb to laugh under pressure, whatever his or her age.

Where Children Can Use This Strategy

Humor is the great equalizer and can be effective in almost any situation. I'd make an exception, though, for truly demeaning, belittling teasing incidents. Bigotry, mocking of physical and mental disabilities, and similar cruelties are never laughing matters, and kids should not be encouraged to smile or in any other way make light of them. Humor should be effective in any case when agreeing, reframing, or complimenting would be suitable. In fact, those strategies already rely heavily on dry humor.

How to Teach Your Children to Use Humor

Wit is a gift, and not all kids have it in equal measure. I'm not sure there is any way you can teach a person to be funny except possibly by providing models. Point out the kind of gentle, undemeaning humor that you would like your child to use when you see it in movies or on TV. Read funny stories and books to impart the subtleties of humor. Lore Segal's *Tell Me a Mitzi* and *Tell Me a Trudy* are great examples of gentle, dry humor that will tickle the younger funny bones. Anything by Shel Silverstein will show kids the humorous power in words. Roald Dahl is another perennial side splitter.

Another possibility is to brainstorm with your child. You can have a lot of fun and take the sting out of teasing just sitting around conjuring up funny responses to the kinds of teasing the child has received and can anticipate.

When to Ask for Help

Most types of teasing can be dealt with effectively by children if it is not chronic or repeated over a long period of time. However, at times it is necessary for a child to seek adult assistance or intervention when the teasing is prolonged, when it occurs frequently, or if the child does not feel emotionally or physically safe. In most bullying situations, a child needs adult intervention.

How to Instruct Your Children to Ask for Help

We must help children understand that asking for help or "reporting" in these situations is not "tattling." Reporting is when a child tells an adult that someone is doing something that is repeatedly upsetting or harmful. Tattling usually occurs when one child is trying to get another's attention or is attempting to get another child "in trouble" for a behavior that is not that significant. Discuss with your child whom he would approach for help, if necessary. When I ask students whom they would turn to for help, the list includes parents, teachers, playground supervisors, the principal, school social worker or counselor, grandparents, baby-sitters, brothers, and sisters. It is also important for children to remember that they can ask friends or classmates for help. There is strength in numbers. Support from classmates can often serve as powerful positive peer pressure that is very effective in easing the teasing. Kids can effectively use the "I" message when they are asking for help. A second-grader said to her teacher, "I feel very upset that a few kids make fun of the way I talk. I have asked them to stop, but they won't. They copy the way I talk. Can you help?"

To Sum Up

The effectiveness and success of the Easing the Teasing strategies generally depend on the child's feeling comfortable and confident in using them. Comfort and confidence develop from "the other 3 R's": rehearsal, repetition, and review. Just as children have to consistently review math facts and spelling words, they must repeatedly practice these techniques. Frequent discussions and role-playing foster and enhance a child's successful use of the strategies.

After I teach students the ten strategies, I devote at least one class session to practicing them. I pretend that I'm the teaser, and the kids must decide which strategy to use. The students are very enthusiastic about this exercise. One student approached me a few days before our scheduled "teasing" discussion with a big smile on her face. She asked, "Mrs. Freedman, are you coming to our class to tease us next week?" When I said, "Of course," she replied, "I can't wait!" The students had fun going home and sharing with their parents that the social worker was coming into class to tease them!

I begin the "teasing" session by asking the kids who would like to be teased and what they would like to be teased about. Most children are eager to volunteer. We role-play the insults and put-downs that are presented. They respond with an appropriate strategy and sometimes want to role-play two or three different responses to the same tease. I teased eight-year-old Cody about his braces. I called him "Brace Face." He replied with three strategies. "Thanks for noticing, but I prefer to be called 'Railroad Track.' I hope that my teeth will look as nice as yours." I find that the continued review and practice seem to desensitize and alleviate some initial and automatic anxiety about teasing.

The Easing the Teasing strategies usually empower kids and reduce feelings of helplessness in teasing situations. Still, children will often go further and try different strategies until they find the one that is the most effective to stop the teasing. Sometimes they succeed. If they don't, and the coping skills in this chapter don't give them the ability to stave off hurt from the teasing, you'll notice that your child is continuing to experience stress or anxiety from chronic teasing. In that case it's important to consult with your child's pediatrician; teacher; or school social worker, psychologist, or counselor for additional guidance and advice.

MY brother was teasing me so I said, "Your Point Being." He got so anowed that he walked away.

Your Point Being!

When I am getting my feelings hurt I ignore the person and play the feelings away.

7

---◆---

Easing the Teasing at School

How Parents and Teachers Can Work Together

The literature confirms what I have heard throughout my work-shops. A majority of schools have not actively, consistently, or effectively dealt with the bullying and teasing that takes place at school every day. It's understandable that they have not. Past conventional wisdom says that kids should "fight their own battles" and work things out themselves. Attempts to be fair caution school employees against being too quick to take sides in conflicts. And even when they do wish to intervene, teachers and administrators rarely feel sure of how to do so.

A fair measure of truth lies in most adages we live by, and the ones stating "boys will be boys" and that behaviors like teasing and bullying are "all just part of growing up" are no exception. But it is also true that a teased child often needs support at school in addition to the coping skills taught in Chapter 6, and I have met hundreds of otherwise well-adjusted children who feel that teachers or other school personnel have not intervened effectively when they have been teased. I've talked to hundreds of parents who are frustrated that schools have been unresponsive to their pleas for help.

In this chapter, you will learn how to form a fruitful partnership with your child's school so that it can work to resolve any teasing your child is suffering while building an environment that is hostile to teasing and tormenting of any child by any other child. The first section of the chapter is devoted to tips for communicating productively with teachers and school administrators. The second section contains tools and techniques that you can offer to your child's school for use with the entire student population.

You might ask why your child's school would welcome this kind of "interference" from you. Naturally, teachers and school administrators will resist parents' attempts to undermine their authority, claim expertise where none exists, or disrupt a carefully planned educational program. But in my experience, school personnel will welcome help with teasing, as long as it is offered tactfully, without accusation, and accompanied by concrete suggestions. In the wake of tragedies like Columbine and subsequent incidents, more and more schools are seriously looking at violence prevention. Character education programs are becoming increasingly popular in classrooms. Schools are also responding to the wake-up call sent by the U.S. Supreme Court ruling on May 24, 1999, in the case of *Davis v. Monroe County Board of Education*. The Supreme Court determined that public schools may be sued and forced to pay damages for failing to stop sexual harassment by students. Public school districts that receive federal monies can be held liable when they are "deliberately indifferent" to the harassment of students. Although we often think of sexual harassment occurring in junior high and high school, it might have its origin in the teasing that occurs between girls and boys in primary grades.

Parents are often instrumental in facilitating more active and effective school intervention in incidents of verbal and physical aggression. Many anti-teasing and anti-bullying campaigns have been implemented because parents have pleaded with school personnel not to ignore this universal problem. It is a logical partnership. Parents often need to rely on teachers for insight and guidance. Teachers need to hear from parents about situations they may not be aware of.

The list of ways to air the issues surrounding teasing in the classroom and how to minimize it is limited only by the imagination of the adults and children involved. The wealth of ideas available empowers parents to approach teachers and principals, and I am finding schools are receptive to listening to and implementing many of these user-friendly activities. It is my hope that schools will proactively teach young children coping skills for teasing situations just as we teach "stranger danger." Teaching these to young children will help them deal with teasers they encounter and better prepare them for the more difficult social challenges that they will encounter in later years. Children who are able to effectively deal with name-calling and ridicule are less likely to become victims of bullies.

Approaching Your Child's School for Help

A parent of a shy fourth-grade boy called to inform me that her son was not eating his lunch because of taunting occurring at his lunch table. A few boys were pretending to take his food. They would stop whenever a lunchroom supervisor came over to the table. I shared this information with the classroom teacher. She spoke with her class about appropriate lunchroom behavior without mentioning specific names. I alerted the lunchroom supervisors, who more closely monitored the situation. The teasing stopped, and the student resumed eating his lunch.

Sounds simple, but you and I know that getting from hearing your child complain about teasing to enlisting the school's help in stopping it requires a big leap—one that demands effective parent-teacher communication.

When Do You Ask for Help?

Usually, parents know when their own guidance or advice is not working and they need to call in the school personnel. If the situation doesn't seem urgent, you can start with Chapter 6 and see if any of these strategies helps your child put a stop to the teasing or at least deflect its harmful effects. If not, ask yourself the following questions, which might help you make the decision to seek assistance.

- How long has your child been upset? Is it a temporary situation or a regular occurrence?
- Does your child not want to go to school?

- Is your child complaining of physical ailments more than usual?
- Has there been a deterioration in your child's academic work?
- Is your son or daughter sad or stressed most of the time?

A simple "yes" to any one question is not necessarily enough to indicate the need for help. If a child is distressed about being teased or taunted, most of these questions will get an affirmative answer, but a child can exhibit the same symptoms in reaction to other problems, such as academic difficulties or health-related issues.

Intuitive and concerned parents usually know when additional help is warranted. When my sons were younger and got sick, I usually knew when they had colds and other minor illnesses that I could handle and when I needed medical assistance. I also knew whether a simple phone call to the doctor would do it or only an office visit would suffice. Calling the doctor was usually motivated by *my* stress level.

I believe you should take a similar approach when trying to decide whether to call for assistance with teasing. Trust your instincts. Base your decision on your own stress level or your feelings of helplessness that result from the child's stress. A call or conference with the teacher or other school personnel can be a big first step in resolving the child's problem and thus relieving your stress.

If your child has been complaining regularly about teasing, start compiling a list of the incidents that she describes. A list of when and where incidents occurred is a visual record that will give you a clearer understanding of the extent of the problem. Seeing how the list "grows" can be the impetus to make the call for assistance.

How Do You Ask for Help?

As noted in Chapter 5, I encourage parents to approach school personnel with the idea that you would like to work *together* to resolve the problem. Parent-school communication is the prerequisite to collaboration and effective problem solving. Some parents are very frustrated and angry that the school has allowed the situation to exist and continue. Although I certainly understand this anger, it can interfere with the meeting's success.

The list of incidents you have compiled can help you stay focused on the facts and keep you from speaking from pure emotion. Taking this list with you also aids your recall. It communicates to the teacher, social worker, counselor, or principal that you are serious and have made efforts to be objective rather than flying off the handle and running to the school at your child's very first complaint.

Where to Take Your Requests for Help

It's important to follow the appropriate chain of command in your school or school district for a couple of reasons. First, it will save you time on potential backtracking or buck-passing. Second, it will generally make school personnel more receptive to your concerns and requests. For example, if the teasing is taking place in your child's classroom and you go directly to the principal instead of approaching the teacher, you might rob yourself of the assistance and goodwill of the teacher by going over his or her head. Many teachers will take this as a sign of lack of trust or confidence in them.

If you don't feel the teacher has effectively addressed the issue, a logical next step would be to approach the assistant principal, principal, or headmaster. Some parents might choose to talk to the school's mental health professional. However, this is not always an option because not all schools provide counseling service. Some parents choose to bypass the principal and go right to the school district's superintendent. I strongly suggest that you follow the chain of command within each district, keeping in mind that it will vary from location to location. To find out the chain of command in your area, ask the school secretary, usually a valuable resource for this kind of information. The school directory or a parent-student handbook will often include a list of administrators in the district.

Another option is to voice your concerns at a school board meeting. Again, however, it's important to understand the protocol before you barge in and demand to be heard. I know one local parochial school where visitors are allowed to state their issues during a short period at the end of an open board meeting. But, they may not speak during the meeting, and they cannot expect a response to their concerns at the meeting at which they express them. Another avenue open to parents at this school is to write a letter to the school board and ask that it be aired at the meeting. Check the school board's bylaws and constitution to see what the sanctioned procedures might be.

In my area, a large public school district also has local school councils (LSCs), established under the School Reform Act of 1988 by the Illinois State Legislature. The philosophy is that site-based management promotes involvement, collaboration, and cooperation among parents, teachers, administrators, and the community. Many LSCs focus on academic issues in addition to safety. The councils have become meaningful and positive partners in children's education.

The problem with airing concerns at a school board meeting is that regularly scheduled open meetings may occur only once a month or so. Also, procedures for getting an issue added to the agenda vary, and some parts of meetings may be closed altogether. If you need a quick response, this might not be the fastest way to get it. You might stick with school personnel for help in resolving the immediate problem and reserve communications with the school board for pursuit of longer-term solutions.

Local parent-teacher organizations (called PTOs, PTAs, or home-school associations, among other names, depending on whether the school is public or private and where it is) are also very active and integral parts of most schools. Their functions vary, though they often concentrate on planning fund-raising events to provide supplemental materials and programs for students, such as cultural arts enrichment, and may not be the right vehicle for getting the kind of help you need. On the other hand, they might be ideal for providing sources of funds for parent and faculty education on teasing, bullying, and other social concerns. Often they will sponsor speakers or pay for extra professional development if the school's budget does not allow for this. In some cases, parents are included in many joint committees with faculty and administrators, which can open up another channel for communication. If your school does not have a PTA because of low numbers and interest, why not explore the idea of starting one yourself?

What Can You Expect from Your Requests for Help?

I would hope that parents could expect at least assurances that their children would be safe, physically and emotionally, at school at all times. Unfortunately, we cannot take this for granted. If you perceive that your child is not feeling safe, it is reasonable to expect the teacher and school administrator to be receptive to your concerns— just like you would attentively listen to your child's concerns. In some schools, the administrator will listen but will also dismiss or minimize a parent's concerns. That's when you take the next step up the ladder of communication and responsibility.

The ideal response would be attentive listening, an understanding of your concerns and feelings, a statement of a plan of action (such as investigating the situation with other school personnel and students), an appreciation for your bringing the issue to their attention, and an agreement to a follow-up meeting.

Several parents from various school districts have told me about their frustration when they independently approached their respective school principals about the teasing their kids were experiencing. They were upset about the lack of responsiveness and the minimization of the situation. One parent decided to share her concerns with the health and safety committee of the school's PTO. The committee took this information back to the PTO's executive board. After some informal exploration and networking with other parents, it was learned that a few other parents had similar concerns about their children. The executive board decided to approach the principal, asking how they could work together to address this issue. The principal agreed to work with them. As a first step, the principal supported the PTO's idea to invite me to talk to the parents about teasing. This well-attended parent education meeting raised the awareness of the parent community and served as an impetus for the school to discuss how they could better address the problem. As a follow-up, I was asked to provide an in-service for the teachers. This is just one example of how a request for help might lead to a positive outcome. There are many other routes by which you might get help from your school. I encourage you to persevere.

Offering the School Tools to Combat Teasing

The following are tools that any school—or, for that matter, Scout troop, camp, or other group setting for kids—can use to fight and prevent teasing. If your child is being teased, you will probably want to be sure that problem is addressed first. But once you've got the ball rolling, you can mention to your child's teacher, principal, social worker, or school counselor that you have some ideas that can help prevent the same situation from occurring in the future. Remember that you're trying to establish a partnership with the school. Offer to help with the implementation of the tools or in any other way that the teacher needs.

Teasing Survey for Classroom Use

Evaluating the degree and nature of teasing that is currently occurring is a good start toward a total anti-teasing campaign in a classroom or other group setting. Many teachers and social workers have used the following survey as a way to gather information to better understand the extent and nature of teasing. It also serves as a way to introduce the topic to students, which then becomes a springboard for further discussion. The survey heightens the awareness of teasing in the minds of students and teachers.

Please be aware that some teachers might resist receiving this survey directly from a parent because it might imply that they are not adequately dealing with the issue, and many teachers resent being told what to do by parents. If that is the case in your situation, my hope is that you will pass the survey (or, better yet, the whole book!) on to the principal or social worker, who could then introduce the ideas to the teachers. This has been the case in many schools where I have given workshops for teachers. In several schools, the social workers began using the survey in a particular grade level or in small groups. Teachers have witnessed the effectiveness of it and then asked to learn more about it. You could present the book to your school principal as a resource for teachers to have rather than insisting that they distribute it ASAP.

Parents may also want to complete the survey with their kids. The completed form may offer interesting information that a parent could share with the child's teacher.

The survey can be utilized by teachers, school social workers, counselors, or psychologists. Most of the small group and elementary school classroom assessments are oral. I believe, however, that a written survey is more appropriate for middle school and junior high school students, who generally are uncomfortable or perhaps embarrassed to share their teasing experiences with their classmates. For a more subtle approach with older kids, math teachers can ask students to conduct a survey about teasing and analyze the results.

In the survey, the choices in Question 3 should be adapted or modified according to the age of the students. The teacher should ask the students to sign their names but explain that he or she will not share the specific information with anyone without their permission, though general results will be discussed with the class. The survey should provide some valuable information about the nature and extent of teasing, but it may also help the teacher identify victims of frequent taunting and ridicule, which could lead to further exploration, investigation, and support. Many students might feel more comfortable sharing this information via the survey than taking the initiative to tell a teacher about their experiences. Children who are teased frequently will probably want the teacher to know who they are.

Teasing Survey

1. What is teasing?_____

_____

_____

_____

2. Have you ever been teased, made fun of, or insulted?

   ☐ Yes
   ☐ No

3. Which of the following have you been teased about? (Please check all that apply.)

   ☐ What you do
   ☐ What you think
   ☐ What you believe
   ☐ What you have
   ☐ What you don't have
   ☐ What you wear
   ☐ What you like
   ☐ What you don't like
   ☐ What you say
   ☐ What you eat
   ☐ How you eat
   ☐ How you act
   ☐ How you look
   ☐ How you feel
   ☐ How you perform in school
   ☐ How you read
   ☐ How you draw
   ☐ How you write
   ☐ How you talk
   ☐ How you walk
   ☐ How you run
   ☐ How you learn
   ☐ Being overweight
   ☐ Being underweight
   ☐ Being tall
   ☐ Being short
   ☐ Having teeth that are not straight
   ☐ Wearing braces
   ☐ Wearing glasses
   ☐ Wearing hearing aids
   ☐ Taking medication
   ☐ Having allergies
   ☐ Having a scar
   ☐ Being the oldest in the class
   ☐ Being the youngest in the class

☐ Being smart
☐ Not being smart
☐ Reading a lot of books
☐ Not knowing how to read
☐ If your parents are divorced
☐ How you sing
☐ How you play
☐ How you kick a ball
☐ How you throw a ball
☐ How you catch a ball
☐ How you jump rope
☐ If a family member has died
☐ Having a single parent
☐ Your hair
☐ Your toys
☐ Other _____

☐ Your clothes
☐ Your name
☐ Your habits
☐ Your mother
☐ Your father
☐ Your sisters
☐ Your brothers
☐ Your friends
☐ Your opinions
☐ Your culture
☐ Your race
☐ Your religion
☐ Your gender
☐ Having a learning disability
☐ Having a physical disability
☐ Having any difference

_____

4. How often are you teased? (Please check one answer.)

☐ Every day
☐ Several times a day
☐ Several times a week
☐ Maybe once a week
☐ Rarely

5. Where does the teasing take place? (Check the place or places where you have been teased.)

☐ In the classroom
☐ In gym class
☐ In the bathroom
☐ At the locker area

☐ At lunch
☐ On the playground
☐ On the school bus
☐ On the way to school

☐ On the way home from   ☐ At home
   school   ☐ On the telephone
☐ In the neighborhood   ☐ Via E-mail
☐ Other places _____

_____

6. What age is the teaser? (Check your answer.)

   ☐ Your age
   ☐ Older than you
   ☐ Younger than you

7. Do you consider the teaser to be your friend? (Check one answer.)

   ☐ Yes
   ☐ No
   ☐ Sometimes
   ☐ I don't know.

8. Does the person who teases you tease other kids? (Check one answer.)

   ☐ Yes
   ☐ No
   ☐ I don't know.

9. How do you feel when you are teased, put down, or insulted? (Check all the feelings that you experience in teasing situations.)

   ☐ Upset
   ☐ Sad
   ☐ Angry
   ☐ Frustrated
   ☐ Helpless
   ☐ Embarrassed

☐ Scared
☐ Guilty
☐ Hurt
☐ Afraid
☐ Stressed
☐ Excluded
☐ It does not bother me.

10. What do you say or do when you are teased? (Check the way or ways you react.)

☐ Yell or scream at the teaser
☐ Hit the teaser
☐ Tease the teaser
☐ Argue with the teaser
☐ Cry
☐ Ignore the teaser
☐ Tell an adult
☐ Other responses or reactions _____

_____

_____

This teasing survey may be reproduced for classroom use.

The following are suggested references that contain additional teasing assessments.

• *Keys to Dealing with Bullies*, by Barry E. McNamara and Francine J. McNamara. This book includes "My Life in School," a questionnaire for the early identification of bullies and victims, which was developed by Sonia Sharp, Tina Arora, Peter K. Smith, and Irene Whitney of the Division of Education, University of Sheffield England (pages 94–97).

- *Counselor in the Classroom*, by Pat Schwallie-Giddis, David Cowan, and Dianne Schilling, includes a "Put-Down Survey," which increases students' awareness of communication that is hurtful to others (pages 141–143).

Classroom Discussion

Does your child's teacher ever talk to the class about teasing? The classroom is a very logical, practical, and effective setting to address and discuss the issue. Class dialogue is the key to increasing awareness of the problem and strengthening children's coping skills. Children are usually eager to participate and receptive to learn. You might suggest that the teacher initiate a discussion after the class completes the Teasing Survey. One discussion is not enough, however. The topic of teasing requires ongoing attention, practice, and review. The outcome should be that students learn that teasing is not acceptable and that there are effective ways to deal with this hurtful behavior.

Research on open meetings in elementary classrooms suggests that discussions allow students to solve problems as a group, see a situation from classmates' perspectives, and increase children's empathy for each other. The researchers studied a class meeting on name-calling that was conducted after a student at a nearby school shot a classmate because he had been called a name. The authors of the study (Lundeberg et al.) concluded that although the open classroom meeting might not prevent violence, "it has the potential to decrease school violence through teaching children the skills to express their own thoughts and feelings, to listen to each other, and to think about their own behavior."

Understandably, middle school and junior high students are reluctant and often embarrassed to share teasing experiences with classmates. However, they are receptive to talking about the issues in the "third person," when it happens to others. Merely addressing the all-too-frequent occurrences of the school shooters who become violent because of ridicule, taunting, and bullying can generate meaningful discussion. I asked fifth-graders the following questions:

- What is bullying? (Define and give examples)
- What is teasing? (Define and give examples)
- What do we know about the school shooters in Santee, California, and at Columbine High School?
- How could these tragedies have been prevented?
- What would you do if you observed someone being ridiculed or harassed?
- What should you do?
- What would you do if someone picked on you?
- How can students reduce harassing and bullying behavior at school?

The powerful discussion heightened the students' awareness and demonstrated that most of them would take an active role in dealing with these issues. Classroom discussion provides the opportunity for students to know that there is strength in numbers. The students who are usually passive bystanders or witnesses may realize that they outnumber the teasers or bullies. Taking an active role takes the power away from the aggressive minority.

The use of literature to discuss teasing, which is described in the following section, is a subtle way to address teasing and integrate the teaching of effective coping strategies for older students.

The following suggestions for general class discussion with elementary school–age children have also been effective in working with older students in small groups or on an individual basis. These can be facilitated by the teacher or school social worker, counselor, or psychologist, depending primarily on the availability of your school's mental health professionals. I conduct the weekly class discussions with the classroom teacher's participation. The teacher's involvement is crucial for the necessary follow-through and reinforcement. My class discussions are usually a half hour long. How much we cover in each session is determined by how talkative the students are and what problems they bring up for discussion. The key to the success of this intervention is *in listening and responding to what the kids bring to the discussion* and helping them find appropriate solutions. The number of sessions often depends on the age of the students, how much time a teacher wants to devote to this, and the very practical matter of how much time the discussion facilitator has in his or her schedule.

The information and material here do not make up a specific curriculum that must be followed step-by-step. Each teacher and mental health professional has his or her own style. These suggestions should be implemented and applied in the way in which the discussion facilitator is most comfortable. My goal is to offer ideas to use and integrate into teaching and daily routines.

Some teachers might prefer to organize the teasing discussion by following the order or format of the Teasing Survey. Teachers can then teach their students the strategies in Chapter 6, after all of the points in the survey have been addressed and discussed.

I usually begin the first session by asking the students to complete the following sentence: "I think teasing is_____."

After several responses, I ask who has ever been teased. In the elementary grades, almost every hand goes up. I proceed by asking what kids are teased about, emphasizing that we are not going to mention the names of the teasers. We record the answers on chart paper or on the board. Usually an extensive list is created. We talk about the differences between good-humored teasing and cruel teasing. With older students, I discuss hostile teasing that includes chronic and persistent taunting, harassment, and verbal bullying.

Assuming we complete the planned agenda in the first session, I begin the second session by quickly reviewing what teasing is and reminding the students that we are not using names of the teasers. I continue by asking children to share specific teasing experiences. If appropriate, I ask for volunteers to role-play. During the role-playing I ask what it feels like to be teased. We list the feelings that most children have in teasing situations. When a student shares his or her feelings, I always convey understanding of the emotions and offer validation. I ask the class, "How many of you would feel this way?" Usually many children share the feelings, which provides wonderful support to the person who has been teased.

After talking about feelings that often result from teasing, we discuss what kids "do" with these feelings. Do they hit the teaser because they are angry, or do they cry? Do they tease the teaser? I talk about how the teasing will usually continue if kids react with anger or tears. We begin to discuss ways in which kids currently deal with teasing, assessing if they are appropriate and successful.

Next, we brainstorm why kids tease other kids. Again, we list all responses on chart paper or on the board. I'm amazed at how much insight young children have into the reasons that kids tease.

This is a good time to read *Let's Talk About Teasing*, by Joy Wilt Berry, to children in kindergarten through second grade. This is a great springboard for discussion of situations in which kids are teased about what they wear, how they feel, or what they can't do. Discussions from the examples in this book may extend for several class sessions.

At this point, I begin to teach and review the strategies in Chapter 6, according to the following plan.

A Plan for Teaching the Easing the Teasing Strategies in the Classroom

Teachers can use the following scheme as a rough framework for teaching the Chapter 6 skills in the classroom.

Self-Talk

1. Ask children if they ever "self-talk." When?
2. Give examples of effective teasing self-talk:
   "I will not react with anger or hurt feelings."
   "Is the tease true?"
   "Whose opinion is more important—the teaser's or mine?"
   "I do not like teasing, but I will handle it."
3. Have them think about positive qualities or special times. Brainstorm other examples.

Ignoring

1. Explain what ignoring is—not reacting or responding to the teaser.
2. Talk about body language.

3. Practice and role-play ignoring.
4. How can a child ignore while riding the school bus?

"I" Message

1. Teach students what the "I" message is.
2. Discuss situations in which the "I" message could be used.
3. Role-play with reminders to maintain eye contact and use a polite voice.
4. Provide a visual reminder in the classroom.
5. Warn children that this most likely will not work with teasers at recess or on the bus.
6. Model the "I" message.

Visualization

1. What is a visualization?
2. Explain the idea of using an imaginary shield to repel teases.
3. Provide opportunity to create (draw) visualizations.
4. Share visualizations with the class.

Reframing—Accept the Tease as if It Is a Compliment

1. Brainstorm reframing comments.
2. Role-play.

Agree with the Facts

1. Discuss examples.
2. Role-play and practice.

"So?"

1. Explain that this is like shrugging your shoulders and that it conveys indifference.
2. Read *The Meanest Thing to Say*, by Bill Cosby.
3. Brainstorm similar responses:
   "Your point being?"
   "What is your point?"
   "Whatever."

Respond to the Tease with a Compliment

1. Brainstorm examples.
2. Role-play.

Use Humor

1. Discuss examples.
2. Role-play.

Ask for Help

1. Discuss the difference between tattling and reporting.
2. Whom can a child ask for help?
3. When is it appropriate to ask for help?

After you've taught all the strategies, pretend you are the teaser and ask children to select a strategy to use.

Continue to review and role-play as necessary.

Literature as a Springboard

Sometimes saying "I have some books that your students might find interesting" is one of the easiest ways to broach the subject of offering the teacher help with teasing. Using literature as a springboard for discussion or writing provides opportunities to review and reinforce what students have learned about coping with teasing, a technique any teacher can appreciate. Reading materials also present subtle and natural ways to address teasing with older students. Reading about teasing experiences helps kids realize that they are not alone in dealing with these hurtful situations. Select books and stories that describe appropriate and realistic ways of handling teasing experiences. Discuss the nature and extent of the teasing, put-down, or ridicule. What was the motivation of the teaser? How did the teaser feel? How did the teasee feel? Were there witnesses to the teasing? What did they do? After the students have read a particular book, the teacher can ask them to evaluate how the teasing was handled.

See "Recommended Books for Children" at the end of this book. According to book reviews, descriptions, and guides, I have added the suggested grade levels for which the books are appropriate. In my experience with reading to students, many books are appropriate for either older or younger grade levels than what is suggested.

Two Role-Playing Scenarios for the Classroom
I've used both of these with great success throughout elementary school.

Name-Calling on a School Bus
During the summer of 1996, I visited the Chicago Children's Museum with my niece and cousin, Sophie and Emily, who were both eight years old at the time. I was particularly impressed with the exhibition about discrimination. Part of it was a simulated experience of name-calling on a school bus. As we entered the bus we saw life-sized photographs of kids, who were the passengers, and heard shouts of taunts and teases. It was a very powerful experience. After we passed through the bus, we participated in an activity that encouraged us to discuss how we felt about the taunting and what we would do in such a situation. After our discussion, we were asked to think about names we have been called. We wrote them down on paper, which we placed in a shredder, symbolizing that one can let go of the name and the accompanying hurt feelings.

Fatso	Idiot
Fatty	Freak
Chubby	Retard
Stick	Fruitcake
Skinny	Brain
Shorty	Goody Goody
Peewee	Wimp
Shrimp	Dork
Four Eyes	Poopoo-Head

Loser

Liar

Tattletale

Sissy

Nerd

Stupid

Smarty-Pants

Dummy

Airhead

Geek

Chicken

Weirdo

Teacher's Pet

Brace Face

Metal Mouth

Tinsel Teeth

Baby

Crybaby

Lunatic

Blockhead

Nut

Dope

Dimwit

Imbecile

Butt Head

Dweeb

Freak

Klutz

Moron

Brainless

Mindless

Peanut Brain

Brat

Show-Off

Hairy

Big Mouth

Fat Face

Carrottop

Bigfoot

Big Nose

Bossy

Reject

Know-It-All

Freckle Face

Pig

My niece suggested that I take the students from my school to see the exhibition. I decided to create a similar experience at the school instead. I elicited the help of several fourth-grade girls, with whom I was working to improve their social skills and self-esteem. With the assistance of our art teacher, the girls created the inside of a school bus and life-sized cutouts of passengers. This experience presented many therapeutic opportunities for the girls to work cooperatively, compromise, and feel proud of their accomplishment.

The girls brainstormed insults, put-downs, and teases and then made an audiotape of these words. No obscenities or swearing were allowed. This list of names was used in our simulated activity.

This activity can serve as an introduction to teaching the strategies in Chapter 6 or may provide an opportunity for review. An additional goal is to raise the awareness of verbally aggressive students, which might decrease name-calling and taunting. This provides a great opportunity for the school principal to remind students and parents of the rules regarding physical and verbal aggression on the bus and what the consequences are.

Some teachers have told me that since they don't have bus service, they have changed the setting to a playground or locker area. The scenario easily adapts to any public area connected with a school.

The following guide was distributed to classroom teachers, who facilitated the discussion after students walked through the bus.

1. Your class will walk through the simulated school bus in my office at your designated time.
2. When your students return to the classroom (before you begin the discussion), ask each child to write down a name he or she has been called, especially a name that was hurtful. Ask the student to put the paper aside. It is important to reassure the class that these names will not be shared.
3. Ask your students how they would feel if they experienced this name-calling or teasing on the bus or elsewhere. If some students respond by saying, "It doesn't bother me," perhaps they can share with the class why it doesn't.
4. A question that often generates interesting discussion is "Why do kids call other kids names?" The likely answers are attention, feelings of power or superiority, revenge, peer acceptance, and judging others' differences in a negative way.
5. Emphasize that although we don't like to be called names, we must remember that we cannot control what other people do or say. However, we can learn to control how *we* react. We don't have to "automatically" have "hurt" feelings.
6. Ask your students to brainstorm some strategies to use in a name-calling situation. This activity can serve as an introduction to teaching the Chapter 6 strategies or provide another opportunity for review.

7. Ask your students what they would do if they witnessed someone calling someone else a name.
8. At the end of the discussion, have each student tear up the piece of paper with the hurtful name written on it and throw it in the garbage. This symbolizes that they can let go of the hurt feelings. This can be quite powerful for some kids.

"I Don't Have to Upset Myself When Someone Teases Me"

I wrote this script for a puppet show that I presented to first-graders. It's been amazing to see how many children remember it years later. It's also helpful for older kids to perform this for younger children. A copy of the script was sent home to parents so that they could either reread it to their children or perhaps "perform" it at home. I hope that your children will enjoy this.

Moderator to audience: You will soon meet Natalie Namecaller. She says mean things to boys and girls. She teases children and makes fun of them. If Natalie Namecaller called you a name and made fun of you, how would you feel? (*Interact with children about the feelings they have when someone calls them a name.*) Let's look at how Natalie acts toward a girl whose name is Hurt Holly, and how her friend, Helpful Helen, helps.

Natalie Namecaller (*yells*): Hey, Holly, you've got glasses . . . Four Eyes! You've got four eyes!

Hurt Holly: That hurts my feelings, Natalie.

Natalie Namecaller: So what? You wear glasses, and you have four eyes!

Hurt Holly begins to cry. Natalie walks away laughing.

Helen enters and approaches Holly.

Helpful Helen: What's the matter, Holly? Why are you crying?

Holly (*tearfully*): Hi, Helpful Helen. Natalie Namecaller called me "Four Eyes." She hurt my feelings. I am so sad. Natalie must not like me.

Helen: I see that you're very upset about this, Holly. Is it true that you have four eyes? I see only two eyes and your cool glasses.

Holly: Well, no. Of course I don't have four eyes.

Helen: If it is not true, then why are you upset? Let's think about it. Why are you upsetting yourself over this?

Holly: What do you mean?

Helen: Natalie Namecaller called you "Four Eyes" because she probably wants to upset you. You can decide if you are going to feel sad, angry, or upset. You don't like it when you have those feelings, do you?

Holly: No, I don't like those feelings, and I don't like it when people call me names or make fun of me. Do you have any advice? What could I do?

Helen: It might help to ignore her—you should pay no attention to what she is saying to you. You should not look at her or show her that you are upset. In fact, you should pretend that Natalie is invisible! While you are ignoring her, you could pretend that the words are just bouncing off you—like a Nerf ball would bounce off of you.

Holly: But what if she doesn't stop calling me "Four Eyes"?

Helen: Sometimes, when ignoring doesn't work, you could try other things.

Holly: What else could I do?

Helen: Maybe you could thank her for noticing your glasses.

Holly: Thank her for noticing my glasses??!!??

Helen: Yes, you could say, "Natalie, it makes me feel good that you noticed my glasses. They help me see as well as you do." Saying "thank you" to Natalie kind of takes the "tease" out of it.

Holly: That's a great idea, Helen. I bet Natalie would be surprised if I thanked her!

Helen: I think she would be very surprised. I think you're really understanding how to react to Natalie's name-calling and teasing so that you're not feeling upset.

Holly: These are really neat ideas. I never thought there was anything I could say or do to help myself feel better. Helen, can I tell you about one more problem?

Helen: Sure.

Holly: There is a boy whose name is Tommy Teaser. He teases me about being short. He said that I am the shortest person in my class and maybe even the shortest kid in the whole school!

Helen: You must have felt bad.

Holly: Well, even though it is true that I am the shortest person in my class—maybe even the shortest in first grade—I feel upset when he teases me.

Helen: What's wrong with being the shortest person in your class?

Holly: I don't like to be teased about it!

Helen: No one ever likes to be teased, but you don't have to upset yourself.

Holly: Upset myself?

Helen: Yes. Remember, you can decide if you're going to be sad or upset when Tommy teases you. Holly, someone is always the shortest person in a class, just like someone else is the tallest, the oldest, or the youngest. Everyone is different. The difference makes you unique and special.

Holly: You think I'm special?

Helen: Of course—and you should think you're special too.

Holly: Should I ignore Tommy?

Helen: Yes, you could ignore Tommy or you could agree with him that you are short.

Holly: Agree with him?

Helen: When he says that you are so short, you could say, "Yes, I am short. I think I am the shortest kid in the whole school."

Holly: Helen, thank you so much for helping me. I now know why your name is Helpful Helen.

Helen: We wish that everyone would say only nice things to us, but that doesn't happen. No one likes to be called names, but it's not the worst thing. I know you don't like it, but I know you can handle it!

Holly: Helen, thank you for all of your great ideas and for being such a good friend.

Continue to role-play the strategies described.

P.S. A social worker who has implemented Easing the Teasing at a K–8 school asked the older students to write their own scripts related to teasing. It was a great way to reinforce the strategies she taught them. The short plays were acted out for the younger children in the school.

Teaching Appreciation of Differences

The underlying cause of some teasing is a misunderstanding or a lack of understanding of differences. Many children who are not familiar with a cultural or ethnic trait may tease because of their own discomfort or fear. A child with a learning, physical, or speech disability may become the target of teasing because his difference is perceived or judged negatively.

The classroom is an ideal setting to promote tolerance of and appreciation for differences and diversity. Following hate crimes in the last several years, community and activist groups have been emphasizing the need for schools to cultivate tolerance and respect. Diversity training is gaining popularity in the school setting. Educators across the country are intentionally teaching lessons about compassion and respect for others. More and more classroom time is being devoted to character education.

I routinely devote a few class sessions to this important topic. I begin by asking the students about their similarities to one another. We discuss basic ones such as age, grade, teacher, neighborhood, gender, and eye and hair color. We then discuss the importance of understanding and respecting each other's different qualities. We brainstorm a list of differences. I ask the students to complete the following sentence: "One thing that makes me different from my classmates is. . . ." We eventually learn one difference for each student. Who is the oldest in the class? Who is the youngest? Who was born in a different country? Who speaks more than one language? Who speaks with an accent? Who was born in a different state? Who is the tallest, and who is the smallest? Who has the most brothers and sisters? Who has the lightest hair? Who has the darkest skin? Who has braces? Who wears glasses? The message conveyed and emphasized is that the difference makes the child special and unique.

During these discussions, many children have shared their significant differences, which was therapeutic for them to do. They revealed differences such as being adopted, living with a single parent or a grandparent, and going for extra help in reading. A child with a hearing aid shared that she has something in common with President Clinton. A seven-year-old boy discussed his significant physical disability and mentioned that at times he is teased about it.

Lori, a third-grader, commented in a class discussion that she was upset about the teasing of a classmate, Dan. She observed that someone was making fun of him because he had been born in India. Dan reluctantly acknowledged that this was happening. I encouraged him to explain to the class some differences in his family because of his cultural background. As he explained some of their customs, I believe that his classmates gained a better understanding of his uniqueness and clearly heard the message that teasing about a difference is wrong. The teaser, who was a student in this class, was never mentioned in our discussion. Without prompting or encouragement, the teaser apologized to Dan at the end of our discussion. A week later Dan's grandmother visited his class and cooked Indian food for the kids.

A second-grade class was taken by surprise when their very loving, nurturing teacher, Mrs. Novak, became quite firm and serious when she asked everyone who was wearing blue jeans to stand in the back of the classroom. The bewildered students dressed in blue jeans followed the directions and reluctantly proceeded to the back of the room. In a stern voice, Mrs. Novak said that they were not going to be allowed to participate in recess anymore. She explained that they would be required to stay in the classroom during recess beginning the following day. The kids looked puzzled, confused, and scared. When asked how they felt about this new rule, most of the students voiced their strong opinions that it was unfair. The entire class was in disbelief. Mrs. Novak then asked the students who were wearing jeans to sit down. She explained that this is how it feels when people are excluded or discriminated against because of a particular trait or difference. She connected this experience with the work of Martin Luther King Jr. The students gained a better understanding of how African-Americans felt when they had to sit in the back of the bus. The students who were wearing jeans were very relieved to learn that they had not lost their recess privilege after all!

Today, most schools actively make an effort to initiate discussions like the ones I just described, but you might pass on this example when you are talking to your child's teacher about ways to prevent or stop teasing in the school. The following are some references that can be helpful too. For more information on helping children develop empathy, see Chapter 9.

Anti-Defamation League. *A World of Difference Elementary Study Guide.* Anti-Defamation League, 1994. An anti-prejudice and diversity awareness program for educators and families.

Canter, Lee and Katia Petersen. *Teaching Students to Get Along.* See "Lesson #1 Appreciating Diversity," pages 13–18.

Hannaford, Mary Joe. *102 Tools for Teachers and Counselors Too.* See "Likenesses and Differences" on page 125 and "Prejudice" on page 126.

Getskow, Veronica and Dee Konczal. *Kids with Special Needs. Information and Activities to Promote Awareness and Understanding.* Santa Barbara, CA.

Schwallie-Giddis, Pat, David Cowan, and Dianne Schilling. *Counselor in the Classroom.* See "The Take on Tolerance" on pages 138–140.

National Crime Prevention Council. *Helping Kids Handle Conflict.* See "Conflict Over Diversity," pages 39–50.

Getting Creative: A Few More Ideas for the School Setting

By and large, teachers tend to be creative people, and most will jump at the chance to try new ways to reach one destination. If you pass this book on to your school's principal, the following ideas may find their way to the individual teachers. I'm betting that the teachers will take these ideas and run with them.

Monitor Unstructured Settings

Many young children complain to me about the teasing that occurs after school in day-care programs. What fertile ground for teasing— it is generally unstructured and has multiaged kids. Most of the kids are either overtired or wound up by the end of the long day. I'm not sure that many day-care personnel take an active role in dealing with or stopping teasing behaviors.

Because teasing occurs more frequently in unstructured settings or situations, such as the playground, locker areas, and the school bus, having adult supervision in these areas is crucial. The bus driver's priority is, of course, to drive safely, not to provide discipline. However, many bus drivers are very aware of the problems that take shape on their buses, and some even take action when they can. I received the following E-mail messages from one bus driver in early 2001:

I wanted to commend you for trying to do something about children teasing and bullying each other in this country and, hopefully, in this world of ours. I'm a school bus driver in a small town west of Chicago, and as much as some of the students I drive every day dislike me for it, I will not stand for anyone talking negative about anyone else on my bus. I was teased as a child for being skinny (wish I had that problem now), and I know how it feels to stand out among other children and feel less of a person because someone else decided to put you down. I won't tolerate it and I always speak up and try to teach them to be nice to each other.

I just wanted you to know I'm happy someone is getting through to children and adults alike, helping them to cope and to respond to these people who put them down and helping them understand that we all have flaws and we all have pluses in our lives.

Keep up the good work and God bless you for it.

Marilyn

I would like to include the fact that I drive middle school students, and some live in more modest homes than others on my bus, and you can see the expressions on their faces some days about how embarrassed they are by not living up to snuff like the other kids. Those kids I try to compliment a couple of times a week on their hair, a piece of clothing they're wearing, or just something to give them a lift. I wish more people would do that for these kids. They need it at this age.

Thanks for your time, for reading my thoughts.

Marilyn

When you don't have a Marilyn to drive your school buses, an extra adult on board is ideal. Some schools provide an aide for the bus ride, while others have parent volunteers. An opportunity for playground supervisors, lunch monitors, and bus attendants to consult with the social worker, counselor, or principal regarding how to deal with aggressive behaviors is generally well received and appreciated. This ensures greater consistency among the adults, who often don't know what to do when faced with teasing incidents. Adequate supervision, established behavioral expectations, and consistent consequences are the keys for dealing effectively with verbal and physical aggression.

Schoolwide Kindness Programs

Promote or increase the awareness of positive behaviors by establishing classroom or schoolwide "kindness" programs. Recognition of positive behaviors on a consistent basis contributes to a healthy emotional climate in the school. Some primary and elementary teachers have a compliment box in the classroom. During the week, students deposit compliments about classmates in the box, which are read on Friday afternoons. In many schools, recognition is given weekly to students for academic work as well as kind and caring behaviors. During class discussions, I often ask students to say something kind to classmates. The compliments bring smiles to their faces. I like to do this activity around holiday time, emphasizing that one of the best gifts to give a friend is a kind word or compliment.

The following are suggested references that can help establish a kindness program in your school. See Bibliography for publication information.

Nass, Marcia Shoshana and Max Nass. *Kindness Makes the World a Happy Place.*

Markova, Dawna. *Kids' Random Acts of Kindness.* Kids from all around the world tell about their acts of kindness.

STOP Violence Coalition. *Kindness Is Contagious, Catch It!* K–12 curriculum for teachers that promotes the principles of respect, empathy, and kindness and how words and actions affect others.

Involve Safety Patrol

Engage older students or the safety patrol to monitor teasing and put-downs in the hallways, in the locker areas, and on the school grounds. Discuss with them their appropriate responses when teasing is observed. But don't just give them the power and leave them alone with it. A parent who works in her children's school said that the older safety patrol kids were actually intimidating and bullying the younger students. So remember that this kind of effort must be monitored to ensure that no one takes advantage of this position.

Involve Student Council

Encourage the student council to sponsor a school campaign to promote respect. Older students promoting, modeling, and teaching
respect to younger kids can be very powerful. I recently helped the
student council at the school where I work with our campaign,
"Respect Rocks." The fourth- and fifth-grade student council representatives led discussions in all of the classrooms about respect.
They asked students, "What is respect?" "How do we show respect
to each other?" "How do we show respect to our school?" Following this discussion, the student council representatives told each class
about the door-decorating activity. Each class was asked to decorate
its door with pictures, poems, posters, collages, and essays that conveyed the message "Respect Rocks." Some of the activities and projects were done individually, some in small groups, and others on a
classroom basis. The creativity was overwhelming. Each class took
pride in their outstanding door decorations.

Student council reps asked students to enter the "Respect Rocks"
bookmark design contest. The winner of the contest had his or her
bookmark used when the safety patrol monitors passed them out
when respectful behavior was observed.

The music teacher joined in the campaign when she taught songs
to the different grade levels about respect. Her selections were from
"A Better You . . . A Better Me!" by Rodger Emerson.

Our physical education teachers participated, as well, as they
emphasized respect with lively posters throughout the gymnasium
and frequent discussions. With the students and teachers participating in an enthusiastic way, respect rocked at Prairie School.

Elicit the Help of Older Kids with Reading

Have older students read relevant literature to the primary-grade students. Younger children enjoy hearing from the older ones, and it
provides a great opportunity for the older students to serve as role
models. Some schools have partner classes. For example, a second-
grade class is paired up with a fifth-grade class for the year. They
work on several projects together. It is a way for the older and
younger kids to get to know each other. Often big brother–little

brother and big sister–little sister pairings can offer mentoring to younger kids who could benefit from positive guidance from older students.

Assignment to Interview Parents

Students can interview their parents or an older family member about their teasing experiences to heighten their awareness of teasing and generate discussion about what people are teased about. Kids find it interesting to hear about their parents' earlier experiences of being ridiculed or made fun of. The interview assignment also serves as a way to open communication between parent and child about this important subject.

- "Tell me about a time when you were teased."
- "What were you teased about?"
- "How old were you?"
- "How did you deal with it?"
- "How did you feel about it?"
- "What advice would you give someone who is being teased?"
- "Do you think the issues are different for kids today?"

Teasing Essay

A seventh-grade language arts teacher heard my Easing the Teasing presentation for staff development at her school. The very next day, she asked her students to write an essay about a time when they were teased. One essay was of great concern to her. She shared it with the school counselor, who met with the student to explore the situation further. Without the essay assignment, the student may have continued to suffer in silence.

Activate Bystanders

Encourage students who witness teasing to intervene either by telling the teaser to stop or by offering support to the teasee. Witnesses and bystanders can assume a very significant role. Chapter 9 includes some ideas for teaching children mutual support.

Teachers Can Determine Groupings

Many teachers like to take an active role in establishing small groupings or partnering in the classroom. They report that this alleviates the anxiety that many children feel when they are not picked or excluded regularly. Some teachers use a lottery to mix up groups, where others use other systematic pairing systems. Liz Androjna, a physical education teacher at our school, offers these suggestions:

- Choose someone from another class.
- Choose someone with the same hair color or style.
- Select a partner who is wearing the same color of clothing.
- Find a partner who has the same number of pets.
- Choose a partner who has the same favorite food.
- Find a classmate who is either the same or different height.
- Using a deck of cards, group students according to the same suit, same number, even or odd numbers, or numbers added together.
- Using cards with words, ask students to find the student holding the card with the opposite word.
- Young children are successful at using cards that have different shapes, such as a triangle, square, rectangle, circle, and half moon.
- Cards that have pictures of animals, birds, or reptiles are great for young children.
- Older kids are able to form partners by matching up states and capitals.

Adult Help for the Frequent Teasee

A classroom teacher, school social worker, or counselor can serve as a "coach" or "tutor" to a child who is a frequent target. Providing positive hints and suggestions often helps the child deal more successfully in peer interactions. Some kids take the advice of a special adult at school in a different way from the same advice often given by parents. I have seen this be especially helpful with young children. Usually the child appreciates the teacher's efforts because it does convey that she cares about him. Note, however, that the child has to be somewhat motivated to stop the behavior that invites unkind remarks. Obviously, too, the agreement has to be made during a private conversation.

A fifth-grade teacher was very concerned about Bryan, a student who was very bossy and often put down classmates about their schoolwork. These behaviors resulted in his being isolated and excluded. Unfortunately, these behaviors were so much a part of how Bryan related to peers, he was often unaware of when he was bossy or putting others down. Bryan and his teacher agreed that she would give him a cue when he was demonstrating these behaviors. The subtle signal instantly alerted Bryan to think about his behavior, which often resulted in an apology or a change in his actions.

Discuss Policy with Staff and Parents

Discuss the policy regarding teasing, bullying, or harassing behaviors with school staff and parents. The policy should include clear and specific behavioral expectations and consistent consequences (otherwise, consequences for student misconduct are usually left to the discretion of the principal or, in some cases, the assistant principal). Clear behavioral expectations should be stated in addition to what the consequences will be for teasing, harassing, or bullying behaviors. Rules and consequences should clearly send the message that these behaviors are unacceptable. Consequences will vary depending on the specific behavior and the student's previous history and might include the following:

- Removal of a privilege such as recess or another special activity
- Parent contact by telephone, E-mail, or formal letter (If this is the student's second offense, our principal asks students to call their parents in his presence. Parents may be called following the first offense; it depends upon the severity of the behavior.)
- A parent conference to discuss the situation further is often necessary if the teasing behavior continues. The teacher and

administrator should be present, and often it is helpful if the student attends.

- Assignment of a detention outside of regular school hours
- Referral to the school social worker, counselor, or psychologist to assess the cause of the behavior
- Parent notification and an in-school suspension
- Parent notification and an out-of-school suspension
- Parent notification and recommendation for expulsion

I recently heard that a parochial school expelled an eighth-grade student (a few months before graduation) because of his persistent harassment of a classmate. (The harassment resulted in the victim's changing schools.) The principal explained that the expulsion of the student had served as a powerful example to other students; in fact, teachers observed an improvement in other students' behaviors toward each other following the expulsion.

Consequences for teasing and harassment on the bus might include:

- Warning
- Assignment to a particular seat (near the bus driver)
- Loss of bus privilege for a limited time
- Loss of bus privilege for an extended time

In response to recent school shootings, many state legislatures are discussing legislation that would require school districts to adopt a policy that addresses bullying behavior. According to the June 4, 2001 issue of *People* magazine, Georgia has an anti-bullying law that allows schools to expel students who have been disciplined three times for picking on classmates. The governor of the state of Washington is pressing for anti-bullying training in his state's schools. A policy adopted anywhere should include systems for reporting and investigating complaints, training of staff and volunteers in conflict management and handling bullying behaviors, notification of parents or legal guardians of the aggressive students, and a requirement for therapeutic intervention. If no plan is in place, the literature suggests that a committee, including school personnel and parents, be designated to develop a policy regarding the physical and emotional safety of students.

A sample policy created by the Illinois State Board of Education can be viewed at isbe.net/bulletins/ED-INSIGHT4-01.pdf. *The board recommends that schools review the policy with their school board attorney before adopting it for their own use.*

Parent Meeting

Provide an opportunity for a meeting where parents can learn how they can help their kids cope with teasing situations and share any concerns that they have. Many parents of kids who are teased feel isolated and helpless. A meeting can provide support as well as establish lines of communication to identify and resolve the existing problems. A parent meeting is a way to begin the process of communication.

Establishing the School Connection and Moving On

I expect that teachers, school administrators, parents, counselors, and other concerned adults will come up with many more innovative ideas for discouraging teasing on a broad scale in the months and years to come. When a spate of violent tragedies struck the nation's schools in early 2001, individuals and institutions responded with ideas and actions on a scale I've never seen before. We can all find hope in the fact that the country's minds and hearts are hard at work on the issue of cruelty among children, inside and outside our schools. You can do your part by helping your child recognize and form healthy friendships, the subject of the next chapter.

8

---◆---

Helping Your Child Form
Healthy Friendships

"Why do you want to be friends with someone who calls you names like
that?"

"What do you mean Lisa went along with it when Lauren made fun of the way
you dance?"

"Why don't you ever invite anyone over anymore?"

A good friend is someone who makes you smile most of the time
and cares about your feelings, but many teased children don't
seem to understand that. They will tolerate humiliating verbal abuse
from a "popular" peer, apparently hoping that any attention will
make them part of the in-crowd. They may not realize that a true
friend won't join in on the cruelty leveled at them or even look the
other way while it's happening. Or, they may go to the opposite, cyn-
ical extreme, isolating themselves because "everyone is mean."

As parents, we are very free with advice like "Just go eat lunch
with someone else" or "I wouldn't be friends with her if I were you."
But we're not always as quick to tell our kids what a worthy friend
is and how to find one. Sometimes we don't fully remember the
importance of friends to developing children, or we think that friendships will just fall into place naturally. Kids who are being teased can
usually inform us otherwise.

Understanding the Allure of Popularity

Jamie came home on Monday complaining that Susie had said mean things to her in the cafeteria and ignored her request to be her partner for an activity in gym class. On Tuesday, Jamie sadly told her mom that Susie had stared at her during class while whispering to the classmate next to her. Jamie came home very excited on Wednesday because she had sat at Susie's lunch table. Her feelings took a downward spiral on Thursday because Susie had told Jamie that her jacket was dorky and had excluded her from a game. Jamie cried herself to sleep, wondering why Susie didn't like her.

Jamie's mother could not believe how dependent Jamie's emotional state was on Susie's actions and attention. She asked her daughter, "Why do you want to be friends with Susie? She hurts your feelings so much." Jamie responded, "Because Susie is popular."

That kind of answer may offend our mature logic, but on a visceral level most of us remember how rational this explanation seemed when we were nine, twelve, or even sixteen. Almost all kids pursue popularity at some time during childhood, and they have a variety of reasons for doing so, all of which seem quite compelling at the time. But some kids go too far, seeming desperate to be popular or to be associated with those who are, to the point of allowing themselves to be hurt. Pursuing popularity too slavishly can cause children to be teased. And children who are already being teased often feel especially driven to make themselves popular. These kids need to be steered gently in the direction of true, healthy friendships. To do that effectively, however, you need to understand thoroughly why they seem so ruled by issues of popularity. Empathy is the best way to gain their attention.

• **We all want to be accepted.** As children mature, their self-worth takes shape with the help of a variety of internal and external influences. It's only natural that feedback from their peers will contribute to how they feel about themselves. Kids who are sought after as playmates and imitated by those around them get the message that they are acceptable and worthy. It's a good feeling that gives children the confidence to face the fears and challenges of growing up. Popularity, to many kids, simply means acceptance by others, which builds their self-worth.

• **The worse we feel about ourselves, the more we let others define our worth.** Popular kids are often idealized by children like Jamie because those on the outside looking in usually don't feel good about themselves. They place popular kids on a pedestal and are always looking up to them. Many children strive to be part of this particular group, so they aren't on the outside looking in anymore. Meg Schneider writes in her book, *Popularity Has Its Ups and Downs*, that "a person is popular because a group of people have chosen him or her to admire, follow, and in some cases even imitate." She discusses the importance of a child's self-esteem in viewing popularity. In fact, she believes that, if a child feels inferior when she is with a popular person, it has more to do with that child's opinion of herself. I agree with Ms. Schneider's conclusion that if a child does not feel good about herself, she will forever be a victim of popularity. Many of the strategies in Chapter 6 are aimed at helping children define and build up their own self-worth so that they can break the popularity-seeking cycle.

• **There is safety in numbers.** Aristotle said that man is a political animal. We tend to congregate with other human beings; we like being in a group. Belonging to a group insulates children from some of the danger inherent in trying new things and making strides toward adulthood. If they make a mistake, they have company, and they can all laugh at themselves. When they're alone, they run the very real risk of being laughed *at* for their mistakes. Children who are teased know this better than anyone else. No wonder the protection of a group appeals to them. No wonder the group they covet is made up of kids who are admired, not mocked. Many insecure children gravitate to these "popular" kids in the desperate hope of being part of the group. They tolerate and accept verbal abuse, ridicule, and exclusion when there are any glimmers of hope for the friendship.

- **Growing independence from parents means growing dependence on peers.** The need to be accepted by others intensifies as children become more independent from their families. Parents are often taken by surprise when an eight-year-old who used to rush out to play without a care in the world turns into a nine-year-old who worries about who will be out there and whether he'll be allowed to join in. I often see more social groups and friendship circles emerging in fourth grade. The groupings become more clearly defined as kids get older. The older kids get, the more important it is to be part of a group—and that doesn't mean the family. Cliques are quite evident in middle school. At this age, children seek a stronger sense of belonging to their peer group as they undergo the normal developmental shift of focus and interests away from their family and toward their peer group. This need to belong may lead kids away from healthy friendships and toward whatever and whomever is defined as "cool" and "in."

- **If you can't beat 'em, join 'em.** Some kids pursue the popular group because they are simply trying to get in good with someone who is potentially hurtful to them in the hope of avoiding such harm. They're not seeking protection from those outside the in-crowd but from the in-crowd itself. They may know very well that the popular but mean kids aren't worthy of their affection. Giving them other ways to protect themselves, such as the strategies in Chapter 6, frees them from trying to align themselves with undesirable kids.

- **Image is compelling.** Growing children tend to believe what they see on the surface. When Jamie looks at Susie and her friends, she sees a group of kids who always seem to be having a good time. She sees the admiring looks that others give them. She sees that these kids aren't bullied, ridiculed, or put down. She automatically assumes that Susie and company have all of the qualities she would want in a friend. She doesn't really know what they are like individually at all except, ironically, for the way they treat her. Most likely, Jamie's desire to be part of the group is based on the *image* of popularity and not the personality traits of Susie and her friends. Many kids learn (the hard way) that once they get to know the popular kids, they don't really like them, or at least they don't necessarily have anything in common with them. They learn to look beyond the surface image to find true friends. (This is not to say that popular kids never make good friends; many kids are both.) But if your child is being hurt currently by efforts to get in with the popular kids, you may not want to wait for this maturity to occur on its own. You'll want to help him or her look more closely at the pursued individuals—see the suggestions later in this chapter.

- **The apple doesn't fall far from the tree.** What's your attitude toward social stature? Not surprisingly, if popularity is important to you, it will be to your children, too. Some children may feel pressured to be friends with the "popular" kids by parents who are very concerned with social status. I know a sixth-grader who invited friends over for a get-together at her house. A couple of the boys got rowdy and began making anonymous phone calls to kids who were not invited. The parents of the child hosting the party did not discuss this behavior with the boys' parents because they wanted to be sure their daughter was invited to the boys' parties. Why? Because these boys are considered the most "popular" kids in the grade.

Many parents obviously remember wounds that they suffered from being excluded by the popular kids, and so they try to "help" their own children by paving their way to popularity. Unfortunately, increasing evidence suggests that popular kids are not always the nice kids, and it's hard to imagine that parents who thought carefully about this would push their kids toward those types of associations. In fact, studies indicate that many popular kids are cruel and aggressive. Researchers at Duke University found that 28 percent of popular boys in elementary school are aggressive, unfriendly troublemakers. According to the study's lead researcher, Dr. Philip Rodkin, "These boys may internalize the idea that aggression, popularity, and control naturally go together, and they may not hesitate to use physical aggression as a social strategy because it has always worked in the past." Dr. Rodkin explains that these socially connected boys and their followers can have large effects in disrupting the classroom environment and taunting other children. William Pollack, author of *Real Boys* and codirector of the Center for Men at McLean Hospital in Boston, states that boys look up to other boys who are aggressive. Michael Thompson, a psychologist and coauthor of *Raising Cain*, discusses how misbehaving helps boys gain respect from their peers.

Many people seem to believe that this is a recent social development, but I cannot find much concrete evidence for this assertion. Aggression is and always has been a fundamental survival skill, and it seems only natural for adults and children to gravitate toward the other survivors of the world. Whether we as a society are encouraging gratuitous aggression is another issue altogether, and the debate over how the media's glorification of violence might be influencing our children continues to rage on. One thing that doesn't seem open to debate is that when aggression is perceived as "cool," it is difficult for parents to explain the difference between a popular child and a potential friend.

What Makes Someone Popular?

Children answer this question in a wide variety of ways. Interestingly, several third- and fifth-grade girls told me that the "popular" students in their grade *think* they are popular but they are not liked by a lot of kids because they are mean. They explained that these girls think they are popular because they wear the coolest and most expensive clothes. I was intrigued with their perception of "popularity." Apparently some children mean "admired" or "envied" when they define someone as "popular." It may have nothing to do with how many people actually want to be the students' friends or even want to be in their company.

When I asked other students, "What does being popular mean?" I got fairly consistent answers to some extent: "Popular kids are cool and smart." "They wear cool clothes." "Popular boys are great at sports." "Popular girls are pretty." On the other hand, their definitions of popularity also varied in interesting ways.

Responses from fifth-grade boys included:

- "Popularity means everyone likes you. In order to be popular, you have to be cool."
- "When I think of popular, I think of cool kids who are good at sports."
- "Popular kids hang out with other cool kids."
- "Popular kids can act like bullies."
- "I don't think the word *popular* should even be in the dictionary! When I think of a popular person, I think of a person who everyone likes, but who is really mean. People might like that person for his athletic ability or his looks, but they really don't care how that person is on the inside."

Responses from fifth-grade girls also included positive and negative perceptions:

- "Many popular kids are funny. Many popular kids make fun of other people. Some popular kids are mean and rude to other kids, so they act 'cool.' "
- "A popular person is liked by many people. A girl might be popular because boys like her. The same goes for boys. Popular girls are usually pretty and popular boys are athletic. Someone who doesn't get made fun of a lot can be called popular."
- "A lot of people think that popular people are pretty and well-known and liked by many. But I think people who are popular are snotty and self-centered. They think they are liked so much that they take it for granted. I think people are popular because they *think* they are!"
- "People think that if they hang out with 'popular' kids they will be cool. In my school, the 'popular' kids are athletic and have lots of friends. I think popular kids are nice, kind, loyal, and honest people."

In my opinion, my thirteen-year-old cousin, Emily, is a perfect example of a popular seventh-grader. She is very pretty, poised, and sweet and has a lot of friends. Emily has great grades and actively participates in school and extracurricular activities. She is president of the school and student council. Emily shared with me that she is not in the "popular" group at school. What is Emily's perception of popularity? With her permission, I am sharing her E-mail:

I would say popular people are in a way exclusive. The popular people I know kinda use people for awhile as friends but then move on to new friends. They also always do stuff together on weekends and don't really allow anyone to do things with them like go to the mall on weekends! But, popular people are just accepted by a lot of people and are looked up to by others a lot. Others think of them as being "very cool" and "perfect." I have gotten to be good friends with a lot of popular girls and they're really "fake." They say really mean stuff about people and then the next thing you know they act like that person is their best friend. Also I've noticed popular girls get in fights more over really stupid stuff and they don't always have the best of friendships between one another. Most popular girls are known to have the coolest clothes, wear a lot of makeup, have good grades, and go out with hot guys, which is very true. They also judge people, too, and are like "get a load of her shirt" or "she wore that last week." Yet not all popular girls are like that. Some are very nice and hate it that they get all the attention, like one of my good friends.

The one idea that all of these definitions of popularity seem to share is that of power. Whether it's through outright aggression or underhanded meanness, many popular kids are perceived as having power to exclude or include others, designate someone as "cool" or "uncool," and define what is "in" or "out." Apparently, some kids come by this power honestly—they are admired because they have a special talent, a social ease, or the charm or charisma that attracts others—and they use it humbly. These kids could be said to deserve their popularity; they are truly desirable as friends. Other popular kids evidently saw an opportunity to grab some power and went for it. Now they misuse it. They may not be so popular as they are envied and even feared.

If your child is bewildered by the injustice of the latter children acquiring their lofty position, remind him or her that it's the other kids who make a child popular. Popularity is bestowed upon them by others; it's not something anyone is born with. Just as it is given, it can be taken away. A child who doesn't deserve the admiration of others will not remain popular if everyone around him stops rewarding his negative behavior and attitudes. That's what the strategies in Chapter 6 are all about—children standing up for themselves and refusing to give cruel and aggressive peers power.

It's just as important, however, to point out to your child why deserving children become popular. Children who become popular and stay popular often seem to be the ones who are self-confident, seem comfortable with who they are, and are not imitators. That attracts others—either because they admire independence and self-confidence or because they are intrigued by someone who doesn't seem to need approval or permission from others. This often makes kids wonder what this confident child has that makes him or her so confident. Here again, Chapter 6 can help, by offering tools that will boost any child's self-confidence and self-determination.

Interestingly, as I think about the most "popular" kids when I was in junior high and high school, I realize that many of them had older brothers or sisters. They seemed to "know the ropes" and were more socially savvy. Some followed in the footsteps of their popular siblings. I am not concluding that having an older sibling contributes to popularity, but it can enhance one's confidence.

Parents and schools can, in fact, take advantage of this principle to help all young children, including those who don't have older siblings. Sometimes the core purpose is academic, but social examples are imparted as well. Here are some ideas:

- Many schools have "reading buddies" or the like, whereby older students go to the classrooms of younger grades and read to them on a regular basis. Often the books give the kids openings to conversation on social subjects.
- In our school, the older grades (fourth and fifth) have partner classes with first- and second-graders. During the year, they participate in various activities.
- I like to suggest to teachers that they involve the older students in role-playing the teasing strategies, perform the script for the puppet show (see Chapter 7), and read books

about teasing. The pre-K–eighth-grade schools love this idea. The responsibility is also great for the older students.

- When my son entered fifth grade (in a 5–8 school) he was assigned an eighth-grade big brother for the year.
- This year, two fifth-grade girls came with me to my weekly sessions in a first-grade classroom. They read stories and helped me facilitate discussions and activities. One day, when I was not at school, they led a discussion about coping. They defined *coping* as dealing with a situation that you don't like without crying or getting mad. They helped the class develop a list of what coping skills they needed to use in class. The first-graders loved the fifth-grade girls.

How to Talk to Your Child About the Difference Between Being Popular and Being a Good Friend

If your child is like Jamie—willing to tolerate teasing and other abuses in the hope of becoming friends with the popular kids—you should take some time to talk about his pursuit of the teaser. Ask why he wants to be friends with this person who does not treat him like a friend. Don't be surprised, especially if your child is relatively young, if he says something like, "I don't know. I just do." Kids often can't articulate why it feels so important to be accepted by the popular kids. In that case, you can segue into a discussion of the difference between being popular and being a friend. Compare the following lists and ask your child which person seems more appealing to have around.

A popular person . . .

is pursued by others.

is admired by others.

has what you want.

A friend . . .

wants to be with you.

likes you and is liked by you.

has things in common with you that you can share.

can do what he wants.	thinks of and cares about your feelings in what he does.
seems better than you.	is the same as you.
thinks she is cool.	thinks you're cool.
waits for you to smile at her.	makes you smile.

What True Friends Have to Offer

The longing to be popular can detour children away from friendships that are healthier and more fulfilling. Fourth-grader Katy had been friends with Allison since kindergarten. They played at each other's houses, and they were on the same soccer team. In first and second grades, they were both part of a larger group of friends. They participated in the same Brownie troop and often walked to school together. By fourth grade, however, Allison had gained power in the larger peer group and often abused it, becoming bossy and verbally aggressive and excluding some classmates. Katy was a frequent butt of Allison's cruelty. But instead of rejecting her former friend, the more Katy was left out, the more she wanted to hang on to Allison. The more she hung on, the more she was hurt. This vicious cycle continued. The fact that Allison's behaviors were very subtle made it difficult for adults to witness and intervene. Katy's mother mustered up enough courage to call Allison's mother to discuss the situation. Allison's mother was defensive and denied that her daughter was doing anything wrong. Katy's mom felt helpless and discouraged and finally called Katy's teacher.

When the teacher consulted me about the situation, I decided to talk to the two girls separately (more on this later in the chapter). Guess how Katy answered when I asked her why she wanted to continue her friendship with Allison? "I don't know, I just do." Even after we had talked about the qualities of a good friend and discussed the fact that other classmates were nicer to Katy than Allison was, I saw her continue to stand by Allison in line and try to sit by her in the learning center and in the lunchroom. When the hurt continued, the teacher intervened and urged Katy to sit at the other end of the table with different classmates. After several days, we observed Katy smiling and laughing during lunch and recess. Although she didn't recognize it right away, Katy was finally reaping the benefits of true, healthy friendships.

In trying to help children understand what a true, healthy friendship is, I ask them to complete the sentence "I would like a friend who. . . ." From the responses they have given me over the years I have compiled the following "ABCs of a good friend."

I would like a friend who is:

Accepting	Honest
Agreeable	Interesting
Believes in me	Jolly
Caring	Keeps promises
Cheerful	Kind
Dependable	Loyal
Doesn't tease me	Makes good choices
Doesn't boss me around	Neat
Enthusiastic	Optimistic
Fair	Polite
Fun to be with	Patient
Giving	Quiet when I talk
Good listener	Responsible
Good sport	Respectful
Happy	Sets a good example
Has similar interests	Shares
Helpful	Sincere

Smart

Sticks up for me

Treats others fairly

Trustworthy

Truthful

Understanding

Very funny

Willing to work out conflicts

"Xtra" special

Your loyal pal

Zany

You can do this activity with your child. Involve the family and create a list of friendship qualities. After creating your own list, you might want to rank the qualities in the order of importance. Some children may need you to create your own list of what you look for in a good friend. You can always describe what you like about one of your good friends whom your child knows.

It is very typical for a six-year-old to say, "I would like a friend who is nice and fun." When I talk to young children, I encourage them to give specific examples of what "nice" and "fun" mean. They often need help in recognizing specific kind behaviors, such as sharing a snack, picking up crayons that were scattered on the floor, or playing a particular game. An eight-year-old boy might respond, "I would like a friend who likes sports, is funny, and is fun to be with." A ten-year-old girl typically looks for a friend who is caring, loyal and honest, keeps promises, and is fun to be with.

Kids often understand how desirable many of the qualities on the ABC list are. But they don't like to delay gratification, and sometimes they can't see beyond what seems like fun and is immediately appealing—such as the perceived glory of eating lunch next to the most popular girl in the class compared to the actual joy of having a "nerdy" best friend sleep over and laugh together until midnight. I tell many children like Katy that as much as they want to be friends with the "popular" child, it may not be the healthiest choice. Sometimes they can develop a deeper understanding when I share the following analogy. There is a girl who loves milk shakes, but she gets sick every time she drinks one. She continues to drink them because she enjoys them so much. After some medical tests, she finds out that the reason milk shakes make her sick is that she is allergic to milk. I ask the child, "Would you continue to drink the milk shakes and get sick, or would you choose another treat that is healthier for you?" You would hope that she would find an alternative treat that she enjoys and does not cause her any adverse effects, just like Katy eventually found friends who made her smile.

For an older child, it may be more effective to explore what the child will get out of a true, healthy friendship compared to mere proximity to a popular child. When Lisa was in fourth grade, she frequently felt left out by several girls she perceived as "popular." I encouraged her to spend more time with two other girls in her class who went with her for special academic help. Although Lisa had fun with these girls, she continued to strive to be part of the "popular" group. Now that she is in fifth grade, she has come to value the friendships she has developed with the two girls. They have established a special bond because they have spent so much time together receiving additional academic support. I recently talked to all three of them about moving on to junior high. Lisa was feeling a lot of anxiety about the change. Her two friends were incredibly supportive and understanding. I was so impressed with how they truly care about each other. I told Lisa that this is what friendship is all about.

Patching Up Good Old Friendships

Sometimes, in cases like Allison's and Katy's, there is hope for patching up a friendship that has fallen apart. Allison could be going through a difficult time and might be capable of becoming Katy's friend again. In many such situations, depending upon the age of the child and the nature of the relationship, a talk with the teaser and teasee about the hurtful behavior may be beneficial. It often helps to have a teacher, social worker, or counselor facilitate this conversation. (A parent isn't always objective.) The meeting may clarify some misunderstandings and allows the teaser and teasee to share both sides of the situation. Many young children don't realize the impact of their words. They don't understand that joking around can be hurtful. This conversation can also provide the opportunity for the teaser to apologize. In many cases, the friendships are mended and the importance of respect is emphasized.

A mother called me to tell me that her daughter, Marie, was very upset because Julie was calling her names as they walked home from school. The girls had been friends the year before but decided to go their separate ways, primarily because of their two-year age difference. The name-calling and teasing began several months earlier. Marie was becoming increasingly upset as the comments escalated and became more hurtful. Marie's older cousin, who attended another nearby school, began walking home with her to "protect" her from Julie's stinging comments. When I talked to Marie about the situation, she told me that Julie was making fun of her weight, hair, clothes, and friends. When I talked to Julie, she admitted that she called Marie names, and she also said that Marie's cousin was calling her names and swearing at her. Both girls were hurt by the taunts and teases exchanged daily on their way home from school. When I brought them in together, I acknowledged that the walk home from school was hurtful and stressful for both of them. They agreed. I told them that the purpose of our meeting was not to place blame or determine who "started it." My hope was that the name-calling and teasing would stop. We talked about respecting each other even if they were no longer friends. They both seemed relieved that I was addressing the situation. They willingly made a verbal agreement to stop using hurtful words. Julie apologized to Marie and Marie even apologized for her cousin's comments.

Finding New, True Friends

"Making friends is not as simple as it used to be," proclaimed a recent *Chicago Tribune* headline. One of the principal messages of this March 11, 2001, article by Mary Ann Fergus was that parents had better be prepared to facilitate children's quests for new friends because the days of making pals out on some open field where all the kids gather after school are long gone. But chauffeuring and becoming your child's social secretary are tasks well worth the effort, the article stated. Friends are critical for many obvious reasons, chief among them is that best friends contribute more to a child's acquisition of social skills than parents, teachers, or even organized groups like Scouts. And in an age when families move around a lot and kids often opt for solitary activities like computer games, far too many kids are becoming deficient in these social skills. As we've discussed, lack of social skills is one factor that can make a child vulnerable to teasing. So please don't underestimate the importance of your child's making good friends or the worthiness of your contributing to that end.

As it turned out, Allison, the girl that Katy was so set on keeping as a friend, really did not want to be Katy's friend anymore. After reviewing the situation, I recognized that I had two choices. I could bring Katy and Allison together for a conversation that could clarify the situation and perhaps mend the friendship, or I could meet the girls individually to assess their feelings and motivation for the friendship. I decided to meet with Katy and Allison individually because I was concerned that it might be too risky to bring them in together. From the fact that Allison had not demonstrated any positive interactions or motivation to continue the friendship, I speculated that Allison would tell me that she did not want to be friends with Katy. Although this was a reality that Katy might have to deal with, I did not want this to occur in a joint meeting with them. So, I decided to have separate talks with them. It was clear in my talk with Allison that she did not want to be friends with Katy. In fact, she found Katy to be annoying and very clingy. She complained that Katy never gave her privacy with her other friends. Although Allison owned up to some of her hurtful behaviors to Katy, she did not appear very remorseful. School personnel can emphasize the importance of being respectful and polite to everyone, which is what I did. At our school, we have the rule "You can't say 'You can't play'" (from Vivian Gussen Paley's *You Can't Say You Can't Play*). Kids cannot exclude anyone from any activities or play. We can't, however, make kids maintain or continue friendships.

Sometimes kids end up with fair-weather friends—kids who are willing to be their friends as long as it serves them well or doesn't cause them too much trouble. Katy had another friend in Allison's crowd, Jenna, who was willing to be Katy's friend most of the time and even commiserated with her about Allison's treatment. But when Allison was around, Jenna would become mysteriously silent. When Katy gave her a beseeching look, hoping she would defend her, Jenna would find somewhere else she needed to go and occasionally even smirked along with the other girls when Allison was making some snide remark under her breath. This confused Katy even more and only reinforced the idea that Allison's friendship and goodwill were extremely desirable. When I talked to Katy, she reluctantly acknowledged that Jenna's friendship was probably not worth trying to keep. Instead, I encouraged Katy to pursue other friendships—kids she could trust and who would be loyal.

So, when the friendships cannot be mended, parents need to help their children recognize whether it was healthy to begin with. Parents, teachers, and other adults in a child's life can help the child understand his or her rights as a friend and how to tell a friend from someone who's not. Whether you're talking about kids who are cruel to your child but still pursued by her or kids who are fair-weather friends of your child's, sit down with your child and discuss the following questions:

- Do your child's friends care about her feelings?
- Do they treat her with respect?
- Do the friendships help your child feel good about who he is?
- Does your child consistently complain about hurt feelings, ridicule, or feeling left out?

If your child has become isolated, forsaking friendships altogether and spending most free time alone or only with family, you'll want to adopt some of the following suggestions right away. A wealth of research supports the fact that children need friends—and good ones.

Children's friendships provide opportunities to develop and strengthen social skills that are important throughout life. Initiating conversation, listening, understanding another person's point of view, conveying empathy, sharing, compromising, resolving conflict, developing trust, and having fun are part of a child's social learning that takes place within peer relationships. Having good friends and feeling accepted contribute to a child's self-esteem. Fred Frankel, author of *Good Friends Are Hard to Find*, explains that researchers have found that children who have difficulties making and keeping friends were more likely to drop out of school and turn to drugs during their adolescent years. He also reports that research findings indicate that children who do not have friends grow up to be lonely adults.

Ask your child if there is a person whom he would like to get to know better. Does he know anyone who would have some of the qualities on the Good Friend ABCs list? Inviting that child over is the next step in the friendship-making process. Playing with a child one-on-one is the best way for kids to get to know each other. Dr. Frankel emphasizes the importance of making play dates for children. He states, "If you don't schedule it [a play date], it isn't going to happen, and if it doesn't happen, you can forget about close friendships." When the play date is scheduled, don't plan the first get-together for the whole day. A shorter period of time after school is the best way to start. It is much better to have kids want more time together than feel like they have had too much of each other. Some kids may want to schedule a particular activity such as bowling, ice-skating, or working on an assignment together. You might want to suggest that your son or daughter invite another child to go along when your family visits a museum or goes to the movies.

Another way to promote different and additional friendships is to encourage your kids to participate in outside activities. Begin by finding extracurricular activities that provide additional opportunities for peer interaction, social success, and acceptance. The Scouts, a park district class, a sports team, a computer club, and a religious class are great opportunities for developing friendships, learning a particular skill, and enhancing self-esteem. Classes, teams, and other organized activities automatically establish a common interest, which is an important basis for friendship. These activities and classes have adult supervision, which makes excluding kids very difficult.

Not all children have best friends at school, as in the case of Melissa, who felt very excluded from the "in-group" in her fourth-grade classroom. She felt quite lonely and spent a lot of time by herself. Fortunately, Melissa had great friends from religious school and camp.

Eight-year-old Tommy was on the fringe of his peer group. He was small and soft-spoken. Although he was not the target of teasing and ridicule, he was not consistently included because he rarely took the initiative to join and interact with others. Tommy's dad decided to coach Tommy's baseball team so that he could facilitate peer interactions in a subtle and appropriate way.

Polishing Up Those Social Skills

Once you have directed your child toward some additional opportunities to meet and make new friends, it might be a good idea to review some basic friendship strategies. Most children learn social skills informally, while others need more specific instruction and guidance. It is easy to tell our kids to "act friendly," but what does that mean? We often need to remind children to greet others with a smile and to make the move to say "hello" first. It is a good idea for kids to ask questions to get to know someone. "What is your favorite sport?" "What games do you like to play?" "Do you have any pets?" Brainstorm with your child a list of questions that would be appropriate. Some children need reminders to listen without interrupting and to look interested when the other person is talking. Acting out a "getting to know you" scenario is a great way to instill confidence in your child as he prepares for the actual situation. Then, the next step is inviting a child over to play, at which time it is important to remind your child about the importance of sharing and cooperating and caring about the guest's feelings. Talk to your child about what he can do to ensure that his guest will have a fun time.

This book can't possibly do justice to the subject of increasing a child's social skills, so the preceding ideas are merely a start. If you are concerned about your child's social acumen, talk to the child's teacher or the school social worker or counselor. In addition, many excellent books can help socially awkward children become comfortable with their peers and others. Among them are *Good Friends Are Hard to Find*, by Fred Frankel, and *Why Doesn't Anybody Like Me?: A Guide to Raising Socially Confident Kids*, by Hara Estroff Marano.

Peer pressure is powerful, and the longing to be popular can detour children away from friendships that will be supportive and nurturing and help the child ease teasing from others. If you are worried about your child's peer relationships, remember the difference between friendship and popularity. Parents can be central to promoting healthy friendships. A big part of a healthy friendship is empathy and mutual support, the topics of the next chapter.

9

All Together Now

Teaching Children Empathy and Mutual Support

There is power in numbers, and peer pressure can be positive. If we adults stimulate children's empathy and help them summon up their courage, bystanders and witnesses can exert powerful peer pressure to stop cruelty aimed at an individual child. But we can go even further. We can help kids integrate empathy and mutual support into their everyday behavior in a way that tends to reduce incidents of teasing in the first place. If your children have been teased, it's important—and surprisingly empowering—to teach them not just to protect themselves from harm but also to translate how they felt when teased into action that discourages others from succumbing to the temptation to tease.

In Chapter 8 we talked a lot about the distinction between being popular and being a good friend with the aim of encouraging victims of teasing to pursue the companionship of the latter rather than the former. Children who are vulnerable to teasing often seek out the popular kids in the hope of becoming acceptable by association. Sadly, many popular kids often take advantage of their status to torment others, and they may pay particularly cruel attention to their weakest and neediest followers. I'm happy to report that it's not always that way.

Michelle is fourteen. She loves to be at the center of the social activity in her eighth-grade class but has always felt that the pinnacle of popularity was just out of her reach. Now she laughingly refers to herself as a "nerd." But at the beginning of seventh grade for the first time in her life she told her parents that she didn't want to go to school. The most popular—and the meanest—boy in the class, it turns out, had chosen her as the new butt of his typical verbal torture. Her sixth-grade boyfriend had dumped her, she was a dork, her hair looked terrible, she had an obnoxious laugh, and so on. "Where were her friends when this was going on?" her parents asked. Full of support and sympathy, Michelle said, but only after the fact, when John was nowhere to be seen. Even her most loyal friends wouldn't risk having his attention turned toward them.

Michelle's parents were dismayed to hear that a small, generally close class was so easily torn apart by one boy. They advised her to take every opportunity to defend the other kids from John's barbs, as publicly as possible. They stressed that Michelle shouldn't demean or attack the boy in return. In fact, if she could respond jokingly in a way that might invite John to laugh gently at himself along with her, he'd be able to save face, he'd know she was trying to be his friend, and at the same time she'd be putting him on notice that she wasn't going to let him get away with meanness.

Right away Michelle came home happily reporting that a boy she had defended had thanked her after school, an incident that was repeated with several other classmates in the weeks to come. John himself started joking self-deprecatingly *with* Michelle, and their on-and-off friendship of many years got more and more solid as he realized that Michelle was one person who could reject his behavior without rejecting him altogether, as many of the other kids had done. By eighth grade, Michelle was called "the nicest person in the class" by another classmate, widely considered the coolest, most sophisticated boy in the grade; and the girl she had always perceived as the most popular wistfully told her she envied Michelle because she was "always surrounded by people." Michelle had become one of the most popular kids in eighth grade not by making other kids feel inferior but by being a good friend to everyone.

Similar examples are all around us, and these are the scenarios we need to make sure our kids notice and remember. Teaching your teased child to be brave in supporting other victims not only helps the child contribute to the worthy cause of discouraging teasing but may even make the child an admired leader. In a candid article on the constant eighth-grade pursuit of popularity, the April 8, 2001, *New York Times Magazine* described how Tory, the most popular girl in her Westport, Connecticut, eighth grade, "performed an act of kindness that served only to make her more popular.

"Out on the blacktop during recess one day, a couple of kids started pegging basketballs at Jason, an eighth grader with few friends. Jason was cornered, alone and defenseless and reduced to tears, while most of the grade simply looked on, not wanting to be associated with someone so obviously unpopular. That is until Tory walked out of the cafeteria.

" 'I went over and took his hand and walked him to the nurse and then the guidance counselor,' Tory says. . . .

"Chris, another popular boy, says, 'I felt a little bad for him, but Tory's the only one who'd stick up for him.'

"In the days and weeks that followed, Tory's act of mercy became the stuff of lunchroom legend.

" 'I think people thought that other people would make fun of them for helping Jason,' Tory says. 'And I think that they thought it was nice of me to do that.' "

Would Tory have had the guts to make that gesture if she hadn't already occupied a lofty position among her peers? Maybe not. As another onlooker explained, " 'Other people think that they might get in trouble for going over to talk to Jason. But for Tory, no one's above her.' " When we try to encourage our children to take a supportive, courageous stand at a time when they are already viewed as unpopular or weak, we have to be sure to let them know that we understand how hard it might be. And then we have to give them as many examples and models as we can come up with to illustrate how worthwhile the effort usually is. You might start with some of the dozens of movies devoted to this subject of triumphant underdog, such as *Freak the Mighty*, *Simon Birch*, *Angus*, *The Sandlot*, and many others. Renting a videotape on this topic is a fun way to spend a family evening together and a great launching point for starting your work toward instilling empathy and courageous support in your child. And pass on any examples of empathy and compassion you've encountered, from the news story about a twelve-year-old boy who opened his own homeless shelter to the glowing reports from teenagers about how good they feel after fulfilling the service requirements that many schools today have established.

Empathy comes naturally to us, and sometimes all we need is a reminder. The American Psychological Association called empathy "the trait that makes us human."

"I Know How You Feel"

Psychologists and social workers make an important distinction between sympathy and empathy. Sympathy means feeling sorry for someone, pitying him for his plight. It's sympathy that makes a child's friends stand around during a teasing incident looking concerned and then rush over to commiserate once the perpetrator has had his fun and left the scene. Empathy means knowing how someone feels, being able to put yourself in someone else's shoes. It's empathy that makes a child's friends act in her defense while the teasing is going on. If we want children to stop tolerating teasing—not just of themselves but of others too—we have to reinforce empathy.

To have empathy, children must recognize and understand the feelings of others. Children begin to have the capacity for empathy when they are three or four years old, and their ability to empathize develops as they mature. For a very young child, empathy might be limited to something as tangible as physical pain. All young kids have experienced bumps and bruises, and because they are so familiar with what hurt feels like, they can show empathy when someone else is hurt. A four-year-old girl, for example, might readily offer a kiss to her mother when she has a sniffle or to her father when he needs a Band-Aid. As they mature, children's ability to look beyond themselves increases, as does their capacity to identify and understand a variety of feelings. Ten-year-old Julia was distracted in class because she was worried about her very ill grandfather. During lunch, her good friend Rachel asked what was wrong. When Julia told her she was sad because her grandpa was very sick, Rachel said, "I understand how you feel; my grandfather died two years ago," and began to cry. Rachel told Julia a little about her grandpa and his illness. She said, "Julia, I am here to listen if you want to talk about your grandpa." Later in the chapter you'll read about two eleven-year-old girls who were moved by compassion and empathy to talk to me about a classmate who was being teased.

How much children are able to call forth empathy when they have strong feelings that might conflict with it or when the situation they're observing is very different from anything they have ever experienced will depend on their relative maturity and also their inherent sensitivity. A child who stands by and lets another be teased may be prevented from feeling empathy if he has never been victimized. Realistically, the older kids get, the more likely it is that they have been in the victim's shoes. Still they may do nothing, however, perhaps because their fear of turning the teaser's attention to themselves is much stronger than their compassion for the victim.

Many factors can influence the development of empathy in an individual child. For example, psychologists have known for a long time that young children whose feelings are not acknowledged or addressed by the adults who care for them have difficulty developing empathy. This may be why abused children sometimes become abusers themselves and why neglected children have trouble making emotional attachments to others as they grow up. I have read that children who witness their mothers being abused by their fathers have difficulty developing empathy. Kids who have experienced harsh punishment also struggle with this issue.

Then there are all the cultural influences that our children are exposed to today. While it is very difficult to prove a definite cause-and-effect connection, many mental health professionals have suggested that the prevalence of entertainment media violence has desensitized children and diminished their capacity for empathy. That is, when very young children see human beings being hurt over and over on a TV, movie, or computer screen, they may lose the ability to feel empathy for a real person undergoing the same harm right in front of them. Add to this possibility the "me first" aggressiveness that is so widely celebrated by American culture today, and it seems little wonder that the empathy that comes so easily to children when they're three could be muffled by the time they're eight.

So, are we raising a generation of cold-hearted automatons? Of course not. But it certainly can't hurt to take advantage of the many opportunities before us to strengthen empathy in our children (and ourselves!). These opportunities are called "teachable moments," a term adopted by millions of parents and teachers looking for chances to introduce important lessons into their children's lives without preaching or lecturing. Parents and teachers can offer children loads of opportunities to increase their sensitivity toward others, to understand how another person is feeling or how it might feel to be in someone else's situation. If kids truly understand what it is like to be the target of ridicule and taunting, they will more likely make a choice to actively intervene rather than just stand by as merely passive observers. The first chapter of 20 *Teachable Virtues*, a helpful resource for parents, is about empathy, which the authors believe is the core virtue around which caring, honesty, trust, and tolerance are built.

Empathy Training at Home

Parents are the logical teachers of empathy. In the family's daily routines, parents have unlimited opportunities to point out or remind their children of other people's feelings. Whether it is a situation occurring in your family, on television, in a movie, or in a book you are reading to your child, look for openings to ask questions like these:

- "How do you think he felt when his friend laughed at him?"
- "How did your sister look when you called her names?"
- "I wonder how Arthur felt when Francine made fun of his glasses. What do you think?"

There are countless teachable moments in our daily lives, and simply training your child's attention on other people's feelings on a regular basis is a great way to start instilling empathy.

Recently, I asked a class of third-graders to record a log of put-downs and mean comments they had heard or observed on TV. The purpose was to raise their awareness of the "funny/hurtful" comments. Following the assignment, we discussed the appropriateness of the teases and put-downs. Many children reported put-downs during various episodes of "Rugrats." Mean comments heard on "Hey Arnold," "The Wonder Years," "Arthur," and "The Simpsons" were also discussed. The students explained that although the put-downs are inappropriate, most of these comments are laughed at by other characters in the show or by the viewing audience, which is cued to laugh. The students discussed their confusion about the double message they receive. They are told they shouldn't tease or ridicule others, yet this behavior must be acceptable behavior because it is portrayed as something funny on television.

The following TV log is a great family activity.

Teasing, Put-Downs, and Insults on TV

TV Show: _____

Date & Time: _____

Characters Involved: _____

Funny/Hurtful Comments: _____

_____

Your Reaction to Comments: _____

_____

So what can you do if you witness or observe a put-down or insult on a show that your child is watching? You can turn this into a teachable moment! When you observe teasing or ridicule while your child is viewing television, you can ask:

- "Was that really funny?"
- "How do you think the character felt when someone made fun of him?"
- "Would you make a remark like that to someone?"
- "How would you feel if someone said that to you?"
- "What would you do if someone said that to you?"
- "How would you feel if someone said that to your friend?"
- "What would you do if someone said that to your friend?"

The lessons from this discussion increase children's sensitivity to others, promote empathy and compassion, and provide an opportunity to think about actions to take in teasing situations. This teachable moment will clarify the confusion that many children experience when they see and hear insulting behaviors in the media. A follow-up lesson can be to look for kindness on television. What shows can kids find in which the characters treat each other with respect and concern?

Everyone Has Feelings
As I mentioned earlier in the book, it's not uncommon for children to automatically feel fearful when they encounter someone who is different. This fear tends to overwhelm empathy. To alleviate that fear, we can talk to our children about differences that they notice in others and create opportunities to clarify misconceptions and provide factual information. That way children can make sense of, understand, and respect the differences they observe in others. The pamphlet *101 Tools for Tolerance—Simple Ideas for Promoting Equity and Celebrating Diversity*, by the Southern Poverty Law Center, is loaded with suggestions for parents. These include attending a play or listening to music by artists whose race or ethnicity is different from yours, shopping at an ethnic grocery store or specialty market, and taking your family out for lunch or dinner at an ethnic restaurant. You can find the pamphlet on their website, splcenter.org.

When you see a person who is different in any way whether it is at the grocery store, the park, or at a museum, take the time to talk about what the difference is. See how many differences your child can identify—whether it is related to the way a person looks, walks, talks, or acts. You can make a game out of it: Who can spot the most differences? What is the most different difference? With older kids, you can take it a step further. If a person doesn't exhibit an obvious difference, imagine what might be different about that person or his or her life. After the differences have been identified, a great discussion can follow regarding how the people might feel. Again, another teachable moment. Another opportunity for valuable discussion would be to talk about how your kids feel when they see people with these differences.

Those of us who were taught not to stare and to avoid noticing differences, lest we make the person with the difference uncomfortable, may feel uncomfortable playing this game. If you're among them, keep in mind that the differences are simply noticed and acknowledged, without judgments or derogatory remarks made. I've found that bringing our natural powers of observation out demystifies differences and makes kids and adults more tolerant and empathic.

The first time my son, Matt, who was quite young at the time, saw a man with only one leg, he could not stop staring. Initially, I thought he was going to say what he was thinking so loudly that the physically challenged man would hear this. I tried my hardest to "shush" Matt so he wouldn't say anything. I later realized that I had not dealt with the situation the way I should have. I decided to bring it up later that day. "Do you remember the man we saw at the grocery store with one leg?" I asked my son. Of course he did. We talked about how that might have caused him to feel scared. I remember telling him that people are different in so many ways. We played a game naming all of the differences people can have. Obviously the list of a small child is more limited than the list created with an older one. Nevertheless, it was a beginning. We talked about why the man might have had only one leg. Was he born that way, or had he been in an accident? We talked about how the man felt. Was it polite to stare at him?

I decided to be proactive in discussing other differences with Matt. The next time we went to the grocery, I said, "Let's see how many people we see who are different in some way." We saw people with different color skin, a lady with a cane, and a man with a hearing aid. The discussion of differences was ongoing throughout his childhood.

Literature is another great way to introduce the topic of differences, or it can serve as reinforcement to issues you have previously discussed. A few of my favorites to read to young children are:

I'm Like You, You're Like Me—A Child's Guide to Understanding and Celebrating Each Other, by Cindy Gainer

The Biggest Nose, by Kathy Caple

Rosie's Story, by Martine Gogoll

Modeling Empathy

The most powerful lesson of all takes place when you model empathy by conveying an understanding of how your kids feel. Whether your child is disappointed because she's sick and can't go to a party, is afraid of thunder, or is upset that she can't go to the mall with her friends, you can say, "I understand how you feel." Although the validation of feelings does not "fix" the problem the child is facing, it is quite reassuring and consoling, which generally helps kids feel better.

Affirming a child's feelings is one way to instill empathy. Another is to speculate about how a child is feeling when the child is not expressing it outright. Tasha seemed glum when her mother picked her up after basketball practice but just said, "Nothing," when her mother asked what was wrong. Changing the subject, Tasha's mom asked about her homework. Tasha ran down the usual list of math, science, social studies, and language arts, and then turned back to the car window.

"What did you say?" her mother asked a moment later, when Tasha mumbled something she didn't quite catch.

"I said, 'I'll have plenty of time to do it all, but I have to call Melissa before 7:00 so we can plan our presentation.'"

Sensing something in her daughter's voice, Tasha's mom probed: "Oh? Why do you have to call by then?"

"Because she and Sue and Jane and Tanya and Cindy are all meeting online then."

"What about you?"

"They didn't ask me to get on with them." Tasha kept her gaze on the car window.

"Oh," said her mother quietly. "I bet that made you feel kind of left out."

"Not really," Tasha answered sulkily.

"Well, when my friends got together without me when I was a kid, I couldn't get my mind off it. I just kept wondering what they'd all be talking about and why they didn't want to include me. Made me feel really lonely."

Tasha finally turned away from the window. "Really? So what did you do?"

That was the beginning of a lively conversation about friends and friendships. Tasha's mother suggested she try calling Sue a little before 7:00, just to talk, and when she did, Sue naturally ended up asking Tasha to go online with the rest of the girls. Tasha had a great time with her teammates, but even more important, at least for the long term, was the fact that Tasha's mother had demonstrated empathy by intuiting what her daughter must be feeling when her daughter wasn't quite up to expressing it.

Children whose parents convey empathy to them are more likely to convey empathy to others.

By the way, when you're conveying empathy, don't forget to notice your child's positive feelings too: "You must have felt so excited!" "I can see how proud you're feeling!" It's important to help kids make the connection between positive actions and behavior and good feelings.

Broadening Horizons

The development of empathy can be slowed when children are exposed to only a homogeneous environment. When everyone they know looks the same, acts the same, has and wants the same things, their ability to understand what different people might be feeling in varying situations is stunted. Parents can make sure that children broaden the information base for their empathy by exposing them to new and different situations.

Volunteering on a monthly basis at a church's soup kitchen was a meaningful experience for the Butler family. The children's work in the kitchen helped sharpen their awareness and deepen their understanding that many people do not have food to eat. It stimulated a short but memorable discussion among the Butlers about what it must feel like to be hungry and not be able to head for the refrigerator as well as how various family members might feel if they had to depend on strangers to feed them.

Doing a favor for an ill or elderly neighbor, donating toys and clothes to charity, and taking canned goods to a local food pantry are acts that help children realize that good deeds can make an incredible difference in the lives of others. These kind actions help kids feel good about what they have done to help others.

Another idea for home or school is to study or read about the achievements of famous empathetic people, such as Martin Luther King Jr., Jane Addams, and Florence Nightingale, to increase the child's understanding of the power of empathy.

Empathy Training at School

The classroom also provides unlimited opportunities to think about and discuss how other people are feeling. Teachers can ask an infinite variety of questions during class discussions or group activities that will help students focus on the feelings of others. The use of literature is a powerful way to address feelings and facilitate the development of empathy. Any book or story that your child is reading offers a great opportunity to assess and understand what the characters are feeling. But some specific books model empathy in particularly powerful ways, such as Harper Lee's *To Kill a Mockingbird* for junior high students. Ask your child's language arts teacher, the school librarian, or the public library's children's librarian for other titles.

We begin the school year by focusing on the feelings of our new students. Over the years, I have seen new kids at school become the targets of teasing. Often, their only local friends are a couple they may have met in the neighborhood when they arrived. When they are different in any way—they have an accent from another country or a different part of the United States, they look or dress differently, they like the "wrong" music or movies—they are easy targets of teasing. To help new students adjust, I have a class discussion introducing the new students and ask the class to think about how the new students are probably feeling. Most of the new students say they feel excited, nervous, or both. Many new students say they miss their old friends, and sometimes they admit they're afraid they won't make new friends. Some younger children feel overwhelmed because the school feels so big.

Once the class has an understanding of how the new students feel, we talk about what everyone can do to help the new kids feel more welcome. Many students volunteer to be the new students' buddy. They are enthusiastic about showing new kids around the school, introducing them to kids in other classes, and of course playing together at recess.

During the discussion, I set aside time for the students to ask the new kids any questions to get to know them. In a short time, the new kids begin to feel connected as they see there are some common interests. *The Brand New Kid*, by Katie Couric, a rhyming story about a new student who is teased because he is different, is a great springboard for discussion for primary and young elementary age students.

If your child is transferring into a new school, talk to the administration and teachers about what kind of orientation they offer for new kids. Suggest something like the discussion I just described if they don't mention taking any special measures to help kids adapt socially.

Marcia Anderson, a counselor serving grades 6–8 in my district, spends one morning with the new students of each grade level for an orientation. The morning agenda includes some testing, a tour of the building, and a question-and-answer period. Current students help with the orientation. The counselor checks with the teams of teachers the first week of school to see how the new students are doing. New students and their parents are asked to fill out a form to provide additional information about the students' prior school experiences and interests. Several weeks into the school year, the counselor arranges a new-student luncheon. The students play a trivia game in which they have to find out personal information about each other, for example, "Which student plays the harmonica?" (The counselor uses the information from the forms completed by students and parents.) They also play a "How well do you know Twin Groves [the school]?" game. Questions included are "Where is the lost and found?" "What is the name of the school nurse?" New students are encouraged to sign up if they would like to continue eating lunch together. A few of the new students have ongoing contact with the counselor or social worker.

The classroom offers additional opportunities throughout the year for learning about others who are different, which increases children's sensitivity to situations different from their own. Field trips to different schools, visits to senior citizen homes, and trips to food pantries to deliver collected goods are memorable learning experiences that expand the world of children. It's important to follow up on these experiences, however, so that the effect endures. After one fourth-grade class went to visit a senior citizens' home to interview seniors and play bingo, the students became pen pals with the seniors. Many schools and religious organizations invite people to adopt a family at holiday time, donating clothing and toys for a specific family whose ages and genders have been supplied.

Teaching Mutual Support

If kids can develop empathy for a child being teased or ridiculed, they will more likely make a choice to intervene actively rather than passively stand by as observers. During the last several years, I have focused more sharply on the role of the bystander or witness to teasing. Obviously, many kids do nothing because they're afraid that they're likely to become the next target. They don't want to get on the bad side of the teaser. However, many kids who don't intervene or show support for the teasee may feel sad or guilty about their passive behavior. We must strongly encourage a bystander or witness to intervene, show support, or ask for help. It is imperative that children take an active role when they witness or observe a classmate being teased.

Reporting Teasing to Adults

Two fourth-grade girls, Sophie and Emily, recently asked to talk to me about a situation they found upsetting. They explained that a few girls in their class were teasing a classmate, Peter. The girls were making fun of him, moving away whenever he sat down, and talking about him to other kids. The girls, who were acting cruel toward Peter, were generally polite and were not perceived as troublemakers. Sophie and Emily talked to the girls about their hurtful behavior toward Peter, but the situation continued. Sophie and Emily did exactly what I encouraged them to do—ask for help.

I approached Peter and told him that I was very upset when I heard that some girls were giving him a hard time. Peter, who is very good-natured, said to me, "I imagine you would be upset." I asked how he felt about our talking about the situation during our regular class meeting. He said that would be fine.

At the beginning of the class meeting, I used the "I" message, stating that I was very upset to hear that Peter was being teased by a few classmates. I emphasized that this behavior was not appropriate or respectful. I did not mention the names of the teasers. I asked Peter how he felt about it. He admitted he didn't like it, but he said he was dealing with it. I asked the class how they felt about the situation. Many kids said it wasn't respectful. When I asked the students how they thought Peter felt when he was teased, one student said, "He probably felt mad or sad, or maybe both." Another classmate thought he might be really annoyed. I could tell that Peter was gratified to hear the support of so many classmates.

Then I asked if the students who were giving him a hard time would like to apologize, noting that I knew this would take much courage. One girl said, "I don't know if I've ever said anything mean to Peter, but if I have, I'm sorry." Peter said that she had never made fun of him.

Another girl then raised her hand very tentatively. She said in a soft voice that she had said things that were not nice and that she was very sorry. I praised her courage and honesty. Three other girls followed suit and apologized to Peter. He was glowing, and the girls exhibited a sense of relief.

The next day as I passed Peter in the hallway, he gave me a thumbs-up sign. A few days later he told me that he was now playing soccer with the "popular" boys in the class.

This was a powerful example for me about the importance of witnesses taking an active and responsible role. The kids who witness verbal aggression and rude behavior must realize the power they have to make a difference. I told Sophie and Emily that they were heroes.

While we naturally want children to feel comfortable reporting teasing to adults, some won't come forward without the protection of anonymity. One school social worker told me she has placed a box in a secure place in her school where students can anonymously submit concerns about specific teasing incidents. This idea is similar to the "Notice of Harassment" form (one for parents and one for students) which was developed by Steve Clinton after his thirteen-year-old daughter's tragic death. The form can be found on the Internet at jaredstory.com/notice2.html.

Intervening Safely When Teasing Occurs

The first thing I tell kids who witness teasing is that the very least they can do is not show any support for the teaser. This includes not spreading rumors started by teasers or telling stories about the latest put-downs. It also means not responding positively while witnessing teasing. Sometimes kids don't understand that laughing, while it seems like a benign response, is humiliating for the teasee and reinforcing for the teaser. Poor Mark was mortified when he vomited in the school hallway before he could make it to the boys' bathroom. He felt even worse when a classmate called him "Barf Boy." But the worst humiliation occurred when several boys stood there and laughed.

Since many victims are not able to defend themselves, witnesses and bystanders can assume a very significant role. Instead of laughing or joining the taunting, the observers can choose to tell the teaser to stop. Tell your child that this doesn't have to be an elaborate rescue attempt. When someone is being teased, your child can say something simple like "Cool it" or "Knock it off." Sometimes teasers are stopped in their tracks when a bystander asks the question that often stumps them: "Why are you saying such hurtful things?"

As an alternative (or in addition) to addressing the teaser and directly intervening in the teasing, kids can offer support to the teasee, either privately or in the presence of the teaser. A bystander can simply say to the victim, "I really think what he said is untrue and disrespectful" or "I really like your glasses. I think they're very cool." A child who is reluctant to speak up in the presence of the teaser can offer support to the teasee later: "I'm not very good at baseball either. Maybe we can practice hitting together." Teasees appreciate support anytime.

Bystanders can also interrupt the teasing without antagonizing the teaser by asking the teasee to join in their activity. Or they can decide to seek help from peers or adults. Meghan and Jill, the two eleven-year-olds I referred to earlier, initiated a series of events that added up to one of the most gratifying professional experiences I have ever had. These two fifth-graders came to my office to talk about their deep concern about what was happening to Ralph, a student new to our school in the middle of the year. In spite of our efforts to integrate new students, Ralph never positively connected with his classmates. He was an easy target for ridicule and teasing. He is smaller than most kids, very smart, and not very polite. A few of the "popular" fifth-grade boys were giving Ralph a hard time, especially in less structured situations such as recess and gym. Their efforts included put-downs, exclusion, and advising fellow fifth-graders to do the same. Meghan and Jill told me that they would like to help Ralph. They said they were comfortable speaking up to the teasers. They realized that they might be the next targets, but that didn't impact their compassion for what Ralph was experiencing. I asked them if any other students shared their concern. They said they would ask their friends. I suggested we all have lunch together in a couple of days so that we could brainstorm some ideas and strategies. Much to my surprise, nineteen students (boys and girls) came to our "brainstorming" lunch. Several kids admitted that they had previously teased Ralph and now felt very bad about it. They all decided to speak up to the teasers the next time they observed any put-downs or teasing behavior.

The very next day, one of the teasers said something to Ralph before gym class began. Two girls, who overheard the comment, went over and said to the teaser that it was not respectful for him to say that to Ralph. Their emphatic statement took the teaser by surprise. Similar situations occurred with the other teasers. After one confrontation, a friend of the teaser said to one of the girls, "Do you love Ralph? Is that why you're standing up for him?" She calmly said, "No, I don't think anyone should treat anyone else that way."

The students met with me the following week and reported that the teasers were now actually acting nice to Ralph. I decided to meet with the teasers one-by-one with their teachers. They admitted that they had teased him but said it had stopped. It was important for them to know that we (adults) knew what was going on and that there would be significant consequences if the behavior occurred again.

The students who came together to support Ralph asked that he join us for our next lunch. They wanted to tell him that they were there to support him. I told Ralph what was happening. Although he did not show much positive emotion, he agreed to attend the lunch. It was amazing. Twenty-two students attended. A few kids expressed how bad they felt about his being teased and picked on. Three of the students apologized for not being nice to him when he initially transferred to our school. Some of the students complimented Ralph for not fighting or teasing the teasers back. Ralph answered questions about how it felt to be a new student, how it felt to be excluded and made fun of.

The following week we had a pizza party to celebrate the remarkable efforts of these special kids. As they enjoyed the pizza, a few kids congratulated Jill and Meghan for their bringing the situation to my attention. Two students commended Ralph on enduring so much this year. A few students thanked me for listening and helping them. When I asked Ralph if he wanted to say anything, I wasn't sure what he might come up with. I held my breath, and finally he said, "I appreciate everyone's support." Hardly effusive, but more positively expressive than this student had been in the past. This was a wonderful example of the power of empathy to activate the "caring" majority. The twenty-two supporters ended up having more power than the three "popular" teasers.

There is power in numbers, and peer pressure can work in a positive way if bystanders and witnesses take an active role. The more children learn to live by "the golden rule" and the more they stand up for each other, the lower their tolerance as a group for teasing, bullying, and other cruelty.

10

Success Stories

Children Speak Up About Coping with Teasing

Over the years that I've been teaching kids strategies for coping with teasing, I've collected a thick file of their writings, most of them describing how they adapted these new tools to handle their own unique situations. Some were unsolicited letters and drawings from individual children, while others were little essays produced by each student in a whole class at the direction of the teacher. Still others were the combined efforts of a couple of children who found themselves inspired by what they had learned—like the butterfly story written by two fifth-graders that appears in this chapter.

Whatever their source, these writings are a testament to the power of the ten Easing the Teasing strategies to motivate, soothe, and empower children struggling with the hurt and humiliation of being teased. If your child feels any hesitation about trying the strategies, these testimonials should reassure him or her that the effort will pay off. Even more, however, these letters and stories are a testament to the creativity and courage of all the children I've met. I hope you'll be as impressed as I have been by the resourcefulness and spirit they represent.

We want to express our feelings about what we did about the teasing for Ralph. At first we felt bad because everyone made fun of him. Then we went to talk to our school social worker, Mrs. Freedman, about what was happening with Ralph. She asked us if other kids felt the same way we did. We talked to our friends and discovered that 19 people wanted to help stop the teasing. We all met during lunch and recess for a few weeks to talk about how we could help. Our teacher helped too. We decided to stick up for Ralph when we saw kids picking on him. The teasers were really surprised when we told them to stop. Mrs. Freedman and our teacher talked to the teasers. The teasing mostly stopped. We then told Ralph about the group. At first he looked embarrassed and nervous, but then he seemed happy. It made us feel great for what we did. Now we are friends with Ralph and are proud of him for taking this so well. We are so glad we did this for him too. We would like to say thank you to Mrs. Freedman for being our social worker at our school and to Ralph for becoming our friend. We are amazed how fast this happened. All in 2–3 weeks.

We hope that kids everywhere will stand up for others who are teased like we did. We call this method "strength in numbers." It is forming a group and sticking up for kids teased or bullied. We have many emotions about this—happiness, proudness, and joyness. Now not many are teased at our school. We both know how it feels to be teased and it doesn't feel good. So treat people the way you want to be treated and they will treat you right too. All this stuff we learned from Mrs. Freedman.

Meghan and Jill

TEASING RAP
By Jessica Brenner, fifth grade

There are some ways to keep your cool,
When you are being teased there are ten simple rules.

1. *Whose opinion matters here?*
   I'm not going to let that teaser create one tear.

2. *I'm gonna use the "So?" strategy,*
   Cause I know Mrs. Freedman would be proud of me.

3. *This strategy is so easy.*
   All I gotta do is simply agree.

4. *I'm gonna answer with a joke,*
   So the teaser will not laugh at me, I hope.

5. *Ignoring is one of those simple rules.*
   Ignoring will help you keep your cool.

6. *"I feel bad when you do this to me.*
   It makes me feel low when you tease me."

7. *I'm gonna use the complimentary,*
   Because the teaser will be stunned and stay away from me.

8. *Reframing is what I gotta do.*
   I will tell the teaser, "I want your opinion too."

9. *If you're gonna use the visualization,*
   You gotta think real hard.
   You have to use your concentration.

10. *If none of these work, you have to ask for help,*
    You have to be real calm and try not to yelp.

    These are some ways to keep your cool,
    When you're being teased,
    Use these ten simple rules! Yeah!

I was teased about my glasses. I felt like I wanted to throw my glasses away. I said to myself, "I like my glasses, and that's all that matters. If they don't like my glasses, they can buy ones they like!"
    Jeff, fifth grade

Someone says the "I" message
He says he feels mad,
The other person accepts it,
Now everyone is glad!

Mrs. Angel's first-graders

My brother teased about my Iowa test score. He said he did better in third grade. I told him that it didn't matter, and he stopped teasing me.

   Bethany, third grade

Teasing is a very bad thing. Once when I was young, 8 years old and 3.2 ft. tall, a big kid in third grade made fun of me because I was short. So, I said, "So? I like to be short." He never bothered me again because he knew that I knew that he knew that I liked when he called me shorty.

   Brandon, fourth grade

I was once teased in kindergarten when I first got my glasses. At first it was annoying, but later on, about 2 weeks later, it just stopped. I got teased again about my glasses 2 years ago in camp. All I had to say was, "Since I have four eyes, I can see in two more directions than you." I really don't tease people because I remember how it felt to be teased.

   Richard, fifth grade

Dear Mrs. Freedman,
I thank you very much for helping me with my school problem (clubs). It is now working out better. I wrote a rhyme-less poem for you. It goes like this:
   They used to make me cry,
   Now they make me laugh.
   They used to make me frown,
   Now they make me smile.
   They used to make me sit at the corner of the lunch-room table,
   Now there is plenty of room for me to sit.
   They used to make me look like a fool.
   Now I'm considered very cool.

   Nina, third grade

I was teased by some of my friends and a few of my cousins about having a lot of freckles. It made me feel bad. I told myself that I like my freckles and that they are cute—then I felt better.

   Meghan, fifth grade

My brother was teasing me so I said, "Your point being?" He got so annoyed that he walked away.

Jessica, third grade

One day I told my friend that my soccer coach called me "short cake." The next day all the boys were calling me "short cake." They were teasing me about it. So, I remembered what Mrs. Freedman, our school social worker, told us about all the different ways to deal with teasers. I used the strategy of turning the tease into a compliment, and then they all just stopped. I was glad that we had a social worker at our school.

Laura, fifth grade

Last year I was teased about being small. I was playing in the snow when someone I didn't like so much said, "You're so small. You're the smallest kid in the class." She then started laughing. So, I just said, "So?"

Liz, third grade

I was teased about my last name, "Lovett." When the person teased me, I felt sad and angry. I used some of the ten ways to solve the problem. When they teased me, I used self-talk. I also told an adult what that person said to me. I also walked away or I turned it into a compliment. Sometimes I would just change the subject.

Heather, fifth grade

Dear Mrs. Freedman,
I enjoyed listening to your talks with our class. I remember when you talked about stress. It was fun to learn about what it means, how to handle it, good stress and bad stress. I also enjoyed solving other students' problems that happened mostly on the playground and at lunch.

I remember a lot about teasing. Now I am an expert on handling stress and solving problems. I will remember to stop teasing by giving the teaser a compliment, using the shield, saying "so?," agreeing with the teaser, saying the I message, or tell an adult. My visualization would be to flip the teases away because I love gymnastics. I hope to see you again next year so you can help me with my problems.

Sincerely,
Josh K., third grade

I was teased when I got my retainer. When I came to school someone said, "Your teeth look very weird." I said, "I know. I just got a retainer to straighten them." That worked very well.

Amy K., third grade

My brother teased me and I just ignored him and pretended I was deaf. I said, "Did I hear something? I don't think I did." If Joy my best friend were there, I'd say, "Did I hear something, Joy?" She'd say, "I don't think so." Then I'd say, "Me neither. I don't think I heard anything." Then my brother stomped off without talking. This is sort of like ignoring. My brother doesn't tease me much now.

Rebecca K., third grade

Dear Mrs. Freedman,

I learned so much from you that it is unbelievable! I learned how to handle teasing, stress, and much, much more. I like when you taught me that I could pretend that I am wearing a shield to help the put-downs bounce off. I thought of the idea that I could think about "erasing" teases away, since I like to write so much. Someone called me "sparks" when I got my braces. I took it as a compliment and he never called me "sparks" again. Mrs. Freedman, you are a life saver! I don't know how you do it. I enjoyed having you come in our class so we could express our feelings out. I liked listening to other people's problems. Your coming in on Tuesdays was a BIG gift. I can't wait to see what you teach us next year in 4th grade.

Sincerely,

Rebecca H., third grade

There are different sides of kinds of teasing. Some people say that teasing really isn't a bad thing and that you can just get over it. Some people take the tease really bad. That one tease could be in your head the rest of your life—whether it is a strong tease which could lead to physical violence or a weak tease like "you're dumb." These words can stay in your head forever.

A fourth-grader

I think teasing is terrible because it hurts people's feelings. If you get teased there are so many things to do. You can walk away, you can say,

"So?," and you ask for help if it keeps up. If someone calls you "four eyes," you could say, "I can see really well now." You could also say the "I" message. "I feel bad when you make fun of me. Please stop."

Lily, fourth grade

One day my friends were teasing me about my shoes. It made me feel bad for a little while, but then I said, "Well, I like them." Then they stopped teasing me because they knew they were not getting to me. It made me feel a lot better.

A fifth-grader

When I got my bangs cut, someone said, "You look stupid." I said, "So what, I like them and what I like on me, I will keep." And then I said, "You have bangs too and if you don't like mine, I don't care."

Michelle, third grade

The Butterfly Who Wore High Heels

By Julie Brontman and Jessica Brenner, fifth grade

There was once a butterfly named Casey. She lived in San Francisco. She was a lovely and kind butterfly. She had lavender wings with periwinkle and baby yellow polka dots. She had gone through many earthquakes in her life. She always wore high heel shoes. But she had a problem. Other butterflies disliked her shoes, so they acted unkindly to her. They also acted unkindly to Casey because she was kind to others unlike herself. When the other butterflies were unkind to Casey, she did nothing but be kind to them! She was kind to every living creature.

Casey was depressed that other butterflies did not like her, but she thought if she was very kind, the other butterflies would like her soon enough. "All in good time," she said to herself. But on the plus side, she had one friend. Her name was Lola—Lola, the cardinal. She always wore a straw hat. She was always very cheerful. They lived together in an old rundown tree house. Lola and Casey were like mother and daughter. Casey's parents died when she was little. They were in a garden and got sprayed with pesticide. Lola helped Casey with her problems, just like Casey's mother would. They were very happy together.

One day, Casey ran into the meanest bully in town! He yelled, "What are you doing here, High Heels?" Soon butterflies were gathering around Casey. She was so horrified she could not fly away. Suddenly out of nowhere, came Lola!! She scooped up Casey and flew away to the tree house together.

As Casey cried, she managed to get her message to Lola. She pleaded . . .

"Please take me away, please. It's not fair that I am treated like this. It has gone on long enough."

Lola asked, "Where do you want us to go? We don't have any money and look at this house! This is all we have for shelter and you expect us to move?"

"But you said you wanted me to be happy. This is a place I will never be happy!" cried Casey.

Lola explained, "I'm sorry I have gotten upset, it's just that we don't have another place to live."

"What about L.A.? I have heard great things about L.A."

"That is an outstanding idea! But I heard it was a little expensive," mumbled Lola.

"Well, we can at least go and see what it is like," suggested Casey.

"Well . . . all right, but we are only looking," said Lola.

As they set off, Lola and Casey were very excited about going to L.A. but a little nervous. They came to L.A. and asked where the apartments were. The kind old butterfly said, "Right over there, 2 blocks down and to the right. You will see the B.B. Apartments for butterflies and bugs."

Lola and Casey went to the B.B. Apartments. They were quite pleased with what they saw. They both decided to rent apartment B68. Lola and Casey moved in right away. It was a peaceful and quiet apartment. The building itself was nice too. Lola and Casey painted the apartment baby yellow. After a while, the apartment was ready. After all of their hard work, they decided to go to the B.B. restaurant inside the apartment building on the main level. They went to a nearby table when they heard someone say, "What are doing here, High Heels?" Lola and Casey turned around and immediately recognized the face. It was the cousin of the bully from home. He was just as bad as the bully. (I guess it runs in the family). "My cousin has told me about you! I can recognize you from the high heels," he said. Lola and Casey left the restaurant as fast as they could. "Well . . . " said Casey with a worried voice, "at least, there are other restaurants in L.A."

"No, Casey. You need to learn the strategies so that you can stand up to all of the teasers," said Lola.

The next day, Lola spent all her time teaching Casey the ten strategies that explain how you stand up to the teaser.

Later in the evening, Lola said to Casey, "Now that you have learned the ten strategies, will you please recite them to me and tell me how they work."

"Sure Lola. Here it goes . . . *So?*, this strategy is used to say to the teaser, 'what is your point?' *Ignoring*, this is the strategy where you don't make eye contact or speak to the teaser. *Humor*, a strategy to make the teaser laugh and to show that you are not letting the tease affect you. The *"I" message*, a strategy that might not always work because it might make the teaser happy to know you don't like the teasing so the teaser might keep teasing you. When it does work, you are explaining to the teaser that you aren't going to take the teasing anymore. *Self-talk* is when you tell yourself that your opinion matters more than the teaser's opinion. Next, umm, I know! Answer with a *compliment*! This makes the teaser feel good about something he did. Another is *visualization*. This is when you visualize the teases bouncing off of you, not letting the teaser get to you. *Agreeing with the facts* is another strategy. This is when you agree with the teaser only if what they say is true. *Reframing* is when you turn the tease into a compliment, like 'thanks for noticing my shoes.' If none of these strategies work, you should *ask for help*. You can ask any adult or friend. There I'm done. Did I leave anything out?"

"Perfect," said Lola.

Afterwards: Casey and Lola decided to permanently live in L.A. From then on, Casey stood up to every teaser that life threw at her. A couple of years later, Lola passed away of old age. Although Casey missed Lola, Casey had wonderful memories of her friend. Everything that Lola taught Casey and all of the times they had spent together, Casey would always remember. Casey would especially remember the very useful strategies on how to deal with teasing. Lola would forever be in Casey's heart.

11

A Little Help for
Parents of Teasers

If your child is being teased, you may wonder what a chapter aimed
at the parents of teasers is doing in this book. Parents of teasers
may not actually buy this book, but the ideas in this chapter may find
their way to them via several routes. For one, you can pass them on
to your child's teacher or to the school's social worker. Or, if you are
a counselor or teacher, you might want to apply them at your school.
If you're a parent, don't offer these suggestions to the parents of a
teaser unless you're asked directly for help or ideas. Parents of teasers
are often already defensive, and being offered assistance by a non-
professional will only make them more so, especially if it's your child
that their child is accused of teasing. Finally, keep in mind that your
child may end up becoming a teaser at some point. Hard as it is to
believe, kids who are teased do turn around and take the role of
aggressor, sometimes out of self-defense, sometimes because they
forget how it felt to be teased and succumb to the appeal of the
power teasing gives them, and sometimes just because children
change over time. At the very least, all kids are likely to engage in
teasing within the family. While most parents tolerate sibling teasing, it can be hurtful, especially when one child is always the victim,
when it occurs over a long period of time, and when there is physical aggression. This chapter may help parents deal with teasing at
home as well as outside the family. In any case, I hope you'll seriously
consider the advice that follows.

If someone complains to you that your child is guilty of hurtful teasing, you have four tasks before you:

1. Knowing how to respond constructively to the accuser
2. Investigating the complaint
3. Identifying the influences that are encouraging your child to tease
4. Putting a stop to your child's teasing

Responding to a Complaint

Unless they happen to overhear or observe their children in the act, most parents don't know their child is teasing until they hear about it from a teacher or another adult. If a teacher, school employee, or adult informs you that your child has been hurting another child (or children) by teasing, your reactions may run the gamut from disbelief to resentment to dismay to guilt to embarrassment. You love your child, and so of course you don't want to believe that he or she is guilty of intentional cruelty to other children. Your instinctive reaction may be to get angry. *Even if you feel indignant, it's paramount that you remain calm.* Resist any knee-jerk urge to deny that your child would ever do such a thing. Step back, take a deep breath, and ask, "Can you tell me exactly what happened?"

If the report is coming from your child's teacher whose fairness or powers of observation have historically been trustworthy, then you may want to give her the benefit of the doubt and assume that what she says happened did in fact happen. If the details provided don't feel like the complete picture, ask probing (but nonaccusatory) questions:

- "Does my child tease more than one person?"
- "Does he [or she] tease more than other kids?"
- "How long has it been happening?"
- "How does my child react to your intervention?"
- "Do you have any insight into why this is happening?"

Just like my recommendation to the parents of teased children, I strongly suggest that you ascertain the accuracy of the reports. Explain to the teacher or parent that you intend to look into the matter to find out exactly what has been happening and why. Do not make any pronouncements or predictions until you have an opportunity to explore the situation, using the suggestions that will be presented in this chapter.

Also don't make any promises about what you will do as a consequence of your investigation. Instead, ask what the teacher or parent wants you to do or thinks you should do about the situation. If you ask this question calmly and openly, you'll be surprised by how often it will defuse a potentially explosive conversation. Parents who call to confront the parents of a teaser often pick up the phone in a fit of anger with the goal of demanding that you "put a stop to" your child's behavior. But when asked rationally what they would specifically like you to do to address the problem, they often have a much less extreme suggestion. Some might say they would like you to talk to their child; others might suggest that the parents get the kids together to work things out.

I once knew two ten-year-old neighbors and former friends who were teasing and treating each other badly, especially on their way to and from school. The situation escalated to physical aggression. The boys' parents sat down with their sons and acknowledged that they were no longer friends but that the put-downs, intimidations, and fights must stop. They encouraged each boy to tell his side of the story. Of course, there are at least two sides to any story. The parents listened and conveyed understanding to both boys. They did not attempt to establish "who started it." Both boys acknowledged their responsibility.

Meetings like this will not be productive if the parents' hurt and hostility interfere with the ability to listen calmly and with an open mind. When parents argue and blame each other, kids are likely to model that behavior. Ideally, parents will come together as caring adults who want to help their children. This willingness to communicate and problem-solve serves as a great example to the kids who are not getting along.

In some cases, of course, by the time the parents call you, they will be angry and frustrated and may stick to their insistence that you put a stop to your child's behavior at once. They may make vague threats about what will happen if you don't or very specific ones about going to the police if the "teasing" is really bullying and involves physical harm, threat of harm, or destruction of possessions. Again, try your hardest to remain calm and repeat that you will look into the situation.

If you're especially lucky, the person who called you might say that each of you should talk to your children about how unacceptable teasing is, and you will agree to encourage your children's school to address it on a more global level, such as in the classroom, with all of the students.

Finding Out What Happened

Please try to suspend disbelief as you go about this exploration. In defense of your child, you are likely to deny that he or she has done anything wrong. And even parents who are inclined to accept a teacher's report would rather believe their child. Parents often feel sure that their children act like all the others and that "kids will be kids." During a conference call with her son's teacher and the principal, Mrs. Pines insisted that her second-grade son, Jake, acted no differently from other seven-year-olds. In fact she was unwilling to come to school for a conference and refused school social work for her son. Jake's verbal and physical aggression, which had spurred many interventions within the school, continued and progressed to the point where kids referred to him as a bully.

After many canceled and rescheduled appointments, Mrs. Pines finally came to school to discuss her son's behavior further. Again, she minimized Jake's behavior, and again, we emphasized that Jake's behavior was much more severe than that of his peers. In fact, the classroom teacher stated that she had received phone calls from many parents regarding their concerns about his behavior on the bus, before and after school, and during recess. Jake's mother angrily accused the teacher of not liking her son. The more examples we gave of Jake's aggressive behavior, the angrier his mom became. She became even angrier when the principal said that the next step would be suspension.

Much to our surprise, Jake's mother pursued outside help for him following our conference. The lesson I hope you'll take from this story is that, even if you are unable to suspend disbelief and remain calm in the face of accusations about your child, you have the opportunity to think about the situation afterward, when you don't feel confronted and defensive. At that time you may realize that the complaint is worth an objective look.

Talking to Your Child About Teasing Others

To find out more about the complaint against your child, the obvious place to start is to ask him. The problem is, of course, that any child accused of wrongdoing, especially when accused by another adult, is likely to deny guilt. Don't be surprised if your child tries to project the blame onto the teasee (*"He* started it. . . . *He* was the one who was being mean to *me!"*) or claims it was all a joke ("I was only *kidding*, Mom. I can't believe he's making such a big deal out of it. What a jerk.")

In fact, if your child is a persistent teaser, you are unlikely to get the full story just by asking. Most kids in this position will deny or minimize their behaviors or make up excuses until they are "caught in the act." As a social worker, it is often difficult for me to uncover the truth when I talk to the teaser who refuses to accept responsibility, when I have not witnessed the teasing myself—when it is one child's word against another's.

Jeremy reported that Mitchell had called him a "homo," taking this as meaning homosexual. When I asked Mitchell about it, he said he meant Homo sapiens, a term that had recently come up in a class discussion. Which did Mitchell really mean? There was no way for me to be sure. In cases like that, when I am unable to ascertain exactly what was said and the intent of the words, I tell the teaser that, if in fact he is making fun of another child, the behavior is unacceptable and must stop. I emphasize that if I find out he is involved in other teasing situations, there will be consequences—such as involving the principal, having a parent conference, or losing privileges.

Eleven-year-old Rob, who initially denied any responsibility for insulting and intimidating a classmate, gave me another opportunity to find out what was happening when, according to reports from many of his fellow fifth-graders, he continued to tease the other boy. I confronted Rob with the information in a caring and concerned way. I emphasized the cruelty of his actions, which he seemed to minimize. He told me that he was "just joking." I equated his cruel remarks with the taunts that have led many school-age children to violence as a way to seek revenge. Rob seemed surprised when I said this. Apparently he had underestimated the power of his words and actions, as do many persistent teasers and bullies. Rob, who had always tried hard to maintain a rough and tough façade, began to cry and finally accepted responsibility for his behavior. This is a first big step in helping the teaser stop. The next step is understanding why the teaser treats others in an intimidating and offensive way, which is addressed in the next section of this chapter.

Parental intervention is essential in helping kids change their verbally aggressive behaviors, and it starts with knowing how to talk to your child about teasing. As with talking to an adult who is accusing your child of teasing, you need to keep cool and not express anger or blame. Becoming angry and "bullying" your child to give the complete story only makes the situation worse. In fact, it gives the child more aggressive behavior to model.

Using the "I" message strategy is an effective way to begin: "I felt quite concerned when your teacher called me about a situation with you and Ashley."

Explain the differences between fun and friendly teasing and cruel and hurtful teasing. Perhaps the child will admit to the fun and friendly teasing—at which time you can talk about how those words might be taken as an insult or put-down.

Ask your son or daughter about the child who is the alleged victim. A discussion of how the teasee might feel could help the teaser develop enough empathy to stop the taunting. Sometimes you might gain some insight into or understanding of the relationship or your child's feelings about the alleged victim that might shed some light on your child's reported behavior. Many children feel totally justified in taunting and teasing a child who has bugged them "forever." Ashley constantly followed Pam around on the playground and always asked to be her partner or part of her group in classroom activities. Pam's exclusion and rejection of Ashley did not deter her. Pam's frustration increased to the point that she began insulting Ashley. When asked about her behavior, she did not regard this as teasing. If a situation such as this comes out in your conversation, you can discuss with your child what other ways she could handle the frustrating situation.

Talking to your child is one way to get information about the teasing from him or her. Another is to use your powers of observation. Once you learn that your child may be teasing others, begin monitoring your son or daughter's behavior more closely. Can you catch her in the act? Listen to see if your child makes fun of others in the car pool or while playing with friends at home. Does he frequently tease his siblings? If so, label the specific behaviors, pointing out examples as they happen. Some kids need to know what teasing is. An important counterpoint to this, of course, is noticing and commenting about positive behaviors toward peers and siblings.

Once you have determined that your child has in fact hurt another child through teasing, you'll want to figure out for yourself why he or she is engaging in this behavior. Again, understanding the motivation behind the behavior will help you zero in on the best possible solution. Then you'll want to find ways to stop the current behavior and deter the child from teasing in the future.

Why Is Your Child Teasing?

Sometimes the reason for teasing aimed at a specific child is pretty easy to pinpoint, as with Pam and Ashley. But in most cases teasing is part of a pattern, in which case you need to identify the influences that are contributing to the behavior. Here too, the "cause" may be fairly straightforward (though it won't necessarily be easy to uncover). Tough-guy Rob, it turned out, was putting on his macho act because his older brother had told him to be tough so that kids won't "mess" with him. But it took us some time and persistent talking with Rob to find that out.

If teasing has become a pattern in your child's peer interactions, it is important to understand why. Is he reacting to the aggressive behavior of other kids? Is the teasing an attention-seeking behavior? Is he modeling behavior of other family members? Does he tease to feel powerful? Is the teasing a result of poor anger control? All of the reasons that children tease, listed in Chapter 3, should be considered. It's entirely possible that your child is hurting others in response to being hurt himself, in which case you need to find out exactly what's going on before you can expect to help him stop teasing. This doesn't mean that your child needn't take responsibility for behaving in a hurtful way toward others. It does mean that most kids aren't inherently bad, and most "bad" behavior can be traced to a tangible cause that can be eradicated. Children are helped when they understand why they behave in hurtful ways. As obvious as it might look to the outsider knowing that a child is exposed to abuse within his family or is experiencing other major family stress, the child may not see the connection between his home life and his behavior at school.

In some situations, teasing is a symptom of children's impulsive or excitable behavior. They may not have malicious motives for their behavior. It might be beneficial to consult with the teacher or the school mental health professional to help with this assessment. Once the cause is determined, an appropriate course of action or treatment plan can be developed and implemented.

Is Your Child Angry or Upset About Something?

In Chapter 3, we talked about the role of anger in children's teasing. Sometimes, angry or hurt kids will strike out at others in a misguided attempt to make themselves feel better. If your child is upset—either at the teaser or at someone or something else—and doesn't know what to do with those feelings, he or she might take it out on someone perceived to be weak and vulnerable. It's your job to find out. When asked about the alleged teasing, if your child responds with "But she made me so mad!" or something along those lines, you need to talk about appropriate expressions of anger. See Chapters 3 and 4.

Sometimes, children develop chronic problems with anger. Some have an innately bristly temperament or "short fuse." Others have been taught, directly or indirectly, that they simply should not get angry, which leaves them with a lot of bottled-up feelings that may demand more and more loudly to be heard. Remember that anger is a perfectly normal and often constructive emotion. Kids should understand the distinction between feeling angry and acting on their anger, as discussed in Chapter 3. Another possibility is that some ongoing, unresolved dilemma in the child's life is leaving him or her with ongoing, unresolved anger. Are there family circumstances that could be making your child angry? Before you say "no" too quickly, be aware that parents are sometimes the last to know when a child is angry over a family problem that he or she feels unable to control. Sadie, her parents were sure to tell her regularly, was "the best big sister in the whole world." She read to Cory and played board games with him whenever his blood sugar was out of control and he had to stay home and rest. Dave and Maggie were mortified when they found out that Sadie had been taunting a sickly child in her class for being a "big sissy." Sadie was angry—at Cory for having diabetes and limiting the family's activities and at her parents for giving her little brother the lion's share of attention.

Tony was angry too, but he didn't dare show it. There was already enough yelling and screaming and threatening at his house, thank you very much, and so at home he was eager to please and always the great peacemaker between his battling parents. At school, though, it was a different story. His parents were shocked when the teacher called and said Tony had been calling the younger kids names on the playground, and now he had escalated to tripping them on the way back into the classroom. Finally, someone had gotten hurt.

I can't give you a quick and easy way to determine whether your child is secretly angry, but if you're stunned to learn that the docile child you see at home is apparently behaving like Attila the Hun at school, do your best to step back and look at the child's life and relationships. Is anything going on that might be making your son or daughter angry? If in doubt, ask your teacher for help, ask the school social worker to interview your child, or ask for a referral to a psychologist or counselor who could talk to your son or daughter in a setting that might make the child feel open enough to be candid. If anger is in fact a problem, you'll find suggestions for helping him or her learn to use it appropriately in Chapters 3 and 4 and also later in this chapter.

Is Your Child Being Influenced Negatively by TV and Other Cultural Messages?

I'm tempted to answer "yes" for you because every day at school I'm hit in the face with the evidence. I've seen kids imitate professional wrestlers, gangsta rappers, heroes of vigilante movies, cartoon villains, and characters in violent video games plainly convinced that belittling others, being aggressive and cruel, and humiliating their peers under the guise of "having fun" is "cool." Do you know what your child is watching on TV, in the movies, and on videotape? Do you know what's in the latest pop lyrics? How about the Internet? TV and films are full of aggressive, vengeful heroes. Plenty of today's music advocates violence of various types. And even when it's just kids talking to other kids, the faceless aspect of socializing on the Internet seems to encourage them to say things they wouldn't say in person. While I don't advocate censorship, I do advocate careful monitoring by parents. My suggestions for doing so are in Chapter 9 and later in this chapter.

What Kind of Model Are You?

"I have met the enemy, and he is us."

So said Pogo in the classic comic strip of the same name, in an ironic send-up of Oliver Perry's famous War of 1812 proclamation

"We have met the enemy, and they are ours." Sad to say, we often are our own worst enemies when it comes to serving as models of compassion and kindness to our children.

Kids learn from what they live with on a day-to-day basis. A child who is physically or verbally aggressive at school is often imitating behaviors and words that he observes or experiences within his family.

Do you model the behavior of a "teaser"? Do you tease your child inappropriately? Do you consistently "put down" your son or daughter? Is your playful teasing perceived by your child as hurtful? Do you often comment negatively about strangers, acquaintances, or family members? Are your jokes filled with sarcasm? Reviewing your own behavior and assessing its impact on your child is crucial if you want your child's aggression to cease. If, as the result of a little soul searching, you believe you could offer your child a better model, you can take some measures to try to change. You've already taken the first step if you're aware of your own negative behavior. The next step is establishing the realistic expectation that this behavior will not change overnight. Once the awareness is there, you will begin to catch yourself when you make an aggressive comment or criticism. Self-talk is an important tool in trying to change these behaviors. It is helpful for some parents to make a list of new ways of reacting to replace old aggressive behaviors. If and when you are aggressive with your children even after you decide to change your behavior, you can apologize and explain that wasn't the best way to handle the situation. Your success in changing behaviors that are ingrained depends on your motivation. If you've ever tried to lose weight, get physically fit, or quit smoking, you know how critical ongoing motivation is to success. In changing how you model respectful behavior for your children, just as in making lifestyle changes to benefit your health, some parents benefit from self-help books, while others pursue professional help.

Remember, actions speak louder than words. I think kids are exposed to so much disrespect that parents need to make very conscious efforts to model respect and kindness. Try making a habit of showing extra kindness to people. Smile and compliment the supermarket cashier; let a driver cut in front of you even when you're in a hurry; make eye contact when you say "thank you," reminding yourself to be patient when you have to wait longer than you expected for something; and show appreciation for a sales clerk's efforts rather than annoyance for minor inconveniences. Hold the door open for an elderly person, talk to a disabled person in line in front of you at the movie theater, and invite people from different backgrounds or cultures to your home. The message to your child will be loud and clear.

Is Yours a Tolerant and Accepting Community?

You don't have to live in Utopia to know how to behave with respect, compassion, and kindness . . . but it helps. What is your community like? Open and accepting of diversity or closed and intolerant? How would you describe your child's friends, as a mini melting pot or an experiment in cloning? What about the atmosphere at school? At some schools, students freely cross racial, ethnic, and economic divides. At others, everyone belongs to a well-defined, if not self-chosen, group. Much depends on the adults in charge and on the resources available. If, for whatever reason, your child must attend school where gang problems exist, violence is an everyday fact of life, or "belonging" involves excluding, you have your work cut out for you. Many of the people, children and adults alike, that your child interacts with every day may be modeling teasing and bullying as a way of life.

In that case, get involved. I know, it's easy for me to say and not necessarily so easy to do. But the news is full of inspiring stories of grassroots efforts made by the "little people" like you and me who have banded together with a few like-minded souls and made a real difference for their children and their community.

Teaching Tolerance is a national education project that helps teachers promote respect and understanding. One of their publications, *101 Tools for Tolerance*, contains simple ideas for individuals, schools, workplaces, and the community for promoting equity and celebrating diversity. For more information, check out their website: splcenter.org.

The Giraffe Project is a program that motivates and recognizes people who "stick their necks out" for the common good. The Giraffe Heroes Program is a story-based curriculum for grades K–12 that teaches compassion, courage, and responsibility. Contact the project at P.O. Box 759, Langley, Washington 98260; 360-221-7989. Or, visit their website: giraffe.org.

According to the information on its website, PeaceBuilders is a community-based violence prevention program for schools. Its goal is to promote and enhance feelings of belonging and safety in schools, workplaces, and communities. Contact PeaceBuilders at P.O. Box 12158, Tucson, Arizona 85732-2158; 520-322-9977. Visit them online at peacebuilders.com.

Community of Caring, founded by Eunice Kennedy Shriver, is a project of the Joseph P. Kennedy Jr. Foundation. The program, endorsed by the National Association of Secondary School Principals, works to implement and encourage the values of caring, respect, trust, responsibility, and family in our schools. Through a total community approach, this program creates a caring, respectful environment and culture in school. Contact the Community of Caring at 1325 G Street, Suite 500, Washington, DC 20052; 202-393-1250. Visit their website: communityofcaring.org.

Character Counts! is quite popular in my area. It is a coalition of schools, communities, and nonprofit organizations that works to advance character education by teaching the Six Pillars of Character: trustworthiness, respect, responsibility, fairness, caring, and citizenship. Contact the National Office/Josephson Institute of Ethics, 4640 Admiralty Way, Suite 1001, Marina del Rey, California 90292-6610; 310-306-1868. Visit them online: charactercounts.org.

What Can You Do to Teach Your Child Not to Tease?

While the task may seem to be an overwhelming one at first, you can teach your child how to interact with other people in a positive and caring manner.

Make It Crystal Clear That Hurtful Teasing Is Not Acceptable

Parents often think that teasing within the family is normal. In fact, many parents tolerate teasing much more than other inappropriate behaviors such as stealing, lying, or physical aggression. Many believe that all brothers and sisters make fun of and laugh at each other, which often contributes to chronic ridicule and teasing within the family. We all know that sisters and brothers are experts at pushing each other's buttons. Generally, parents repeatedly ask their kids to stop. When they can't take it anymore, they lose their temper and often overreact with verbal, and sometimes physical, aggression. In many families, parents reprimand their kids' verbal aggression with aggression.

The first step toward stopping your child from teasing is to establish the family rule that cruel teasing and put-downs are not acceptable and will not be tolerated. The expectation should be clear and specific. Saying "I want you to act nice to each other" is not as specific as saying "Teasing and making fun of each other are not allowed." Examples of teasing and belittling behaviors should be explained so that your children understand what is unacceptable. Kids should learn that making fun of, insulting, and ridiculing others is wrong. Family members should laugh with each other, not at each other. If you see or hear your son or daughter saying or doing anything mean or hurtful to siblings or friends, intervene immediately. Be sure that you convey your disapproval about your child's behavior, not about your child.

I suggest that you also hold a family meeting to talk about teasing. Discuss what it is, giving recent examples of put-downs and insults of family members, and how it makes people feel. Younger children can help you create a list of words and names that are hurtful. Depending upon the age of the kids, a discussion of the teasing and taunting that led up to several school shootings can emphasize the harmful effects of prolonged insults and harassment.

At this point, state that you no longer will allow your children to ridicule or put each other down. Again, give examples of what will not be allowed. Merely stating "Don't be mean to each other" is not specific enough.

Impose Consequences for Teasing

Along with the rule that teasing is not acceptable, children should know the consequences for cruel or hurtful teasing. Consequences must be meaningful, within your control, consistently enforced, and stated clearly. They are easier to enforce if clearly understood ahead of time. If parents are not committed to this change, it will not work!

Parents ask me all the time, "What is the best consequence?" What is a meaningful consequence for one child may not be for another. Meaningful consequences usually vary with the age of the child. The loss of privileges, such as television, computer games, the telephone, or playing with friends, is often effective. An earlier bedtime or the loss of dessert is very meaningful to some young children. Both parents should agree on the consequence and jointly enforce it. If you are aiming at teasing that occurs at school, you'll have to enlist the aid of the teacher or other school staff members in reporting on the child's behavior.

Whether the teasing is taking place at school, at home, or elsewhere, a verbal or written apology to the teasee is an appropriate part of the consequence. For teasing between siblings, try requiring that the teasing sibling give the teased brother or sister a compliment. Sometimes the incidence of teasing will be greatly reduced because the teaser does not want to compliment his sibling! I met a mother who devised a creative plan for dealing with sibling teasing. If one of her kids puts down another, he or she must do the teased sibling's chores for a day. Be sure to teach your children the strategies in Chapter 6 if they are sensitive and react easily to tougher or older siblings, so they are prepared in the event of teasing when you are not around.

Train Your Child to Be Empathetic

Some kids who tease simply don't realize the impact and power of their words. If your child responds to your queries about reports that he has been teasing someone with "I was just kidding," it's important to determine whether that is in fact the case. You'll probably be able to tell by the look on the child's face and what else he has to say. If he seems concerned or sad and says, "I didn't mean to hurt his feelings," there's a good chance that his teasing was not meant to be intentionally hurtful. If, on the other hand, he gets defensive and starts blaming the teased child for being "touchy," he may just be making excuses. Either way, pointing out that some words can be perceived as hurtful can help a child realize how powerful his words can be. Beyond that, many kids need additional training in the art of empathy, discussed fully in Chapter 9.

"How would you feel if you were in that person's situation?" is an all-important question in teaching kids to recognize, understand, and care about another's feelings. Kids can and need to learn how to see things from another child's point of view. They need to understand how another person is feeling so that they will know what to say or do in a particular interaction or situation. It may be necessary to increase the teaser's awareness of how teasees feel. A child should ask himself, "How would I feel if I were teased?" We hope the answer would be "I would feel bad if someone teased or made fun of me, so I won't tease other kids."

"Treat others the way you want to be treated" is a modified golden rule, which implies empathy. Young children are capable of feeling and showing empathy. However, we need to teach, reinforce, and model this important skill. Barbara C. Unell and Jerry L. Wyckoff write about ways parents can teach empathy in 20 *Teachable Virtues*.

I taught the concept of empathy to a second-grade class and was gratified to see the students successfully apply this skill in a different situation, when a classmate returned to school following the sudden death of her younger sibling. Before her return, we discussed how she was probably feeling and what the students could do to help her when she came back. The students' friendly hellos, invitations to play at recess, and nonverbal expressions of understanding (giving her space if she wanted to be alone and listening to her if she wanted to talk about her brother) eased her transition back to school.

Unfortunately, some kids lack the capacity for empathy, especially when they're getting something out of the teasing. Many persistent teasers and bullies either do not care or are not able to understand how their victims feel. This can happen through a variety of paths. Ten-year-old Dana was verbally aggressive with her peers. Being an only child, she was used to getting her way. In fact, she seemed to have the control within her family. Whenever she wanted something from her parents, she would rant and rave until she got her way. The same patterns were observed at school. She was bossy, intimidating, and argumentative when she did not get what she wanted. She displayed little if any empathy for classmates. Her needs were more important than the feelings of her classmates.

Some teasers are motivated by the emotional reactions of others. They are very gratified and may feel victorious when they realize the impact of their cruel words. Their payoff of power or gratification means more to them than having empathy for the victim. (These kids should be considered bullies because of the repeated and prolonged nature of their behavior.) SuEllen Fried and Paula Fried state in their book, *Bullies and Victims*, that 25 percent of adults who were bullies as children had a criminal record by the time they were thirty years old. Many of these children had little or no remorse for their behavior, and therefore it continued. Let's hope that we can reach these kids at an early age and provide the appropriate help for them. Teachers and parents can identify these children early. Once they are identified, a psychological evaluation can determine the cause of the aggression, resulting in an appropriate treatment plan, whether that is learning to manage their anger, developing social or conflict resolution skills, improving their self-esteem, providing family counseling, or something else.

Promote and Practice an Appreciation of Differences

Because we live in a world with people who are different colors, speak different languages, practice different customs, and adhere to different beliefs, parents should consistently encourage tolerance for and the appreciation of differences. If your child remarks about a person who exhibits a difference, take the time to explain what it is. Many young children are afraid of the "unknown." Emphasize that judgments and criticisms are not appropriate. Parents can promote a healthy curiosity, which can lead to an appreciation rather than fear. It's crucial that parents model and practice respect and understanding of physical, racial, ethnic, and religious diversities. Modeling appropriate behavior is the most powerful way to teach our kids.

Respecting differences of each family member is great training for respecting the differences of others. If you hear your kids saying something unkind to someone who is different, tell them firmly that it is disrespectful to say those things. State what the child has done wrong and why it is wrong. The Anti-Defamation League's *Hate Hurts: How Children Learn and Unlearn Prejudice*, by Caryl Stern-LaRosa and Ellen Hofheimer Bettmann, is an excellent resource that gives parents sample dialogues for kids of different ages. See Chapter 9 for more ideas. The suggestions for school use in the "Teaching Appreciation of Differences" section of Chapter 7 can also be adapted easily and effectively for home use.

Monitor TV Viewing

It is very difficult to totally control our children's television viewing. Unfortunately, many programs that are geared toward children include put-downs and inappropriate ridicule. If you happen to observe a teasing remark on television, don't hesitate to talk to your child about the comment. See Chapter 3 for more on the broad influences of the media on our children's attitudes and Chapter 9 for suggestions for instilling empathy and a rejection of teasing.

Help Your Child Get Angry Appropriately

Besides the ideas I offered in Chapters 3 and 4, you can help a child who is having problems with anger by investigating whether there is an anger management class at school or at a local mental health agency. I know two good books that could be helpful. Adolph Moser's *Don't Rant and Rave on Wednesdays* is an excellent resource for parents and kids. *Stick Up for Yourself!*, by Gershen Kaufman, Lev Raphael, and Pamela Espeland, teaches kids how to express their feelings effectively—how to be assertive, not aggressive.

Compliment and Praise Positive Behavior Changes

If you observe or hear from your child's teacher that your child's verbal aggression has decreased or stopped, acknowledge the positive behavior changes. Praise and compliments contribute to the continuation of the appropriate behavior and boost self-esteem. Most children actually feel better about themselves when these negative behavior patterns change. Praising our kids serves as a model for them to praise others.

When you observe a change in your children's teasing of each other, praise, praise, and praise again. An unexpected trip for an ice cream cone or to the video store is a nice reward to recognize the changed behavior.

Teach Valuable Lessons

Although most parents do not have a degree in education, all parents are "teachers." We teach our children valuable life lessons every day. We teach our kids what is safe and what is dangerous, what is right and what is wrong, and what is good and what is bad. We instruct our sons and daughters in how to take care of themselves, how to fulfill daily household responsibilities, and how to treat others. The life lesson of treating others with respect is crucial. We must emphasize that making fun of others, using cruel and hurtful words, and other verbally abusive behaviors are wrong. We must teach through both words and actions.

Recommended Books
for Children

───◆───

In the following list, *preschool* means ages 3–5, *primary* means grades K–2, *elementary* means grades 3–5, and *intermediate* means grades 6–8.

Alexander, Martha G. *Move Over, Twerp*. New York: Dial Press, 1981.
(Preschool/Primary)

Berenstain, Stan, and Jan Berenstain. *The Berenstain Bears and Too Much Teasing*. New York: Random House, 1993.
(Preschool/Primary)

Berry, Joy Wilt. *Let's Talk About Teasing*. Chicago: Children's Press, 1985.
(Primary)

Brown, Marc Talon. *Arthur's Eyes*. New York: Little, Brown, and Co., 1979.
(Primary)

Burnett, Karen. *Simon's Hook: A Story About Teases and Put-Downs*. Roseville, CA: GR Publishing, 2000.
(Primary/Elementary)

Caple, Kathy. *The Biggest Nose*. New York: Houghton Mifflin, 1985.
(Primary)

Carlson, Nancy. *Arnie and the New Kid*. New York: Penguin, 1990.
(Primary)

Christopher, Matthew F., *Johnny Long Legs*. New York: Little, Brown, and Co., 1988.
(Elementary)

Cohen, Barbara. *Molly's Pilgrim*. New York: Lothrop, Lee, and Shepard Books, 1983.
(Intermediate)

Cole, Joanna. *Bully Trouble*. New York: Random House, 1989.
(Elementary)

Cole, Joanna. *Don't Call Me Names*. New York: Random House, 1990.
(Preschool/Young Primary)

Cosby, Bill. *The Meanest Thing to Say*. New York: Scholastic, 1997.
(Primary)

Couric, Katie. *The Brand New Kid*. New York: Doubleday, 2000.
(Primary/Young Elementary)

Crary, Elizabeth. *Heidi's Irresistible Hat*. Seattle: Parenting Press, Inc., 2001.
(Primary/Elementary)

Crary, Elizabeth. *My Name Is Not Dummy*. Seattle: Parenting Press, 1983.
(Primary)

Cumming, Carol. *Tattlin' Madeline*. Edmonds, WA: Teaching, Inc., 1991.
(Primary)

Cushman, D. *Camp Big Paw*. New York: Harper & Row, 1990.
(Primary/Young Elementary)

dePaola, Tomie. *Oliver Button Is a Sissy.* San Diego: Voyager/Harcourt Brace Jovanovich, 1979.
(Primary)

Dube, Pierette. *Sticks and Stones.* Buffalo, NY: Firefly, 1993.
(Primary)

Duncan, L. *Wonder Kid Meets the Evil Lunch Snatcher.* Boston: Little, Brown, 1988.
(Elementary)

Estes, Elinor. *The Hundred Dresses.* San Diego: Voyager/Harcourt Brace Jovanovich, 1972.
(Older Primary/Elementary)

Gainer, Cindy. *I'm Like You, You're Like Me—A Child's Guide to Understanding and Celebrating Each Other.* Minneapolis: Free Spirit Publishing, 1998.
(Primary/Young Elementary)

Gogoll, Martine. *Rosie's Story.* Greenvale, NY: Mondo Publishing, 1994.
(Primary/Young Elementary)

Grant, Eva. *I Hate My Name.* Orlando: Raintree/Steck-Vaughn Publishers, 1980.
(Primary)

Henkes, Kevin. *Chrysanthemum.* New York: Greenwillow Books, 1991.
(Primary)

Hoffman, Mary. *Amazing Grace.* New York: Dial Books for Young Readers, 1991.
(Primary)

Hogan, Paula Z. *I Hate Boys, I Hate Girls*. Orlando: Raintree/Steck-Vaughn Publishers, 1980.
(Primary)

Hurwitz, Johanna. *Aldo Applesauce*. New York: William Morrow, 1979.
(Older Primary/ Young Elementary)

Kaufman, Gershen, Lev Raphael, and Pamela Espeland. *Stick Up for Yourself!* Minneapolis: Free Spirit, 1999.
(Elementary/Intermediate)

Keller, Holly. *Cromwell's Glasses*. New York: Greenwillow Books, 1982.
(Preschool/Primary)

Laird, Elizabeth. *Secret Friends*. New York: Putnam's, 1999.
(Elementary)

Lee, Mildred Scudder. *The Ice Skating Rink*. New York: Houghton Mifflin Co., 1979.
(Intermediate)

McCain, Becky Ray. *Nobody Knew What to Do*. Morton Grove, IL: Albert Whitman and Company.
(Primary/Elementary)

Moser, Adolph. *Don't Feed the Monster on Tuesdays*. Kansas City, MO: Landmark Editions, 1991.
(Primary/Elementary/Intermediate)

Moser, Adolph. *Don't Rant and Rave on Wednesdays*. Kansas City, MO: Landmark Editions, Inc., 1994.
(Primary/Elementary/Intermediate)

Muir, Stephen, and Mary Jane. *Albert's Old Shoes*. Toronto: Stoddart, 1997.
(Primary)

Paterson, Katherine. *Flip-Flop Girl*. New York: Puffin Books, 1994.
(Elementary)

Phillips, Barbara. *Don't Call Me Fatso*. Orlando: Raintree/Steck-Vaughn, 1980.
(Primary/Young Elementary)

Rathman, Peggy. *Ruby the Copycat*. New York: Scholastic, 1991.
(Primary)

Reider, Katja. *Snail Started It*. New York: North, South Books, 1997.
(Primary)

Rosner, Ruth. *I Hate My Best Friend*. New York: Hyperion Books for Children, 1997.
(Older Primary/Young Elementary)

Sachar, Louis. *Marvin Redpost: Why Pick on Me?* New York: Random House, 1993.
(Older Primary/Elementary)

Shreve, Susan. *Joshua T. Bates Takes Charge*. New York: Knopf, 1993.
(Older Primary/Young Elementary)

Shriver, Maria. *What's Wrong with Timmy?* Boston: Warner Books and Little, Brown, and Company, 2001.
(Elementary/Intermediate)

Slap-Shelton, Laura, Psy.D. and Lawrence E. Shapiro, Ph.D. *Every Time I Blow My Top, I Lose My Head.* Planeview, NY: Childswork Childsplay, 1999.
(Older Primary/Elementary/Intermediate)

Venokur, Ross. *The Amazing Frecktacle.* New York: Delacorte, 1998.
(Elementary/Young Intermediate)

Waber, Bernard. *Ira Sleeps Over.* Boston: Houghton Mifflin, 1972.
(Primary)

White, E. B. *Charlotte's Web.* New York: Dell, 1952.
(Older Primary/Young Elementary)

A Few Videos

But Names Will Never Hurt Me (Grades 3–5)
In the beginning Rebecca is the subject of exclusion and ridicule by some of her classmates. This inspiring story teaches students the importance of treating each other with respect.

A Kids Hope and Summerhill Productions, 1997
A Thomas Brown Film
1-800-465-4758
AKidsHope@aol.com

I Was Just Kidding (Grades 4–6)
Students will observe and learn the keys for empathizing with the feelings of others, being sensitive about their choice of words, and respecting others. It emphasizes that words can hurt more than sticks and stones. Accounts of children at the end of the video are very powerful. (From the Respect series)

Peer Power Productions, 1995
AGC/United Learning
1-847-328-6700

No More Teasing (Grades 2–4)
This video helps students understand the impact teasing has on children. It illustrates the strategies of ignoring and the assertive expression of feelings. The importance of self-confidence and the power of the peer group to stop teasing are addressed.

Sunburst Communications, 1994
1-800-431-1934
sunburst.com

Stop Teasing Me! (Grades K–2)
This video helps young children learn that "it is better to please than to tease." A robot who speaks in rhyme adds to the video's appeal.

Sunburst Communications, 1995
1-800-431-1934
sunburst.com

Sooper Puppy—Words Can Hurt (Grades K–3)
Baxter, a puppy, learns how to have consideration for others and to appreciate his individuality. Students will see the importance of understanding feelings, controlling hurtful anger, respecting others, and learning to apologize.

J. Gary Mitchell Film Company, 1995
1-800-301-4050
empowerkids.com

Bibliography

American Psychological Association (APA) Public Communications "Antisocial Behavior by Boys Often Rewarded by Peers." 16 January 2000. Available at apa.org/releases/popularboys.html.

Anti-Defamation League. *A World of Difference Elementary Study Guide*. New York: Anti-Defamation League, 1994.

Beane, Allan L. *The Bully Free Classroom*. Minneapolis: Free Spirit Publishing, 1999.

Berger, Deborah. "Respect—The Key to Stopping Hurt and Harassment." *Parenting Insights* (Issue 15, 1996), 12–13.

Biren, Richard. *Nah, Nah, Nah!* Warminster, PA: Marco Products, 1997.

Biskupic, Joan. "Schools Liable for Harassment." *Washington Post*, 25 May 1999. Online. World Wide Web. 31 August 1999. Available at: washingtonpost.com/wpsrv/national/longterm/supcourt/stories/court052599.htm.

Bloch, Douglas. *Positive Self-Talk for Children*. New York: Bantam Books, 1993.

Canter, Lee, and Katia Petersen. *Teaching Students to Get Along*. Santa Monica, CA: Lee Canter and Associates, 1995.

Chance, Paul. "Kids Without Friends." *Psychology Today*. (January/February, 1989), 29–31.

Cohen-Posey, Kate. *How to Handle Bullies, Teasers, and Other Meanies*. Highland City, FL: Rainbow Books, Inc., 1995.

Dolan, Deirdre. 2001. "How to Be Popular." *New York Times*, 8 April.

Dube, Jonathan. "High School Hell." ABC News. 23 April 1999. Online. World Wide Web. 13 April 1999. Available at: http://204.202.137.114/sections/us/DailyNews/littletonboys990423.html.

Frankel, Fred. *Good Friends Are Hard to Find*. Los Angeles: Perspective Publishing, 1996.

Fried, SuEllen, and Paula Fried. *Bullies and Victims*. New York: M. Evans and Company, Inc., 1996.

Froschl, Merle, Barbara Sprung, and Nancy Mullin-Rindler. *Quit It! A Teacher's Guide to Teasing and Bullying for Use With Students in Grades K–3*. New York: Educational Equity Concepts, Inc., 1998.

Garrity, Carla, Michael Baris, and William Porter. *Bully-Proofing Your Child*. Longmont, CO: Sopris West, 2000.

Getskow, Veronica, and Dee Konczal. *Kids with Special Needs. Information and Activities to Promote Awareness and Understanding*. Santa Barbara, CA: The Learning Works, 1996.

Giancetti, Charlene C., and Margaret Sagarese. *Cliques*. New York: Broadway Books, 2001.

Gordon, Thomas. *Parent Effectiveness Training*. New York: Peter H. Wyden, 1970.

Hannaford, Mary Joe. *102 Tools for Teachers and Counselors Too.* Doylestown, PA, 1991.

Ireland, Karen. *Boost Your Child's Self-Esteem—Simple, Effective Ways to Build Children's Self-Respect and Confidence.* New York: Berkley Publishing, 2000.

Kaufman, Gershen, Ph.D., Rachel Lev, Ph.D., and Pamela Espeland. *Stick Up for Yourself!* Minneapolis: Free Spirit Publishing, 1999.

Kindlon, Dan, and Michael Thompson. *Raising Cain: Protecting the Emotional Life of Boys.* New York: Ballantine Books, 1999.

Lansky, Vicky. *101 Ways to Make Your Child Feel Special.* Lincolnwood, IL: Contemporary Books, 1991.

Leman, Kevin. *Bringing Up Kids Without Tearing Them Down— How to Raise Confident and Successful Children.* Nashville: Thomas Nelson Publishing, 1995.

Lundeberg, Mary A., Judy Emmett, Patricia A. Osland, and Nancy Lindquist. "Down With Put-Downs." Educational Leadership (October, 1997), 36–37.

Marano, Hara Estroff. *Why Doesn't Anybody Like Me?: A Guide to Raising Socially Confident Kids.* New York: William Morrow, 1998.

Markova, Dawna. *Kids' Random Acts of Kindness.* Emeryville, CA: Conari Press, 1994.

McCoy, Elin. *What to Do . . . When Kids Are Mean to Your Child.* Pleasantville, NY: Reader's Digest, 1997.

McNamara, Barry E. and Francine J. McNamara. *Keys to Dealing with Bullies.* Hauppauge, NY: Barron's Educational Series, Inc., 1997.

Nass, Marcia Shoshana and Max Nass. *Kindness Makes the World a Happy Place*. King of Prussia, PA: The Center for Applied Psychology, 1996.

National Crime Prevention Council. *Helping Kids Handle Conflict*. Washington, DC: National Crime Prevention Council, 1995.

Nowicki, Stephen and Marshall P. Duke. *Helping Your Child Who Doesn't Fit In*. Atlanta: Peachtree Publishers, 1992.

Olweus, Dan. *Bullying at School: What We Know and What We Can Do*. Cambridge, MA: Blackwell, 1993.

Paley, Vivian Gussen. *You Can't Say You Can't Play*. Cambridge, MA: Harvard University Press, 1992.

Pollack, William. *Real Boys*. New York: Random House, 1998.

Romain, Trevor. *Bullies Are a Pain in the Brain*. Minneapolis: Free Spirit Publishing, 1997.

Ross, Dorothea M. *Childhood Bullying and Teasing: What School Personnel, Other Professionals and Parents Can Do*. Alexandria, VA: American Counseling Association, 1996.

Schneider, Meg. *Popularity Has Its Ups and Downs*. Englewood Cliffs, NJ: Julian Messner, 1991.

Schwallie-Giddis, Pat, David Cowan, and Dianne Schilling. *Counselor in the Classroom*. Spring Valley, CA: Innerchoice Publishing, 1993.

Shakeshaft, Charol, and others. "Boys Call Me Cow." *Educational Leadership* (October, 1997), 22–25.

Stein, Nan, and Lisa Sjostrom. *Bullyproof—A Teacher's Guide on Teasing and Bullying*. Wellesley, MA: Wellesley College Center for Research on Women and National Education Association, 1996.

Stern-LaRosa, Caryl, and Ellen Hofheimer Bettmann. *Hate Hurts: How Children Learn and Unlearn Prejudice*. New York: Scholastic Inc., 2000.

STOP Violence Coalition. *Kindness Is Contagious, Catch It!* Kansas City, MO.

Unell, Barbara C. and Jerry L. Wyckoff. *20 Teachable Virtues*. New York: Perigee, 1995.

Webster-Doyle, Terrance. *Why Is Everybody Picking on Me? A Guide to Handling Bullies*. Middlebury, VT: Atrium Publications, 1991.

Zarzour, Kim. *Facing the Schoolyard Bully*. Buffalo, NY: Firefly, 2000.

Index